# Architecture in Detail II

# Architecture in Detail II

**Graham Bizley**

Architectural Press

Routledge
Taylor & Francis Group

LONDON AND NEW YORK

Architectural Press is an imprint of Routledge
2 Park Square, Milton Park, Abingdon, Oxon OX14 4RN
711 Third Avenue, New York, NY 10017, USA

*Routledge is an imprint of the Taylor & Francis Group, an informa business*

*Notices*
Practitioners and researchers must always rely on their own experience and knowledge in
evaluating and using any information, methods, compounds, or experiments described
herein.

Product or corporate names may be trademarks or registered trademarks, and are used only
for identification and explanation without intent to infringe.

British  Library Cataloguing-in-Publication Data
A  catalogue record for this book is available from the British Library

Library  of Congress Cataloging-in-Publication Data
A  catalog record for this book is available from the Library of Congress

ISBN 13: 978-0-08-096535-2 (pbk)

Typeset  by MPS Limited, a Macmillan Company, Chennai, India

# Contents

## Civic and Leisure

## Schools

## Education

## Health

## Residential

## Housing

## Offices

## Transport

# Preface

Since April 2004 working details from contemporary building projects have been published in Building Design. This book collates 35 of these studies as a continuation of the series begun by *Architecture In Detail*. In 2006, The Concrete Centre also began commissioning working detail features for their journal *Concrete Quarterly*, which promotes innovative use of concrete in construction. Five of these are included in this volume. In response to feedback received from the first book, the projects have been classified according to the type of building. There is also an index matrix at the back so the projects can be searched by criteria such as structural system, budget or whether work to a listed building was involved.

The purpose of the details is not to provide ready-made solutions but to add to the resource base and stimulate thought. There are aspects of them all that can be criticised. Although the principles applied in solving different problems may be similar, the final details are always specific to the conditions of the particular situation. The projects are presented here in the belief that, by offering a tentative, analogous solution that can then be criticised, we gain insight into our own problem and find fresh strands of thought to follow.

I would like to thank all the architects, engineers and photographers who have allowed their work to be reproduced in this book. A full list of credits for each project is given at the end.

# About the author

Graham Bizley studied architecture at Bath University and ESTAB in Barcelona. He has worked for various architects in the UK, India and Zimbabwe. In 2005, he set up Prewett Bizley Architects with Robert Prewett. He is a regular contributor to Building Design and since 2004 has prepared a regular working detail feature under the title 'In Detail'. A first volume of *Architecture In Detail* was published by the Architectural Press in 2007.

# Thoughts on Construction

It is difficult to identify in the work of one's own time what will be viewed in the future as significant development and what will be forgotten or dismissed. What is lauded is often that which is novel and novelty immediately invites suspicion that an achievement has not been sufficiently interrogated to merit such attention. The buildings in this book have not yet stood the test of time, but rather than try to be judgmental my intention is to attempt to understand the conditions and ideas that make them the way they are. By their inclusion here all the buildings can be assumed to exhibit some innovation or at least to have some design ambition to distinguish them from the norm. To get beyond personal prejudice and establish a critical view it is necessary to see them in the context of their creation and to take a longer view of the trends prevalent when they were made.

Architecture's basic functions of providing shelter from the elements, an ergonomic environment and emotional stimulation have not changed. The ways in which they can be accomplished however are constantly evolving and the balance between the different aims shifts in response to technological, cultural, political and economic trends. An analysis of construction or detailing inevitably becomes a wider discussion because choices of materials and techniques are bound up with more complex issues.

In many fields, not least in politics, the latter half of the 20th Century saw a gradual retreat from dogmatic positions towards more inclusive viewpoints that take in the nuanced, often contradictory nature of situations. Grand philosophical ideas no longer seem credible as all-encompassing solutions. We no longer believe that technology alone will solve our problems or that one lifestyle or belief is objectively superior to another. In architecture a truce has been drawn in the tedious conflict over style that dominated debate in the 1970s and 1980s. The city is appreciated as a dynamic patchwork of diverse, interrelated communities where a variety of architectural expression is desirable to express individuality or collective identity. Meanwhile we find ourselves drawn together by the ever more urgent need to use resources more carefully and reduce the energy demand of our buildings.

Public interest in architecture has never been so high. The Sterling Prize is shown on prime-time TV and architects no longer struggle to persuade unwilling clients to choose modern over traditional design. Public buildings such as Tate Modern, Walsall Art Gallery or the Scottish Parliament have demonstrated the capability of innovative design to make awe-inspiring and accessible civic spaces. In the process materials such as concrete and steel, for so long associated in the public perception with drab post-war housing estates or industrial sheds have been rehabilitated as symbols of urban sophistication. Grand Designs and numerous makeover shows have empowered ordinary home owners to use modern design as a way of improving their quality of life, turning the natural tendency to project individuality and aspiration through the home into a consumer leisure activity.

While public interest in design must be a good thing, the media's obsession with novelty encourages the view that architecture has to be new or radical to be interesting. The day-to-day work of most architects who struggle with limited means to create a well planned environment, appropriate for its use and specific to its users is devalued by the emphasis on visual appearance. Rather than the traditional role as a team leader with a strategic overview of a project the architect is increasingly pushed to one of two extremes,

occasionally that of the figurehead providing a glamorous front for the project or that of the technician merely making sure it complies with the various rules and regulations. In the commercial environment the architect may only be given liberty where it is perceived design will add financial value. In public and commercial projects procurement systems often severely restrict the influence of the architect who is seen as a cause of risk and expensive design 'changes'. The role of the architect has been undermined by a loss of faith in their ability to manage cost and time, responsibility for which is often passed to project managers or contractors. To satisfy clients' demands for proven performance to eliminate risk architects are likely to become increasingly specialised in more technical roles. The split in the profession between building technicians and so-called 'design architects' is likely to widen further.

All but five of the buildings in this book are in the UK and only three were designed by architects based outside the UK. Comparing these examples with the projects that attract most press coverage globally there would seem to be limited correlation, pointing to the widening gulf between the work of the typical practice, particularly outside large urban centres and the pre-occupations of the global architectural elite. It also suggests that there may be something specifically British about this body of work. Are these just the High Street, poor man's versions of international haute couture designer brands or is there something more distinct about them?

Globalisation is often blamed for a loss of local variation. Images of new buildings are published simultaneously around the globe and the dominance of multi-national companies in the construction industry allows the same products to be used in vastly differing situations. Such concerns are not new. John Summerson for example, writing in 1941, pointed out the same phenomenon in relation to the spread of the International style. He was dismissive of the notion that wide dissemination of ideas encourages a ubiquitous response because design is produced by individuals who, despite the effects of globalisation still have vastly different influences making up their view of the world. According to Summerson, 'Architectural change occurs as the result of the irregular and incalculable incidence of men [sic] of genius – innovators'.[1] The schools that form around them through their teaching and former employees inevitably tend to evolve on a regional basis. In one sense the emphasis on the individual neatly side-steps the issue of a national or international style. It also avoids the suggestion that regionalism is inherently conservative or parochial. Valerio Olgiati, working from the small Alpine town of Flims concurs that 'Looking at the world in an individual way is the only way to make an architecture that has character. At the same time we also have to find something general in the individual so that it is understandable in a globalised world – it has to be contradictory'.[2]

Modernism in its pure form never achieved widespread public acceptance in Britain. Those buildings that have won affection tend to exhibit a softening of the orthogonal grid, a response to context and a human scale. The Royal Festival Hall was the first post-war building to be listed grade I. As the centre-piece of the 1951 Festival of Britain it was designed as a symbol of a brighter future amongst the ruins of London. Conceptually the idea of the 'egg-in-a-box' auditorium protected from external noise by the surrounding cascades of public foyers is functional, democratic and entirely Modern but the purity of the diagram is softened by the gentle curve of the river façade, high quality materials and careful detailing. Bespoke elements such as the cast bronze door handles, Wilton carpet and timber handrails are found at the interfaces where people come into contact with the building. Between 2005 and 2007 it underwent a £117 million refurbishment to correct its poor acoustics, re-organise the foyers and introduce more commercial functions around it. The esteem in which it

*Royal Festival Hall – detail of balustrade*
*Photo: Denis Gilbert/VIEW*

*Rich Mix – new louvres on south façade*
*Photo: Morley von Sternberg*

is held is partly a function of its architecture, but also of its symbolic role as a 'people's palace' on the river, a phenomenon enhanced by an 'open foyers' policy adopted since the late 1980s that has opened up the internal spaces to the public throughout the day and evening.

Most of the projects in these pages could comfortably be grouped under a banner of neo-Modernism, where formal manipulation, colour or regional materials have been used in a way that is not purely functional to make them more 'friendly' or give them a specific relationship to their location. The Rich Mix is an arts centre that occupies a converted 1950s garment warehouse on the edge of London's east end. The original structure was unremarkable but architects Penoyre & Prasad have re-clad the concrete frame with a bank of adjustable coloured louvres on the south-facing street façade that provide both solar shading and give the institution a dynamic, contemporary identity. Inside, finishes are modest and the services are left exposed. Rich Mix proudly wears its industrial heritage, playing on associations with spaces artists often chose as studios and with the 'street' culture of the post-war urban landscape.

Historian Alan Powers points to an inherent pragmatism in English culture which is suspicious of intellectual ideas. We rely on our foreign-born architects for free-forms and expressionism. When British architects break from the orthogonal it is with the firm justification of engineering or the givens of the site.[3] It is certainly true that most discussions with clients hinge around cost, programme and what the end product will look like rather than architectural concepts. The idea that architecture should have a theoretical basis or could achieve any political aim has slipped off the agenda, as Alejandro Zaera-Polo pointed out in a recent interview. 'Our generation of architects has not been politically active', he said. 'Architects' traditional role as visionaries and ideologists has become redundant as the shear speed of change overtakes their capacity to represent politics ideologically. We have been consumed in the means of production and in simply making buildings'.[4] The contemporary city is built and run by corporations for multi-national shareholders' interests and the opportunity for representation of any off-message political ideal is limited. Politics itself has shifted away from a polarised left-right debate to a more nimble, issue-based discussion capable of engaging with independent individuals across a field of disparate issues.

Openness and accessibility, by-words in the political arena in the new-labour years have found a literal expression in the use of glass and voluminous entrance halls in public buildings. Middlesbrough's Institute of Modern Art for example addresses a new public square with a wall of glass in front of a dramatically lit, fractured stone wall, a powerful gesture visible from across the square. On its other three sides the building presents unarticulated walls of white render, giving quite the opposite message, suggesting cheapness and alienation. The primary idea is a theatrical gesture rather than a material or constructional idea about the making of the building itself. Manchester's Civil Justice Centre achieves a better resolved relationship to the public realm in the round with a 12-storey atrium allowing views from the street of people moving around inside. Different cladding treatments are used to articulate distinct volumetric elements of the building so it reads as a sculptural assembly of forms with a tension between them. All you can see from outside in either example, however, are the circulation areas and a reception desk. Security and privacy concerns mean that the activities that are the building's purpose remain hidden. Transparency is used as a metaphor for democracy offering a sense of inclusion while actually establishing a tightly controlled series of barriers.

*Manchester Civil Justice Centre*
*Photo: Tim Griffith*

Whatever their flaws, both these buildings suggest a strong belief in a public role for architecture to represent the values of society and to influence people's feelings about its institutions. For such gestures to succeed the emotions they evoke must correlate with people's feelings about those institutions, or at least express an ideal which is not beyond the realms of belief. In the 20th Century a crisis arose in the representational image of public buildings because the associations of a classical language no longer represented the mood of a more socially mobile public in a post-colonial age of mass communication, yet the functionalist alternatives often lacked the familiar imagery, spatial drama and crafted detail to inspire civic pride. As the population becomes more diverse, both ethnically and culturally, it becomes more difficult to provide something that will hold meaning for a wide domain of people. If an institution is to seek public attention with monumentality then there must be sufficient shared belief in the ideas it is vaunting or the gesture will just seem pompous.

*Angel of the North, Gateshead*

Outside the sphere of architecture a public art project that has found a place in the public affection is the Angel of the North, a 20 m high steel figure by the sculptor Anthony Gormley which overlooks the A1 near Gateshead. Gormley uses the human form, stripped of all identifying features so that it might relate to anyone, and invites a very direct interaction with the work so that the individual can feel a personal relationship with it. The monumentality it achieves through its scale and form is enhanced by the use of a single material, Corten steel, which has a timeless quality in its surface variation and the way it weathers.

A building has much more complicated functional demands upon it so such simple gestures are seldom possible. The building envelope, and more particularly the surface are where much recent architectural innovation has been focused. The St John's Therapy Centre in Wandsworth is clad in a single material, timber veneered panels which give it the distinctive identity of a special object like a chestnut or a violin. Bigger elements of the programme were deliberately located at the front of the building so that their large windows could give a civic scale to that elevation, an effect enhanced by an integrated, super-graphic sign at roof level. It achieves a civic presence on the street by its materiality and scale. Apart from the joints between the panels the detailing of construction is not expressed, emphasising the sense of the building as a whole rather than an assembly of parts.

*St John's Therapy Centre – south elevation*
*Photo: Nick Kane*

The 50 mm thick steel ribs and visible welds on the Angel of the North express the taut equilibrium between the structural endeavours of man and the forces of nature. The joints in the cladding of the Therapy Centre are suppressed and instead the thinness of the veneer is expressed by mounting the windows flush with the cladding and introducing a different coloured material where there are recesses. Long horizontal openings suggest structural daring although no elements of structure are directly visible. Without a visible structure the fabric can only communicate formal and sculptural articulation. With a design and build contract procured by a public body there is limited room for manoeuvre. The architects, Buschow Henley have understood well that attention has to be focused on a few strong moves that are robust enough to withstand the limitations of the budget.

The Manchester Civil Justice Centre achieves its monumentality through structural and compositional daring without reference to traditional symbols, achieving a presence in the city appropriate to its programme through sheer size. The programme has been manipulated to exaggerate the proportions of the building using different materials for the vertical elements containing circulation areas and the courtrooms. The glazing support metalwork and the joints between adjacent cladding elements are visible, but the articulation is at such a relatively small scale that it does not distract from the bigger

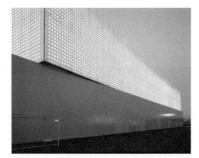

*Multi-purpose hall, Aurillac
Photo: Brisac Gonzales Architects*

*1 Coleman St, London
Photo: Hélène Binet*

*Midland Bank, Cheapside, London*

gestures. Holes in the cladding panels and compositions of colour behind the glass introduce further human scale elements that work as patterns on the larger surfaces.

A building that does achieve a civic identity through a singular gesture is the multi-purpose hall at Aurillac in France. It is clad in a ribbon of precast concrete panels backlit by LED lights. The volume is too big to express its function in a literal sense and relieved of the duty of relating to any neighbours by its edge of town location, the façades have been turned into a giant light sculpture. Whereas traditional articulation fails to deal with the scale of such a structure the lights can be programmed to change colour and pattern to create effects that wrap around the entire building. The construction supporting the ribbon is functional and unimportant as it is not visible to observers of the effect it is sustaining.

In the corporate world innovative architecture has frequently been used as a symbol of dynamic and positive thinking to set a company apart from its rivals. The prime agenda of the developer is to maximise lettable area so the domain of architectural expression is often limited to the building envelope, but the high budgets involved put these envelopes at the forefront of façade technology. 1 Coleman Street in the City of London is an interesting example where a standard steel frame has been clad in a system of precast concrete elements and identical windows. The building has a curved form and the floors bulge out in section. By faceting the precast elements and alternating the angles of the windows between floors an illusion of movement is created by the reflections as one moves around the building, an effect enhanced further by cladding the top floor in polished stainless steel. What is actually quite a simple, repetitive system has been turned into something more engaging by adding a virtual element to the way it is perceived.

It is worth comparing 1 Coleman Street with the nearby Midland Bank building designed by Edwin Lutyens from 1924-39. Its appearance is of a classical, load-bearing stone building but it too has a steel frame and Lutyens' manipulation of the detailing creates intrigue and ambiguity in the façade. In the ground storey a Doric column base and capital are set into the rustication so that the wall can be read simultaneously as a colonnade or a wall. The proportion of these 'phantom columns' has been thickened beyond the normal Palladian proportions to give the building a more massive appearance at the base. Higher up, the wall undergoes a number of setbacks and actually tapers back in section. Each stone course is shorter than the last and there is no cornice so not only is the weight of the façade distorted but the elements by which its scale might be determined are omitted towards the top.[5] Through tricks of perspective, distortion or reflection both buildings manipulate a reading of form and scale to create effects which are more than a simple sum of their parts.

To a Modernist's eye Lutyens' cladding of a steel frame with what looks like a load-bearing masonry façade is all wrong. As Lutyens himself pointed out many Modernist buildings did not express their actual structure and were more interested in appearing to tell a clear story even if that story were not actually true. The issue of honesty in structural expression was an ideal of the Modern movement but no longer appears to be of much concern in the contemporary debate. Of the projects in this book only a few gain their architectural expression from a literal expression of their structure. Southern Cross Station in Melbourne is the clearest example, where every component and connection of the steel roof structure is on view. As it does not require a lined interior the railway station is one of the few building types suited to exposing the structure in this way. The use of a highly engineered structure as an expression of a belief in progress and technology goes back to the roots of Modernism in the 19th Century engineering structures that inspired the writing of Viollet-le-Duc.

For a number of reasons it has become increasingly difficult to build using a monolithic masonry structure. Laying brick or stonework requires skilled labour and is time-consuming as only a certain height can be built in one day. To prevent heat loss insulation is required and a cavity has to be incorporated to prevent water penetration. It is therefore cheaper and quicker to use framed construction. If brick or stone are used it is in a reduced role as an outer cladding to represent security or quality, a thin skin in front of the true structure.

*Southern Cross Station, Melbourne*
*Photo: Markus Bachmann*

This issue has been addressed in different ways in two educational buildings where higher than normal budgets have allowed the architects to build load-bearing masonry walls. Ann's Court is a new administration and residential building for Selwyn College in Cambridge. It has load-bearing cavity walls with the inner leaf taking the weight of the floors. The outer leaf is a whole brick thick, laid in Flemish bond to show its thickness which is a purely aesthetic luxury. In the ground floor arcade where thermal bridging is no longer a problem stone piers and arches carry the load of the whole wall. The building has the appearance and external detailing of a traditional brick and stone structure but to achieve this effect the overall wall thickness is 545 mm and a concrete beam is hidden in the wall above the arcade to tie the piers together. The façade appears to tell a neat story but the true version of events is slightly more complex. At Bryanston School the new science block has a load-bearing brick wall facing a central courtyard which is 1½ bricks thick with no cavity or insulation. The brick is laid in English bond, again to express the thickness of the masonry. Thermal performance has been sacrificed for the architect's desire for an honest structure. Since the time the decision was made energy conservation has become more of an ethical issue and with hindsight perhaps the priorities would have been different. Between the second floor and the roof the piers have concrete cores concealed within them to help resist wind loads and to tie down the roof.

*St Ann's Court, Selwyn College,*
*Cambridge*
*Photo: Morley von Sternberg*

It is in no way my intention to be negative about these deceptions. The demands on buildings are in most cases far too complex to achieve a pure expression of everything that is going on. The architect's task is to create a convincing story by choosing which issues to express and which to conceal as I discussed in the introduction to Architecture in Detail Volume 1. In most buildings a hybrid approach is taken where structure is expressed if it is appropriate to the performance requirements and the architectural intent is to some extent determined on a pragmatic basis. The demands on the building envelope include supporting the floors and roof, exhibiting an appropriate external appearance, thermal insulation, air tightness, solar control, security, and contributing to an appropriate atmosphere in a range of different internal spaces. Every building could therefore be said to have a layered construction with various elements or surface treatments carrying out different roles.

*Sanger Building, Bryanston School*
*Photo: Anthony Weller*

As the level of environmental performance of buildings increases building envelopes are likely to become more complex and will have to be built to more exacting standards. If there is a single issue that unites all aspects of the construction industry it is that of reducing the energy demand of buildings, both in the embodied energy of construction and in their energy

*ARC, Hull*
*Photo: Niall McLaughlin Architects*

consumption in use. Designers and contractors alike are having to consider every decision as part of a more holistic understanding of how construction can be made less harmful to the environment. Technology is moving quickly and we cannot be sure how the balance will play out in the long term. A building that has been designed to adapt to such changes is the ARC, a movable pavilion engineered to be carbon neutral by generating the same amount of energy as it uses through renewable sources. It has a programme of events demonstrating environmental issues and will be relocated to different locations in the Humber region. Architect Niall McLaughlin has committed to a long term relationship with the project. 'Each time we'll redesign it as necessary. I'd like to think that in 20 years time it might not look remotely like this', he says.[6]

Some building envelopes incorporate elements that can be adjusted by the occupier to affect the performance of the envelope. The louvres on the south façade of the Rich Mix are controlled manually in banks of twelve from inside each room to control how much direct sunlight reaches the glazing. The east, south and west courtyard elevations of the EMV Social Housing in Vallecas have external balconies with sliding screens which can be moved by each resident to block direct sunlight. In both cases the choices made by different occupiers creates a dynamic pattern that adds interest and human scale to the elevations. Low-technology solutions like these are robust as they do not rely on electronic control or complex maintenance regimes. Most importantly they allow the individual some control over their environment.

For a number of years 'green' architecture had a certain look characterised by clip-on gadgets such as solar panels and ventilation cowls. As low-energy construction is being adopted more widely, integration of energy-saving measures is becoming more subtle. In terms of saving energy the most effective measures can be invisible. The concrete used for the office building at 1 Coleman Street has a 50% recycled content by mass compared to a typical level in a commercial building of 5%. The steel used for the reinforcement was made from 100% scrap metal, the basement and upper floor slabs incorporate 100% secondary coarse aggregate in the form of china clay stent and the aggregate in the precast elements is 100% from secondary sources (by-products of other extractive industries).

Experimentation in low-energy and low-carbon construction is being led by private home owners who are prepared to use their own money to push the available technology and test new ideas. The Focus House in north London is built using a solid timber panel system that, rather than causing carbon emissions, has extracted and stored approximately 30 tonnes of carbon from the atmosphere. It has a very high level of air-tightness and uses a mechanical ventilation system with heat recovery to supply fresh air. For a given expenditure increasing the amount of insulation in the building envelope and making the construction air-tight can save a much greater amount of energy than can currently be produced by on-site energy generation at the level of the individual dwelling.

In contrast the house building industry and landlords are reluctant to deviate from tried and tested methods unless they can see a direct financial advantage. A number of experimental houses have been built at the Building Research Establishment (BRE) in Watford. In 2008 Barratt completed a house there which is claimed to be the first house in the country built by a volume house builder to achieve level 6 under the Code for Sustainable Homes. To achieve this level, however, the house is reliant on a bank of photo voltaic panels mounted next to it which stand in for the energy that would be supplied by a central biomass plant were the house part of a larger development.

*Focus House – solid timber panels*
*being craned into position*
*credit: Bere Architects*

The BRE has come under criticism for focusing on individual buildings rather than a holistic approach and allowing itself to be used as a marketing device by the private companies that provide the majority of its funding rather than carrying out independent scientific research.[7]

*Clay Field Housing, Elmswell*
*Photo: Riches Hawley Mikhail Architects*

Innovation in larger scale housing developments has so far been limited. Working on a one-off house contractors will not be able to get to grips with new construction techniques quickly enough to represent their actual efficiency at a larger scale or benefit from economies of scale in purchasing components and materials. Clay Field Housing at Elmswell in Suffolk is a development of 23 affordable houses and flats carried out by a housing association but part-funded by a grant from the Housing Corporation. Domestic hot water and heating are provided by a central biomass boiler and materials with low embodied energies have been used throughout. The houses are grouped in threes and clad in cedar shingles and clay render. Although they look distinctive there is no gadgetry on show. Instead their character comes from their integration with the landscape, their materials and a sectional form designed to maximise passive solar gain.

*80% House – rear elevation*

New housing only represents a small part of the UK housing stock. The replacement rate for the existing stock is less than 0.1% per annum so buildings that exist today will account for over 70% of the total building stock by the year 2050. It quickly becomes apparent that a bigger problem is what to do with the millions of existing houses that are uninsulated and poorly sealed to significantly reduce their energy loss. The 80% House is a typical Victorian terraced house in Hackney that has undergone an 'extreme' environmental refurbishment, carried out by my office. Using the maximum possible carbon reduction as the primary criteria it was found that the best use of the available budget was to use as much high-performance insulation as possible and make the house air-tight. The additional embodied energy of the insulation is soon offset by its better performance in use. The refurbishment has achieved an 80% reduction in carbon emission from the house and it is calculated that the carbon emitted in the refurbishment work will be offset after six years. Refurbishment of existing houses is not cheap and is complicated by the fact that every house is different. Some are listed or, like the 80% House are in conservation areas where there are planning restrictions on what can be done. In some areas the cost of refurbishment will be hard to balance with what the house is worth so research must concentrate on finding mass-market, low cost ways of improving energy performance. Workers will have to learn new skills as the industry gets to grips with the necessary techniques for low carbon construction. The challenge is to see how quickly low-carbon construction can become the norm and will simply be known as construction.

Sixteen of the projects in this book are either extensions or incorporate elements of existing buildings. The Siobhan Davies Dance Centre in London and the North Wall Arts Centre in Oxford are both built on top of Victorian buildings. Newlyn Art Gallery in Cornwall and The Bluecoat in Liverpool are both extensions to important listed buildings. Each of these examples is characterised by respect for the existing building and a modest but distinctive expression of the new work. There is evidence of a deeper investigation and understanding of the urban fabric than has happened in the past and a resistance to approaches that ignore context. At Newlyn the old and new buildings are pulled apart and articulated with a glazed slot but the other three exhibit a more relaxed attitude that expresses a

*Vernon Street offices*
*Photo: Terry Pawson Architects*

*Sean O'Casey Community Centre,*
*Dublin*
*Photo: Terry Pawson Architects*

*Herringbone Houses, Wandsworth*
*Photo: Cristobal Palmer*

confidence in the architect's ability to knit the old and new together to their mutual benefit.

This approach has been taken to a magnificent extreme in one of the most daring restoration projects undertaken since the Second World War. The Neues Museum was one of five institutions on Berlin's Museum Island, now a world heritage site. It lay in ruins for 50 years after being destroyed by allied bombing. David Chipperfield Architects and Julian Harrap Architects have painstakingly constructed a new museum through a combination of repair, refurbishment, reconstruction and new building work. The symbolic significance of the project has been immense in Germany, particularly as it was carried out by British architects.

It must be said that in most of these cases the existing building has been preserved for its historical importance rather than as an energy saving measure. The fact that VAT (currently 17.5%) is payable on refurbishment but not on new-build work encourages destruction of perfectly serviceable structures. If the government is serious about reducing the embodied energy of construction, not to say the waste it generates, then the rates of VAT must be equalised.

Perhaps one reason why low-carbon construction has not become a general concern until recently is due to preconceptions about its aesthetic. Style-conscious architects and clients alike have been more interested in what a building looks like than how it performs and prefer to spend money on things they can see rather than on hidden insulation. A continuing preference for clean lines and light, open-plan spaces is evident in contemporary architecture, although the first decade of the 21st Century has also seen a resurgence of interest in decoration and ornament. The Vernon Street offices in Kensington fall firmly the first camp, with flush mounted glazing, invisible means of fixing, and suppression of detail. Rather than articulating the traditional elements of roof, walls and windows the architectural expression comes from the cubist idea of a composition of abstract forms. The heights and volumes relate to those of its neighbours but otherwise the crisp, smooth volumes make a stark contrast with the Victorian and Edwardian brick buildings near-by.

From a distance the volumes of the Vernon Street offices appear homogenous but on closer inspection a subtle grain is apparent due to the surface quality of the material and the fact that the walls are made up of multiple elements. The proportions of the precast concrete pieces are long and squat, emphasising horizontality and the surfaces have been acid-etched to expose the aggregate, making them matt with a slight texture. The overall effect is subtle but does give some articulation to the surface. It would be fanciful to call this decoration, but how far can the necessary elements be manipulated before it becomes decoration?

Two buildings on which the boundaries have been pushed a little further are the Sean O'Casey Community Centre in Dublin and the Herringbone Houses in south London. Like the Vernon Street offices both are composed of quite abstract forms, detailed to avoid expression of traditional elements like copings and architraves. The Community Centre has concrete walls, cast in-situ with a vertically corrugated surface. The corrugations give texture but also make the building more abstract as they do not reveal where the joints were in the materials that made up the formwork. The Herringbone Houses are clad in ipe, a hardwood which can be left unsealed to fade to a silvery-grey colour. The individual pieces of timber have been cut to identical sizes and fixed in a herringbone pattern. The horizontal bands catch the light

*Islington Square housing, Manchester*
*Photo: Tim Soar*

*Regent's Park Open Air Theatre –*
*female wash area*

*Maryland Early Years Centre*
*Photo: Morley von Sternberg*

differently, introducing another pattern the scale of which is bigger than the individual building components.

A more extreme approach is shown by a development of 23 social housing units at Islington Square in Manchester. Except for their front elevations the houses are timber-framed with flat roofs and are finished in white render. The front elevations are load-bearing brick cavity walls but the form of the façade does not follow that of the houses behind. The parapet steps and swoops to form a series of Dutch style gables with occasional openings revealing the sky behind like a stage set. Several colours of brick have been used in a large scale graphic pattern that works to tie the whole terrace together but also makes each house distinct by the way the pattern falls across its façade. Balconies, window boxes and brackets for hanging baskets have been made from timber cut in stylised shapes to evoke ideas of domesticity in an unashamedly kitsch way. FAT's design was chosen by the residents in a competition which suggests they are offering something that was lacking in the other proposals.

The most radical aspect of the New Islington development is its use of decoration in a way that goes beyond surface modulation into a realm of whimsical expression, but not without purpose. Form is certainly not following function but the form is serving a function, that of engaging with the residents and passers-by in a way that is playful but also serious.

Many architects are reticent about using colour unless it is the natural colour of a material. Green is a crucial part of the identity of the Information Commons building in Sheffield for example, but the colour comes from the weathered copper cladding rather than a treatment applied to the surface. Using a material's natural patina as the surface finish is very sensible as it will not require any maintenance whereas a painted or artificially coloured surface will deteriorate and fade over time.

In my office's design for the toilets at the Regent's Park Open Air Theatre we used colour to create an atmosphere one would not expect in such a prosaic facility. The ceiling, walls and doors are made from different timbers and plywoods. The floor is a poured red resin and in the female wash area the ceiling is painted a glossy pink. On one side the facilities are open to external gardens so the spaces also borrow greens from the plants and pinks and blues from the evening sky. Colour here has been used as part of a palette of materials and textures to build up richness and warmth.

In two projects applied colour has been used in a more decorative way to modulate the surface and add another level of interest. The Bellingham Gateway building in south London houses a nursery, sports and community facilities. It is clad in translucent polycarbonate behind which some of the plywood sheathing has been painted in yellow, pink and green. The effect is slight and not always apparent in certain lights, but the uncertainty creates a level of intrigue a more obvious scheme would not have. The Maryland Early Years Centre is also clad in translucent polycarbonate but here the colour comes from the material itself. Two colours are used and there is no strong logic to where the transition occurs between them. The choice does not articulate a particular volume or component, it is simply a playful gesture.

It has become common in façade design to use multiple colours for repetitive components within a single system like the multi-coloured louvres on the Rich Mix or the brickwork pattern at New Islington. There is still a line however which has not been crossed in any of the examples here. Colour is always used within the confines of a particular building element like the brick wall at New Islington or a component like the copper cladding on the

Information Commons building. A pattern of colour never crosses from say a wall to a roof and a change in colour never occurs in the middle of a cladding panel. A few architects have bucked the trend, such as Surface Architects in their Centre for Film & Media at Birkbeck College but these are interiors where the colour has been applied on site as paint and does not have to resist the elements. As well as reflecting architects' adherence to an ingrained decorum the reasons for this may be partly practical. Production processes make it much more expensive to have bespoke components with different colour patterns and the systems used for walls have different characteristics than those used for roofs. The performance requirements of the building envelope make it costly and risky to deviate from the available systems.

Some degree of surface articulation is inevitable in any building as there will always be joints between components or different materials and all materials have their own qualities which are affected by how the surface is treated and finished. The modulation of surface is an unavoidable issue and one that has a prominent effect on the appearance of the building so there must be a positive strategy for its expression.

A strong desire has been evident amongst certain architects to break the constraints of the traditional building elements by making the envelope into a continuous surface. Although there are no examples in this book it is one of the most powerful trends of recent years and presents a fundamental challenge to the construction industry and to our preconceptions about how buildings are made. Built examples would include the Phaeno Science Centre in Wolfsburg by Zaha Hadid and the Selfridges department store in Birmingham by Future Systems. In these projects technology is being pushed to bridge the gap between the idea of an abstract entity with no relation or association with other objects and the conventional demands on a building.

*Phaeno Science Centre, Wolfsburg*

Self-compacting concrete was used extensively in the construction of the Phaeno because it can be used to make complicated shapes in single pours without the need for vibration. The construction joints in the concrete are deliberately mis-aligned with changes in geometry to enhance the sense of the building as a singular entity and to express its dynamic form. In comparison, if we look at the Information Commons building in Sheffield, all the construction joints in the concrete, the glazing mullions and the joints in the copper cladding can be seen to align with one another. The copper cladding wraps around corners and under soffits but the obsessive adherence to the rigour of the grid makes for a much more static composition.

*Information Commons Building,
Sheffield
Photo: Hufton & Crow*

Hadid describes her work as a continuation of 'the incomplete project of Modernism',[8] in the sense that Modernism was an attempt to express in built form the advances in technology that were occurring in the 20th Century. 3-dimensional computer modelling software is crucial to such experimentation but Hadid uses these techniques in conjunction with hand drawing and physical modelling to help maintain control of the process. Technology is merely a tool in the drive for formal invention.

The buildings produced in this way may well let us experience spaces which are unfamiliar and exciting but it is hard to see how the advances made might usefully be applied in the wider industry struggling with the more pressing issues of cost and time. In 1998 the Construction Task Force, led by John Egan produced a report called Rethinking Construction which encouraged the industry to make radical changes to the processes through which it delivers projects. The report made a comparison with the car industry where standardisation and pre-assembly are critical to achieving efficiency and quality. The construction industry has finally taken up this challenge with some enthusiasm in a number of projects, particularly in the housing sector. Complete pre-fabrication of houses is too restrictive in terms of transportation and the vast differences in specific site conditions and occupants to which they would have to be applicable. Instead it has proved efficient to prefabricate certain elements, particularly where wet-trades can be eliminated. If the building can be erected and made weather-tight quickly then work can commence on the internal fit-out at the same time as the external cladding is being applied.

Timber construction affords particular advantages in the UK climate and has the advantage that carbon is captured in the wood so offsetting the carbon footprint of the development. The Focus House in north London was built using a solid laminated timber panel system which is estimated to have locked up 42 tonnes of carbon. Each panel was precisely cut directly from the electronic drawing files by a CNC cutter and erected in a few days on site. For the Maryland Early Years Centre the walls and floors were fabricated offsite as timber framed panels with sheathing and insulation already in place.

Prefabrication works most efficiently where there is repetition which, on irregular urban sites or sloping ground is often difficult to achieve. Computer controlled fabrication machinery is making bespoke or irregular components easier to make but such systems need to be designed at an early stage of the project. Clients are usually reluctant to commit to a certain system prior to tender as it may restrict the number of contractors willing to bid for the work and hence the pricing will be less competitive. Over the past decade a huge variety of systems, materials and techniques have been tried out and no dominant approach has emerged. Whatever cost advantages it might have there is a public revulsion to the idea of standardisation in the built environment. The construction industry needs the skills to take advantage of prefabrication and standardisation where they are appropriate but also the flexibility to respond to the specific requirements of each building.

When modern design began to regain popularity in the UK in the mid-1990s high quality materials were an important factor in its acceptance. Projects like David Chipperfield's shop interior for Issey Miyake (1985) which used veined white marble and wide timber floorboards to make a rich, sophisticated environment, showed how modern design could be seductive and desirable rather than drab and functional. The work of Swiss architects like Peter Zumthor and Herzog & DeMeuron illustrated what can be achieved in a country which still has a highly skilled, craft-based construction industry. In popular culture the materials of Modernism were initially appropriated as a backdrop of gritty realism in film or for aspiring bands to express both alienation from society and a rebellious ability to survive in the aggressive post-war urban landscape. Art galleries such as the Lisson and nightclubs like the Hacienda recreated the atmosphere of the found industrial spaces used by artists as studios or where illegal raves took place. Since the late 1990s we have seen these materials, admittedly in a more bespoke, scrubbed-up state, creeping into expensive restaurants and corporate office buildings. In some cases they are there to lend an edge of cool to otherwise sanitised environments but more and more they are appreciated for their own intrinsic qualities.

*Emmaus School, Sheffield*
*Photo: DSDHA*

Very few buildings have the budget for high quality materials or for bespoke fabrication. Furthermore procurement systems for commercial or public works often restrict the materials that can be used to tried and tested products on which a guarantee is available. A division has opened up between buildings made from products or systems and those made from crafted materials. The Emmaus School in Sheffield for example has a simple palette of white rendered walls and proprietary grey aluminium-framed windows. The architects, DSDHA realised the need to make the details robust so it could be built economically without the need for highly skilled labour. The refurbishment of the Wolfson Building at Trinity College, Cambridge on

*Halligan House, St Albans*
*Photo: Steve Ambrose*

*Thermae Bath Spa – stone cladding*

*Ruthin Craft Centre – detail of concrete*
*Photo: Ioana Marinescu*

the other hand features two new glass seminar rooms suspended beneath the existing concrete structure. The quirks of the existing building and the accuracy of bespoke construction required would have made the project very labour intensive on site for both the architects and the contractors.

The character we discern in a material is intrinsically linked to the level of craft which has been devoted to it. If detailed and built with sufficient care our perception of even quite humble materials can be raised. This is the approach we took with our additions to the Open Air Theatre in Regent's Park where bespoke toilet cubicles were made from inexpensive spruce panels detailed in a way that makes the material feel more refined. A similar approach is apparent in the Halligan House in St Albans where a bespoke glazing system was made very simply using standard double glazed units silicone-bonded to a folded piece of stainless steel on the front of a timber mullion. By using the limited budget carefully, in a targeted way Simon Conder Architects have achieved a quality usually only seen in projects with a much higher budget.

Our appreciation of a material can also be affected by the appropriateness of the way it has been used. If we look at the way Bath stone has been used in the Thermae Bath Spa for example, the pieces of stone are larger than in the surrounding Georgian buildings and are stack bonded. The detailing is well resolved and crisp but the stone is reduced to the role of cladding which removes some of the qualities which make it a desirable material. The stones are all the same size so there is less natural variation between the individual pieces than in the adjoining buildings. Because the stones are stack bonded there is not the sense of them acting together is lost. In a traditional masonry wall, made up of similar but not identical pieces, we may sub-consciously perceive an analogy with the relationship between the individual and society, which in a small but comforting way invokes empathy within us.

There has been a noticeable improvement in the level of craft in certain buildings. Often where an extremely high quality has been achieved it is through the involvement of a specialist sub-contractor who has a close working relationship with the architect and contractor. This trend could be described as a new Arts and Crafts tradition where specialist manufacturing skills form an inseparable part of the architectural intent. The precast concrete elements for the office building at 1 Coleman Street for example were made by Decomo in Belgium. The means of fabrication, transportation and installation were worked up by the sub-contractor with the design team to ensure each piece was prefabricated to precisely the right size and could be installed without damaging the finish.

The surface itself has become a focus of particular attention. A subtle change in the texture, sheen or colour of the material can have a big effect on the character of the building. The Ruthin Craft Centre is a single storey building made from full-height concrete slabs that were cast flat on the ground and then tilted up into position. The concrete is pigmented a similar red to the colour of the local stone from which several prominent public buildings in the town are made. While still wet, part of the surface of each slab was rolled to give it a lined finish above dado height. The architect and contractor experimented on site until they achieved an effect they were happy with. The lines work with the visible joints between the panels and shifts in geometry to break down the scale of the walls, but crucially they add a hand-crafted element to the construction which is both specific to that building and to its function.

Richard Sennett has defined craft as 'an enduring, basic human impulse, the desire to do a job well for its own sake'.[5] As well as a self-indulgent satisfaction for the maker there is also a sense of altruism in the term, an offering of something special to the community that harbours the maker.

If the opportunity to do a job well is denied then the result is frustration. Traditionally craftsmen were held in high esteem and played a part in the rituals of a town in an almost mystical way. The tendency towards anti-elitism, suspicion of authority and a de-skilling of the workforce marginalises the knowledge of the craftsman and erodes the motivation to do something for the greater good.

There is a need in a healthy society for spiritual compensation for the alienation of people from nature and the lack of control they feel over their own destinies. Once this was the role of religion alone but we now seek it in a variety of spheres, including buildings. Wonder can be inspired by the apparent magic of a floating roof, a flying cantilever or expanses of unusual materials with no visible fixings. Magical objects carry out a crucial role in a community of arousing emotions and in focusing those emotions into a useful agent for that community. According to the philosopher Robin Collingwood, 'magical activity is a kind of dynamo supplying the mechanism of practical life with the emotional current that drives it'.[9] The scale and public presence of architecture make it a natural provider of icons, a potential symboliser of the collective will. The difficulty is that many large buildings symbolise the will of corporations rather than that of a wider society, further alienating ordinary people rather than binding them together. Projects like the Angel of the North or the refurbishment of the Neues Museum in Berlin have achieved this role and in both there is a very strong element of craft.

I suggested in the introduction to *Architecture in Detail volume 1* that the buildings we find most satisfying are those which we feel empathy, those which are tuned in to human emotions. If a building conveys joy, pathos, humour or serenity it is communicated in the making of a joint, the way mass is expressed or the manner in which a material has been treated. Perhaps to accept a building as a shared symbol we need to feel strong evidence of the human endeavour that made it and sense that the task was undertaken at least in part for the greater good.

The construction industry has gone through a questioning phase as it tries to get to grips with its inefficiencies and reducing its impact on the environment. Each generation likes to think it has an architecture of its own, one that represents its superior achievements over what went before. If it is impossible to identify a single dominant approach it must mean that some thinking has been going on and we have not completely succumbed to superficial stylistic temptations or easy answers. Perhaps that is an architecture to be proud of.

## References

1. The Mischievous Analogy by John Summerson, written in 1941 and published in Heavenly Mansions, p 211, Norton, 1963.
2. Valerio Olgiati – Architecture Today no. 200, p 28, July 2009.
3. See Britain – Modern Architectures in History by Alan Powers, Reaktion Books, 2007.
4. Alejandro Zaera-Polo (interview with the author, 8 July 2009). See also The Politics of the Envelope in Log issue 13/14 (Autumn 2008) or issue 17 (November 2008).
5. See The Details of Modern Architecture by Edward Ford, p 118, MIT Press, 1996.
6. Niall McLaughlin quoted in A lean-to to learn from by David Littlefield, Building Design, 11 March 2005.
7. See Building Design, 27 June 2008. The BRE is currently 40% publicly funded and 60% privately funded.
8. Quoted in Digital Hadid: Landscapes in Motion by Patrik Schumacher, Birkhauser, London 2004.
9. The Principles of Art by Robin Collingwood, Oxford University Press, 1938, pp. 66–69.

*Photo: Dennis Gilbert/VIEW*

# Royal Festival Hall, London

Architect: Allies & Morrison
Acoustic Consultant: Kirkegaard Associates

The Royal Festival Hall was the centrepiece of the 1951 Festival of Britain on London's South Bank. Its acoustics have always suffered from 'dryness' due to an excess of absorbent surfaces and performers found it difficult to hear themselves on stage because the hall is designed to project as much sound as possible away from the stage to reach the back of the vast 3000 seat space.

In a controversial refurbishment quite a bit of the interior has been altered. The walls around the stage have been re-angled and the plywood canopy removed to project less sound away from the stage. Almost all the surfaces have been altered to decrease their acoustic absorbency and increase the reverberation time.

Legroom in the stalls has been increased by 80 mm involving replacing the precast concrete step units that form the raked floor. The new units span between existing saw-tooth concrete beams, modified for the wider steps by breaking out or building up mass concrete on top of the beams. The existing carpet has been replaced with reclaimed teak strip flooring with vents in the risers for a displacement ventilation system.

The walls at the sides of the stalls, known as the Copenhagen walls are clad in knuckle-profiled elm strips, originally used in Copenhagen's Radiohusets Concert Hall to diffuse sound. They originally had gaps between them and were mounted on a hollow studwork wall which distorted the sound. All the timber was stripped off and the existing studwork infilled with dense plasterboard. New timber profiles were made with walnut infill strips between to seal the gaps whilst maintaining a dark shadow-like appearance.

Seats were moved to make new aisles adjacent to the Copenhagen walls with new mahogany handrails that have bronze brackets with a nickel additive to give a silver finish matching the existing handrail brackets. Where the handrail meets the existing balustrade handrail at the top of the stalls the existing mahogany handrail has been cut away and re-shaped to integrate with the new rail.

According to critics the refurbishment has dramatically improved the clarity and vibrancy of the sound.

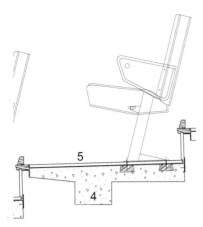

Section through typical row in stalls – 1:20

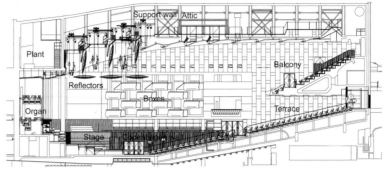

Section – 1:600

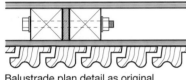

Balustrade plan detail as original (1951) – 1:5

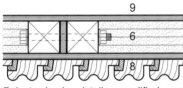

Balustrade plan detail as modified (2006) – 1:5

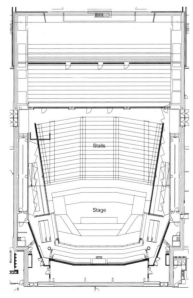

Level 4 plan – 1:800

Drawing labels:

1. Side annexe floor
Existing 160 mm reinforced concrete slab retained.
Existing 60 mm foamed slag screed retained.
Existing carpet and felt underlay removed.
65 × 15 mm tongued and grooved teak parquet floorboards adhesive bonded to existing screed.

2. Side annexe support wall
Existing 230 mm brick walls supporting concrete slab and precast floors.

3. Raked floor to stalls
840 mm deep precast concrete step units with 200 × 200 mm integral beam spanning from masonry wall at perimeter onto existing concrete saw-tooth beams.
Integral beam stopped 140 mm short of end of precast unit so that flat underside of unit bears on saw-tooth beam.
Precast units bedded on 50 mm grout with 20 mm tolerance between adjacent units.

4. Floor sub-structure
Existing 230 mm wide reinforced concrete saw-tooth beams cut back as necessary to support new precast step units.
New mass concrete built up on existing beams to increase depth of each step.

5. Floor to steps and stalls
Treads formed from 65 × 15 mm tongued and grooved reclaimed teak parquet strips screwed to timber battens cast into tops of precast concrete step units.
40 × 40 × 4 mm mild steel angle fixed to front edge of precast step unit.
75 × 25 mm reclaimed teak nosing screwed to angle from underside and grooved to take tongued ends of floorboards.
Risers formed from 65 × 15 mm tongued and grooved reclaimed teak parquet strips with ventilation slots to plenum beneath floor for displacement ventilation system.

6. Balustrade structure
Existing 50 mm wide softwood carcass fixed to concrete slab and masonry walls retained.
All existing timber cladding stripped off.

Carcass infilled with 50 mm thick plasterboard to increase density for sound absorption.

7. Lining to stalls
9 mm elm veneered plywood backing screwed and glued to carcass.
9 mm elm veneered plywood skirting, head trim and end panel screwed and glued to backing ply.

8. Timber lining
47 × 32 mm solid elm strips with curved sound-diffusing profile screwed and glued to ply backing.
18 × 18 mm solid walnut strips screwed and glued to ply backing between elm strips to give shadow effect.

9. Lining to side annexe
9 mm elm veneered plywood panel screwed and glued to carcass.

10. Balustrade capping
Existing 95 × 25 mm solid elm capping to top and end of balustrade retained, sanded and re-sealed.

11. Existing handrail
Existing 305 × 57 mm mahogany handrail retained, sanded and re-sealed.
Existing 95 × 10 mm mild steel stiffening plate set into underside of handrail.
Existing 50 × 10 mm mild steel vertical support bolted to softwood balustrade carcass.
Existing 80 × 45 mm oval profile silvered bronze sheath to vertical supports retained and polished.

12. New aisle handrail
60 × 50 mm mahogany handrail to match edge profile of existing handrail.
Silvered bronze fixing brackets with 60 × 30 mm fixing plate screwed to plywood backing on balustrade.

13. Modified existing handrail
1700 mm end section of existing 305 × 57 mm mahogany handrail cut back and new mahogany piece attached to make junction with new handrail to aisle.
50 mm wide × 20 mm deep finger groove in top of new handrail section.

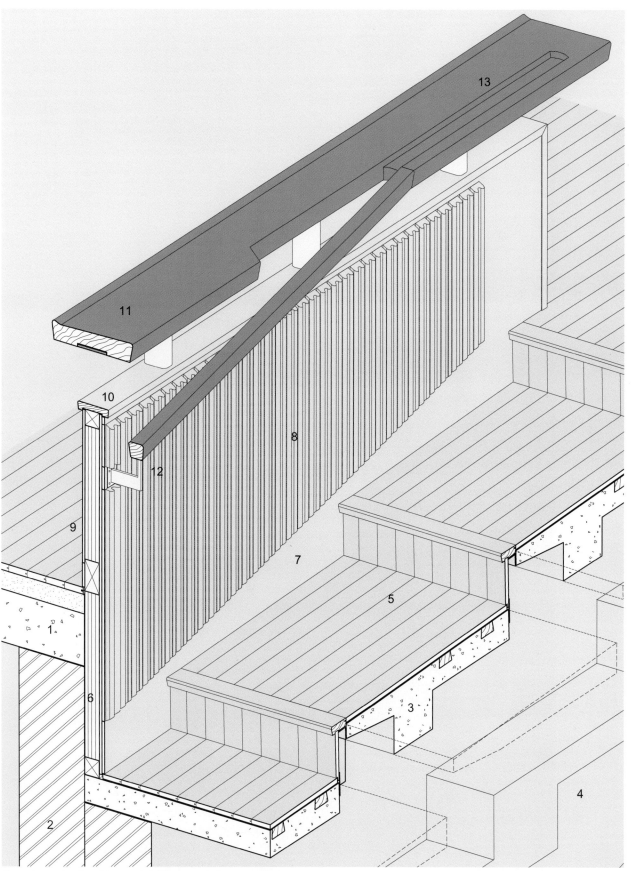

Copenhagen wall and handrail detail section at top of stalls

Photo: Ute Zscharnt

*Photo: Ute Zscharnt*

*Photo: Ute Zscharnt*

# Neues Museum, Berlin

Architect: David Chipperfield Architects
Restoration Architect: Julian Harrap Architects

Designed by Friedrich Stüler, the Neues Museum was the second of five museums to be built on Berlin's Museum Island, now a world heritage site. It was completed in 1855 but was severely damaged in the Second World War and lay derelict for many years. After five years of meticulous work, costing £210 Million, the Museum reopened in 2009.

*Photo: Ute Zscharnt*

The task was defined by the architects as one of repair rather than restoration. Stüler's interiors were highly decorated and any remaining fragments of the surviving fabric have been conserved. Large missing sections of the building have been infilled with new construction using precast concrete to distinguish it from the existing.

The most dramatic interventions inevitably occur where wartime damage was greatest such as in the Egyptian Courtyard where sculptures will be displayed in eight vitrines beneath a flood of natural light. Only two walls of the courtyard are original and the other two have been constructed in reclaimed brick to match. The glass courtyard roof has a lattice structure of concrete beams supported on ten incredibly slender 24-metre high concrete columns. A free-standing platform divides the space in two vertically sheltering a 9-metre high gallery beneath.

All the structural elements are precast concrete. The floor edge beams are L-shaped to support precast floor slabs which are left exposed to the spaces below. The columns and beams have been sandblasted so they have a matt, stone-like surface. In contrast, the floor is paved with the same concrete but with a polished finish so the stone aggregate is much more apparent.

*Photo: Christian Richters*

Services such as air supply ducts have been integrated into the new construction so as not to disturb the existing fabric. Air is supplied via bronze grilles set into the floors to rise and be extracted at roof level.

Around the platform laminated glass balustrades extend up three metres to define a more intimate space within the larger volume. The edges of the glass are protected with bronze T-sections that frame each side of the space.

The warm colour of the concrete tones with the buff brick walls, softening the light and making a serene centrepiece to the Egyptian collection.

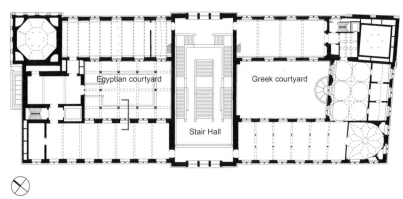

Level 2 plan – 1:1000

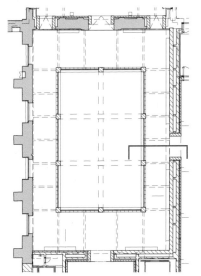

Level 1 courtyard plan – 1:400

Rendering of section through Egyptian Courtyard

**Drawing labels:**

1. Basement floor
60 mm concrete paving with sandblasted surface.
35 mm strips of mortar supporting paving.
Proprietary raised floor system with varying
height void.
Damp proof membrane turned up walls to finished
floor level at perimeter.
1250 mm thick in-situ concrete floor slab.

2. Basement wall
150 mm precast concrete wall slabs with sandblasted
surface, packed level on concrete plinth and fixed to
in-situ wall with stainless steel ties.
40 mm cavity.
In-situ cast concrete structural wall from basement to
ground level.

3. Typical column
500 × 500 mm precast concrete column with
sandblasted faces.

4. Ground floor
60 mm concrete paving with polished surface.
35 mm strips of mortar supporting paving.
Proprietary raised floor system with 250 mm
height void.
170 mm precast concrete ceiling slab sandblasted on
underside.

5. Ground floor edge beam
775 mm high × 500 mm wide × 235 mm thick
precast concrete edge beam with sandblasted faces
spanning across ground floor columns.
Thickness of beam widens to 500 mm at column
positions to form continuous bearing for columns
above.

6. New courtyard wall
380 mm (narrowing to 240 mm at high level) face brick
wall to courtyard made from reclaimed bricks, free-
standing and tied to ribs of the concrete wall with
stainless steel ties.
350 mm cavity.
300 mm in-situ concrete structural wall with
330 × 160 mm vertical ribs.
90 mm cavity.
180 mm (150 mm above picture rail level) precast
concrete wall panels with sandblasted surface fixed
to concrete wall with stainless steel ties.
Precast elements stand on the in-situ floor and on
one another.

7. Wall opening
1270 mm deep × 315 mm thick precast concrete
jamb with polished faces fixed to concrete wall with
stainless steel ties.
1270 mm deep × 370 mm thick precast concrete
lintel with polished faces supporting brickwork only
bearing on jambs and fixed to jambs with stainless
steel pins.

8. Platform beams
500 × 495 mm precast concrete beams with
sandblasted faces.
Perimeter beams have 60 × 235 mm upstand at edge
to conceal in-situ floor.

9. Platform floor
60 mm concrete paving with polished surface.
35 mm strips of mortar supporting paving.
Proprietary raised floor system with 350 mm height void.
Composite ceiling made up from 80 mm precast
concrete ceiling slabs sandblasted on underside
spanning between beams with 150 mm in-situ
concrete structural topping.
In-situ concrete perimeter upstand to support
balustrade.
500 × 490 mm precast concrete edge coping with
sandblasted faces fixed to floor with stainless steel pins.

10. New exhibition rooms (Greek Hall) at second floor
60 mm concrete paving with polished surface.
35 mm strips of mortar supporting paving.
Proprietary raised floor system with 100 mm height void.
Composite structural floor made up from 50 mm precast
concrete ceiling slabs spanning between beams with
150 mm in-situ concrete structural topping.
480 mm void for services.
Ceiling consisting of 80 mm thick sandblasted precast
concrete ceiling slabs with 120 × 150 mm ribs
spanning between beams, movable on rollers to allow
access to services later.
The gap between these elements is closed with
30 mm thick sandblasted precast concrete slabs or
panels for lights and air grilles.

11. Ground floor balustrade
1279 mm high × 49 mm thick toughened and
laminated glass panels with satin-treated surfaces,
clamped in a 245 × 99 × 15 mm thick steel channel
welded to 325 × 16 mm plate bolted to precast edge
beam.
49 × 10 mm bronze flat bar frame to three sides of
glass with 10 × 3 mm central downstand to engage
with recess in glass.

12. Platform balustrade
3400 mm high × 49 mm thick toughened and
laminated glass panels with satin-treated surfaces,
clamped in a 364 × 99 × 15 mm thick steel glazing
support channel welded to 410 × 16 mm continuous
steel plate bolted to edge of in-situ concrete upstand.
49 × 10 mm bronze flat bar frame to three sides of
glass with 10 × 3 mm central downstand to engage
with recess in glass.

13. Air supply
20 mm thick cast bronze grating.
33 × 25 mm bronze angle frame for grating fixed to
plenum channel.
Galvanised steel plenum channel supplied by
ductwork beneath raised floor.

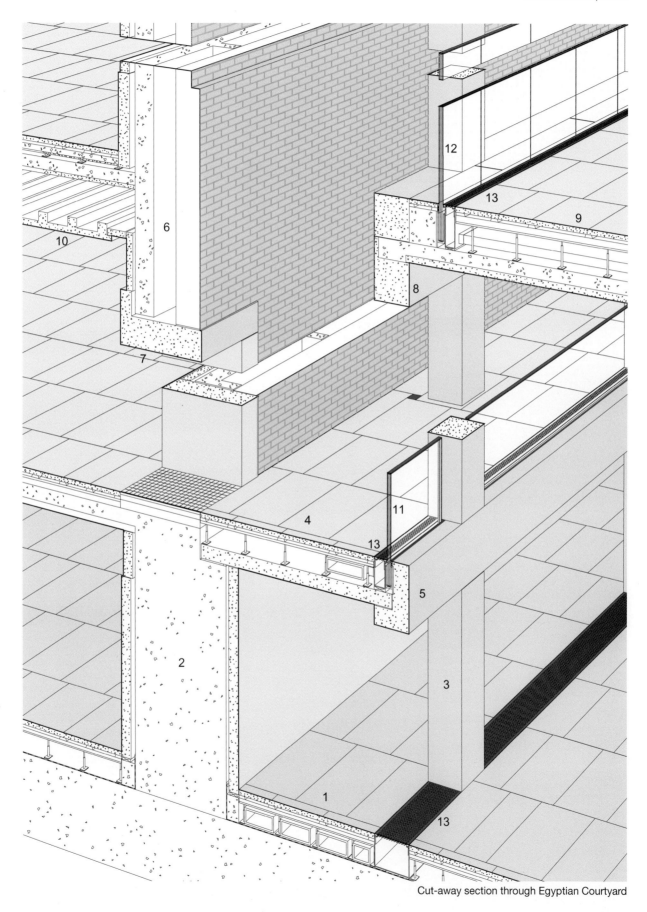

Cut-away section through Egyptian Courtyard

*Photo: Allan Williams*

*Photo: Allan Williams*

# Newlyn Art Gallery
# Cornwall

Architect: MUMA
Slate Consultant: Viv Stratton
Roofing Subcontractor: Forrester Roofing

*Photo: Allan Williams*

*Photo: Allan Williams*

*Photo: MUMA*

Newlyn Art Gallery was designed by local architect James Hicks and opened in 1895. It occupies an enviable position at the end of a public promenade overlooking Mounts Bay. MUMA's refurbishment has created a new education room and entrance in a new building at the rear facing the sea. The new extension is clad in Trevillett slate hung in the traditional Cornish manner. A 'scantle' was used to set out the battens and slates to achieve a continuously diminishing coursing without any banding. A scantle is a length of timber, usually one of the roofing battens, marked up as a gauge to locate each course.

Concrete ground beams and a concrete floor slab sit on pile foundations. The first floor is also concrete with a perimeter ring beam supported on four internal circular concrete columns that allow the ground floor shop and café to be surrounded by continuous silicone jointed glass. Above the first floor the structure is steel with timber studwork infill. The highly insulated walls have an inner and outer leaf of studwork with a 175 mm services zone in between. Both roof and walls are clad in slate and the coursing has been carefully set out to ensure the courses on the gable end line through with the courses on the roof.

The slates have been wet-laid with a minimum triple lap (3½; gauge) on the walls and a quadruple lap (4½; gauge) on the roof to resist the severe Atlantic weather. Stainless steel screws have been used to secure the slates rather than the traditional oak pegs. Hydraulic lime mortar in a 1:2 lime:sand ratio was used without any cement, which might have caused efflorescence and staining of slates. The mortar was laid in a horseshoe-shaped bed to form voids so water cannot be drawn up into the roof by capillary action.

Integrating the roof and walls into a single material idea gives the extension a scale appropriate to its civic function. From the first floor education space, a 9-metre wide strip window gives a sweeping view of sea and sky, a reminder of the qualities that attracted artists to this part of the world.

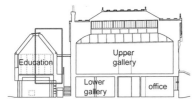

Section – 1:500

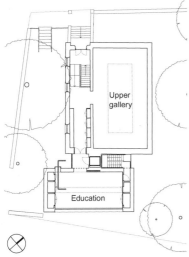

First floor plan – 1:500

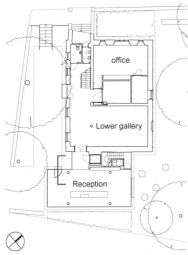

Ground floor plan – 1:500

Site location plan – 1:2000

Drawing labels:

1. Structural frame
Steel frame above first floor level with
203 × 203 mm × 46 kg UC (universal column)
primary members.
300 mm thick reinforced fair-faced concrete
first floor slab with 725 × 575 mm downstand
perimeter ring beam.
Four 300 mm diameter in-situ fair-faced
concrete columns supporting first floor.

2. Typical wall
Wet 'scantle' laid random width Trevillett slate
laid in diminishing courses.
25 × 50 mm horizontal tanalised softwood
battens spaced to suit slate coursing and fixed
to vertical battens with 25 mm stainless steel
nails.
50 × 50 mm vertical tanalised softwood battens
at 400 mm centres coinciding with studs behind
to provide continuous ventilation gap.
Breather membrane.
18 mm WBP plywood sheathing.
100 × 50 mm tanalised softwood studs at
400 mm centres with 100 mm mineral wool
insulation between.
175 mm services zone with mineral wool
packed in voids.
75 × 50 mm tanalised softwood studs at
600 mm centres with 75 mm mineral wool
insulation between.
Vapour barrier.
Two layers 12.5 mm plasterboard with skim coat
and paint finish.

3. Slate cladding
Wet 'scantle' laid random width Trevillett slate
laid in diminishing courses.
Slate to walls laid at 3.5 scantle and slates to
roof laid at 4.5 scantle.
Slates fixed with stainless steel screws through
pre-drilled holes, two holes for wall slates and
one hole for roof slates.
Hydraulic lime mortar laid in horseshoe pattern
between slate courses.

4. Corner junction
Code 4 lead soakers extending full height of
each slate and 225 mm either side of corner.
Slate edges to be mitred at corner.

5. Roof
Wet 'scantle' laid random width Trevillett slate
laid in diminishing courses.

25 × 50 mm horizontal tanalised softwood
battens spaced to suit slate coursing and fixed
to vertical battens with stainless steel screws.
50 × 50 mm vertical tanalised softwood battens
at 400 mm centres coinciding with studs behind
to provide continuous ventilation gap.
Breather membrane.
18 mm WBP plywood sheathing.
60 mm mineral wool insulation fitted over
rafters.
200 × 50 mm tanalised softwood rafters at
400 mm centres.
200 mm mineral wool between rafters.
65 mm phenolic foam-backed plasterboard with
integral vapour barrier taped and skimmed with
paint finish.

6. Roof eaves
203 × 203 mm × 46 kg UC steel eaves beam.
75 × 50 mm tanalised softwood upstand built
off top of wall to support gutter.
Code 4 lead flashing fixed to plywood below
breather membrane and lapped over gutter
lining.
Black insect mesh to cover ventilation voids.

7. Gutter
Fleece-backed reinforced PVC membrane
gutter lining.
175 × 60 mm box gutter made from 18 mm
WBP plywood.
Continuous EPDM membrane to external face
of gutter.
Zinc alloy facing (coated on the underside with
a protective layer) folded over external face
and ends of gutter with drip to line through with
slate coursing.

8. Window
Prefabricated box frame welded up from
550 mm wide × 12 mm thick mild steel plate
fixed to steel structure at jambs.
18 mm WBP plywood external sheathing on
tanalised softwood subframe.
Continuous EPDM membrane to external faces
of projecting sheathing lapped behind breather
membrane behind slates.
Folded zinc surround to front face of window.
Window frame made from 60 × 60 × 4 mm
stainless steel angles.
Window casement made from 50 × 50 × 3 mm
stainless steel box sections.

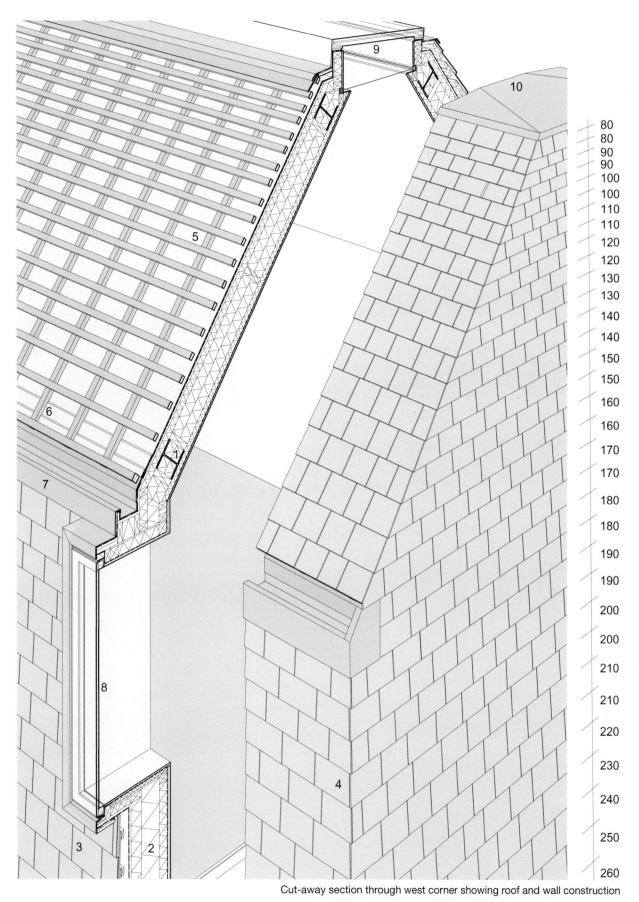

Cut-away section through west corner showing roof and wall construction

Stepped double-glazed sealed unit silcone-bonded to frame consisting of 6mm toughened outer pane, 12mm air gap, 6.4mm laminated inner pane with low-E coating.
Removable zinc-clad WBP plywood panels to head, cill and jamb external reveals.
12mm thick Corian internal cill with 20mm thick leading edge.

9. Rooflight
120 × 120 × 10mm RSA (rolled steel angle) welded to 203 × 203mm × 46kg UC steel ridge beam.
Tanalised softwood carcassing to form 9000 × 900mm rooflight opening.
Stainless steel rooflight frame.
Double-glazed sealed unit consisting of 10mm self-cleaning toughened outer pane, 16mm air gap, 12.8mm laminated inner pane with low-E coating.
Electric roller blind.

10. Ridge flashing
Zinc alloy sheet (coated on the underside with a protective layer) flashed over heads of slates with mastic seal in between and held down with zinc clips at 400mm centres.
Code 4 lead soaker behind zinc and slate junction.
Continuous EPDM waterproof membrane beneath zinc lapped over soaker.
25mm thick tanalised softwood square-edged board deck at 5 degree pitch.
50 × 50mm tanalised softwood firings at 400mm centres to provide continuous ventilation gap.
Breather membrane.
18mm WBP plywood sheathing.
Roof construction as 5.

*Photo: Philip Vile*

*Photo: Philip Vile*

*Photo: Philip Vile*

*Photo: Philip Vile*

# The North Wall Arts Centre, Oxford

Architect: Haworth Tompkins
Structural Engineer: Price & Myers

St Edwards, a boarding school in Oxford, has constructed a new Arts Centre on the edge of its grounds so that it can be used by both the pupils and the wider public. The Centre is a conglomerate of old and new elements. A Victorian swimming pool has been converted for use as a 250-seat theatre at one end, the slope in the pool itself forming the seating rake. At the other a foyer, gallery, drama studio and dance studio are housed in a new structure. The north wall itself is an old brick boundary wall to the road that has been preserved and penetrated to make the entrance.

The new building sits on concrete strip footings. A 300-mm thick reinforced concrete first floor slab spans 10 metres between a concrete beam on the north side and a load-bearing concrete blockwork collar wall on the south side.

In the drama studio, the particle board floor is fixed to isolating battens with mineral wool between to restrict noise transfer to the dance studio below. The dance studio has a floating sprung floor consisting of several layers of flexible material with a vinyl top layer.

English oak shingles have been used to clad the upper storey and roof, while the lower storey and gables are clad with narrow oak slats. A full height oak-slatted screen can be slid across a large sliding window, which looks out over the school grounds from the dance studio. Sliding MDF blackout doors are hung internally across the windows on both floors.

Two floor-to-ceiling windows light the drama studio. Aluminium angles bonded to the rear of the inner pane of the double-glazed unit carry the load of the glass via galvanised angles back to the floor and wall. The outer pane oversails the inner pane, smeared with black silicone around its perimeter on the rear to conceal the means of support. A pressed aluminium flashing seals all four edges of the window. The flashing was made in two pieces with a horizontal joint at mid-height where the two pieces interlock. The suppression of the frame makes the glass appear to float outside the oak shingle cladding.

*Photo: Haworth Tompkins*

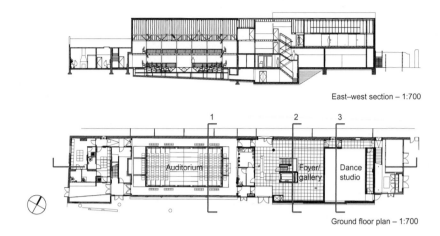

East–west section – 1:700

Ground floor plan – 1:700

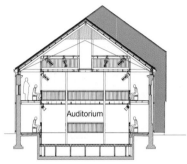

North–south section 1 through auditorium – 1:300

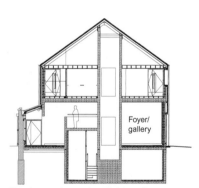

North–south section 2 through foyer – 1:300

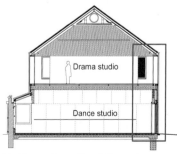

North–south section 3 through new building with detail section shown red – 1:300

Drawing labels:

**1. Foundations**
Minimum 900mm deep mass concrete strip footings.

**2. External paving**
200mm wide gravel strip along edge of building. Black tarmac with white chippings.

**3. Ground floor**
45mm composite sprung floor system with vinyl surface.
75mm floating screed with mesh reinforcement.
20mm rigid insulation.
DPM dressed up over plinth and under door frame.
235 × 38mm concrete paving cill.
150mm reinforcement concrete slab with 600 × 300mm thickening at edges.
225 × 90mm reinforced concrete plinth along south edge.
50mm blinding.
150mm compacted hardcore.

**4. First floor**
3mm sacrificial MDF top layer sealed with black emulsion paint.
Acoustic semi-sprung floor comprising two layers 18mm tongued and grooved chipboard screwed to 50mm isolation strips supported on 50 × 50mm softwood battens.
Services zone for horizontal distribution.
50mm mineral wool acoustic insulation between battens.
300mm thick reinforced concrete slab left exposed on underside.

**5. Typical ground floor wall**
210mm thick load-bearing concrete blockwork collar wall comprising two leaves 100mm blockwork tied together with stainless steel wall ties.
60mm rigid foil-faced insulation.
Prefabricated timber cladding panels fixed through insulation into blockwork with Helifix stainless steel wall ties at 400mm centres.
Panels comprise vertical sawn 40 × 15mm unsealed oak slats at 30mm centres fixed from rear with stainless steel screws to 50 × 25mm horizontal sawn oak battens at 600mm centres fixed through three layers of grey fibreglass mesh to 50 × 25mm vertical softwood battens at 400mm centres.

**6. Typical upper floor wall**
210mm thick load-bearing concrete blockwork collar wall comprising 2 leaves. 100mm blockwork tied together with stainless steel wall ties.
60mm rigid foil faced insulation.
50 × 25mm vertical softwood battens at 400mm centres fixed through insulation into blockwork with Helifix stainless steel wall ties at 400mm centres.
50 × 25mm horizontal softwood battens at 127mm centres.
Unsealed oak shingles fixed to battens with stainless steel nails.

**7. Glazed door**
210 × 460mm deep reinforced concrete beam over opening.
120mm wide PPC (polyester powder coated) aluminium door frame with two sliding aluminium-framed glass doors with double-glazed sealed units.
150mm deep × 2mm PPC folded aluminium flashing with extruded polystyrene insulation bonded to inside screwed to blockwork and concrete beam.

**8. External sliding timber screen**
Painted galvanised steel door frame welded up from 70 × 70 × 8mm equal angles.
Galvanised steel track cast into concrete for sliding door roller.
48 × 38mm galvanised steel head restraint track bolted via brackets to continuous 100 × 100 × 10mm galvanised steel angle welded to 150 × 150 × 10mm galvanised steel angle bolted to concrete beam.
Prefabricated timber panels comprising vertical sawn 40 × 15mm oak slats at 30mm centres fixed from rear with stainless steel screws to 50 × 25mm horizontal sawn oak battens at 450mm centres fixed to 50 × 40mm vertical softwood battens at 400mm centres adhesive fixed to steel frame.

**9. Roof**
Oak shingles fixed to battens with stainless steel nails.
50 × 25mm horizontal softwood battens at 127mm centres.

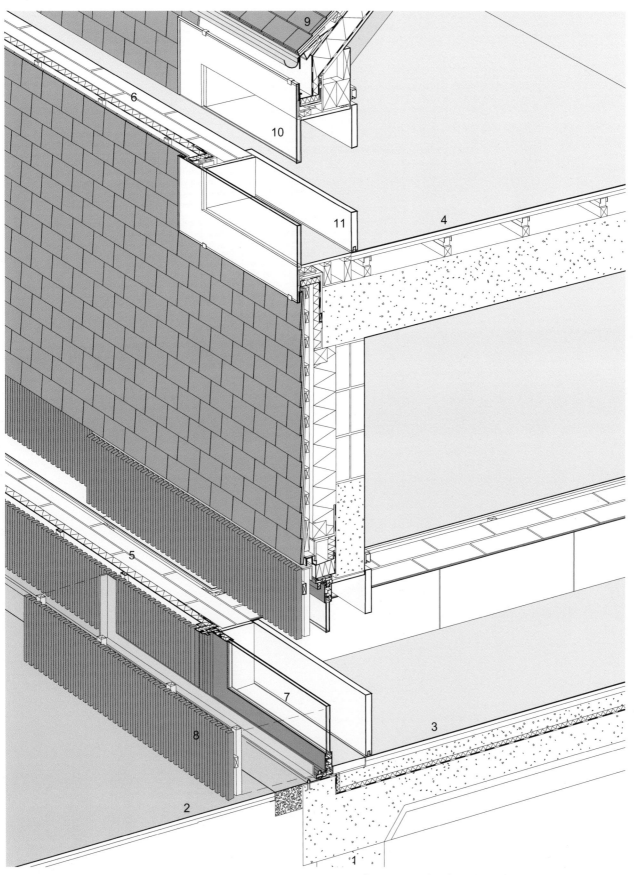

Cut-away section through south elevation of new building

50 × 25mm vertical softwood battens at 400mm centres fixed through insulation into blockwork.
Breather membrane.
105mm rigid foil faced insulation.
18mm WBP plywood deck fixed to rafters.
150 × 75mm softwood rafters at 600mm centres.

10. Window
2515mm high × 1800mm wide double-glazed sealed unit consisting of 6mm clear toughened low E inner leaf, 16mm cavity, 6mm clear toughened outer leaf with black silicone butted oversails.
20mm wide × 2mm thick PPC aluminium glazing clips at 500mm centres across top and bottom of glass.
Continuous back-to-back 127 × 51 × 6mm and 38 × 19 × 6mm mill finish aluminium angle frames silicone bonded to rear of glass.

Angle frame bolted to continuous vertical 125 × 75 × 8mm galvanised steel angles fixed to blockwork with resin anchor bolts at 500mm centres.
Continuous horizontal 200 × 150 × 12mm and 150 × 75 × 8mm galvanised steel angles fixed to first floor edge with resin anchor bolts at 500mm centres.
PPC folded 2mm aluminium flashing with pre-welded corners made in two pieces with joints in vertical lengths screwed to blockwork.
25mm extruded polystyrene insulation bonded to inside of flashing.
18mm Douglas fir faced plywood internal lining screw and plug fixed to blockwork.

11. Black-out shutters
56mm thick painted MDF solid core top-hung sliding black-out shutter on galvanised track bolted to concrete beam over opening.

*Photo: Prewett Bizley Architects*

*Photo: Kilian O'Sullivan/VIEW*

*Photo: Prewett Bizley Architects*

# Regent's Park Open Air Theatre, London

Architect: Prewett Bizley Architects
Structural Engineer: Price & Myers

Hidden amongst the trees in the grade 1 listed landscape of Regent's Park, The Open Air Theatre is a much loved London institution. During the summer months the Theatre puts on two Shakespeare plays, a musical and a children's production in a 1200 seat outdoor amphitheatre hidden amongst the trees in the picturesque park landscape.

The project includes new toilets for the theatre itself and a new bar/rehearsal area attached to the Robert Atkins Studio, a space for small performances and corporate events. The new facilities are conceived as an extension of the romantic landscape of the theatre, a series of magical grottoes and hollows surrounded by hedges and trees.

The toilet areas have red resin coated concrete floors spanning above the ground between mini-piles to minimise the impact on the roots from a nearby plane tree, a survivor from the original planting of Regent's Park in 1811. The toilets use water from a borehole in the Park for flushing and all the rainwater from the roofs is distributed via land drains into the surrounding planting.

The walls above ground are all timber studwork on a primary steel frame, sheathed with birch plywood. The roof is made from Douglas fir joists and Douglas fir faced plywood, exposed on the underside. Following the English tradition of park buildings the external elevations are clad with green stained tongued and grooved softwood boards and concealed by planting.

The cubicles themselves are made from 42 mm laminated spruce panels, opening directly onto the landscape. Internally, the walls in wet areas are clad with phenolic-faced birch plywood so they can be easily cleaned. Elsewhere the walls are clad in laminated spruce panels. The female washing area has a glossy pink painted ceiling and its own window out into the park, a boudoir amongst the trees. Over the winter period and at night it is possible to close the whole facility up with roller shutters. Using lighting and simple materials in unusual ways the new interventions extend the magical atmosphere of the performance into areas of the Theatre which are usually more functional.

*Photo: Prewett Bizley Architects*

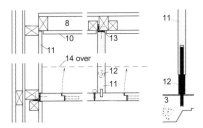

Cubicle partition plan & section
details – 1:20

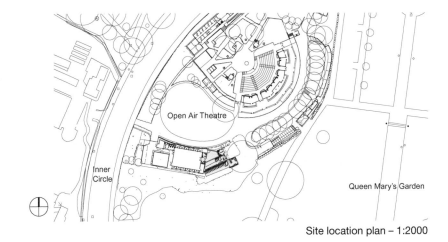

Open Air Theatre

Inner
Circle

Queen Mary's Garden

Site location plan – 1:2000

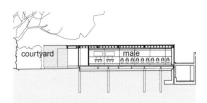

courtyard

male

East–west section – 1:500

Male Female

Bar/rehearsal

North–south section – 1:500

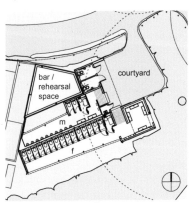

bar /
rehearsal
space

courtyard

m

f

Upper level plan – 1:500

Drawing labels:

1. Foundations
250 mm diameter reinforced concrete piles.

2. Floor structure
Galvanised UB (universal beam) frame (sizes
vary) bolted down to tops of piles.
Galvanised 150 × 75 × 10 mm RSA (rolled steel
angle) welded to tops of beams where floor
edges exposed.

3. Floor
5 mm coloured epoxy mortar finish with 95 mm
coved skirtings.
140 mm concrete slab.
Profiled galvanised steel deck with angle
upstands at edges bolted to steel frame.

4. Columns
Galvanised 80 × 80 × 5 mm SHS (square hollow
section) steel columns with painted finish.
Guide tracks for roller shutters bolted back-to-
back to columns.

5. Roof structure
Galvanised 203 × 102 mm × 23 kg UBs
(universal beam) generally.
Galvanised 200 × 90 mm PFC (parallel flange
channel) edge beams to provide flat face for
fixing roller shutter.

6. Roof
Bituminous felt waterproof membrane.
18 mm plywood screwed to firing strips.
Douglas fir firing strips screwed to tops of joists
to create fall.
225 × 50 mm Douglas fir joists at 400 mm
centres bearing on flanges of steel beams.

7. Roller shutter
Electrically operated hollow-core aluminium
roller shutters bolted to steel frame.
250 × 250 mm pressed galvanised steel box
cover.

8. Spine wall
Two parallel timber framed stud walls with air
gap in between for services and sound isolation.
Each wall made from 75 × 50 mm softwood studs
with 75 mm mineral wool insulation in between.
Joints between sheathing boards, skirting
and roof joists sealed with mastic for acoustic
insulation.

9. Timber carcass
Timber carcasses made from softwood
studwork to form frames for WCs, cisterns,
urinals and wash troughs.
Softwood painted matt black where visible
between wall panel boards.

10. Wall panels in wet areas
18 mm phenolic faced birch plywood panels
secret-fixed to studwork with lost-head nails.
18 mm phenolic faced birch plywood removable
panels secret-fixed to studwork using plastic clips.
Edges of all panels stained to match phenolic
face.
10 mm shadow gaps between panels for
tolerance and to facilitate removal.

11. Cubicle partitions
1900 mm high × 42 mm thick laminated
spruce panels cut to form doors and partitions
between cubicles, all secret-fixed.
Door frames jointed to partitions using full-
height 40 × 12 mm hardwood strip routed and
glued into both panels.

12. Partition support
310 mm long turned stainless steel rods with
brushed finish resin-bonded into concrete
floor 100 mm back from door to support each
partition (thickness 35 mm where exposed,
12 mm where embedded in panel and floor).
Partition panel drilled and dropped onto support
rod prior to rod being epoxy bonded into floor.

13. Partition brackets
40 × 40 × 3 mm galvanised steel angles
screwed to back edge of partitions for fixing
into studwork wall.

14. Female lighting trough
250 × 95 mm lighting trough made from two
42 mm spruce sides and 19 mm laminated
spruce panel bottom.
Trough secret-fixed down into cubicle partitions
to tie partitions and door frames together.
Fluorescent batten luminaires laid continuously
in trough to up-light ceiling.

15. Male lighting trough
125 × 95 mm lighting trough formed behind
plywood wall panel.
Fluorescent batten luminaires laid continuously
in trough to up-light ceiling.

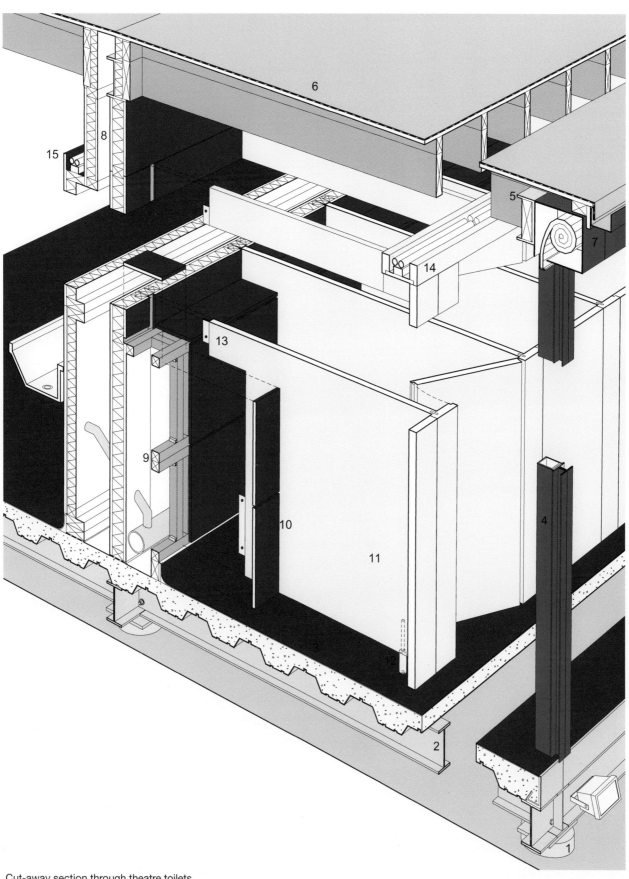

Cut-away section through theatre toilets

*Photo: Stephan Muller*

*Photo: Stephan Muller*

*Photo: Stephan Muller*

*Photo: Biq Architecten*

*Photo: Stephan Muller*

# The Bluecoat Arts Centre, Liverpool

Architects: Biq Architecten
Executive Architects: Austin-Smith Lord
Structural Engineer: Techniker

The Bluecoat Arts Centre has been refurbished and extended with a new wing housing a performance space and four galleries. The core of the complex is Bluecoat Chambers, a school building dating from 1716, which is arranged around two courtyards. The new wing replaces some nineteenth century buildings in the south-east corner of the site.

Wire-cut bricks have been used as a deliberate new texture in the historic development of the original grade 1 listed school building. Every brick is laid in the same orientation such that only stretchers are visible on the long sides and only headers are visible on the cross walls. The bricks are stack-bonded and were intended to be load bearing but the contractor chose to construct the building with a concrete frame. The cross walls above first floor level are still load bearing but the rest of the brick walls are tied to in-situ cast concrete walls that have been left exposed internally.

The 7.4 m high cloister piers have concrete cores and the brickwork contains no reinforcement. A capping beam ties the piers together at the top and they are tied back to the main building at roof level by timber rafters. Areas of wall with no concrete core have been constructed with bed joint reinforcement in every third course.

At first floor the exposed concrete walls define a performance space. Vertical recesses in the brick end walls and cast into the concrete flank walls contain metal channel track ready for mounting performance lighting. Glazed openings to the cloister below have independent inner and outer frames with laminated glass to provide acoustic separation.

The roof and upper level walls are clad in pre-patinated copper on a plywood deck. A secret gutter lined with a single-ply waterproofing membrane runs along above the cloister piers. The brown copper, bronze anodised window frames and burnt orange bricks harmonise with the existing buildings to complete the garden courtyard.

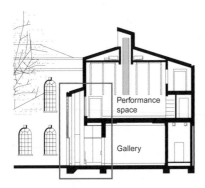

East–west section through new
building – 1:400

North–south section through east wing – 1:750

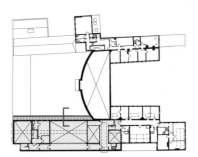

Second floor plan 1:1500

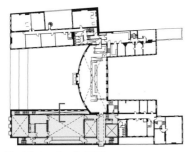

First floor plan 1:1500

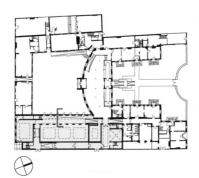

Ground floor plan (new building shaded
grey) 1:1500

Drawing labels:

1. First floor beam
1575 × 440mm exposed in-situ reinforced
concrete beam spanning between piers.

2. Ground floor internal pier
1115 × 328mm stack-bonded brickwork pier
with 8mm raked mortar joints painted white
internally.
665 × 215mm in-situ reinforced concrete
column exposed internally.

3. Internal doors
1565mm wide × 2990mm high white painted
timber doors in two pairs sections folding back
onto internal face of piers on offset floor pivots.

4. First floor
22mm thick oak board floor on 45 × 48mm
softwood battens at 360mm centres on 5mm
impact absorbing foam.
Stainless steel tray containing underfloor
heating pipes suspended between battens.
Mineral wool insulation between battens.
300mm thick in-situ reinforced concrete slab
exposed on underside in ground floor gallery.
Proprietary suspended ceiling system over
cloister gallery with sprayed rough-cast
acoustic plaster on 12.5mm plasterboard.

5. Ground floor cloister pier
1565 × 553mm stack-bonded brickwork pier
with 8mm raked mortar joints.
1115 × 215mm in-situ reinforced concrete
column concealed inside pier.
123mm cavity with 75mm partial-fill mineral
wool insulation.
Vertical DPC lapped into window frame
with mastic seal and dressed 150mm over
insulation.
25mm mineral wool insulation to jambs behind
DPC.

6. External glazing
1135mm wide × 2900mm high bronze
anodised aluminium framed glass door with
window above.

7. Glazing head
225 × 150mm in-situ reinforced concrete
capping beam spanning between piers.
Pre-oxidised copper fascia with welted seams
on geotextile layer.
18mm WBP plywood deck on 80 × 50mm
softwood carcass with 80mm rigid urethane
insulation.
225 × 150mm folded copper sheet secret
gutter prefabricated with 60mm rigid insulation
fixed to back and underside.
18mm WBP plywood soffit with weep hole slot
against fascia board.

8. Cloister roof
Pre-oxidised copper roof finish with welted
seams on geotextile layer.
18mm WBP plywood deck.
110mm rigid urethane insulation.
Vapour barrier.
18mm WBP plywood deck.
150 × 50mm treated softwood rafters at
450mm centres.
Sprayed rough-cast acoustic plaster ceiling
on two layers 12.5mm plasterboard on 30mm
battens fixed to rafters.

9. First floor external wall
120mm thick rigid urethane insulation between
treated softwood ladder frames made from
50 × 50mm battens to avoid cold bridge.
Vapour barrier.
215mm thick in-situ reinforced self-compacting
concrete wall.
122 × 56mm vertical recesses cast into
concrete containing galvanised steel channel
fixed via acoustic resilient layer at 1350mm
centres to support performance lighting.

10. Performance space internal windows
Back-to-back 100 × 60mm stainless
steel window frames to form 2085mm
high × 665mm wide acoustic glazed partition
with internal blinds.
Laminated acoustic glass in each frame.

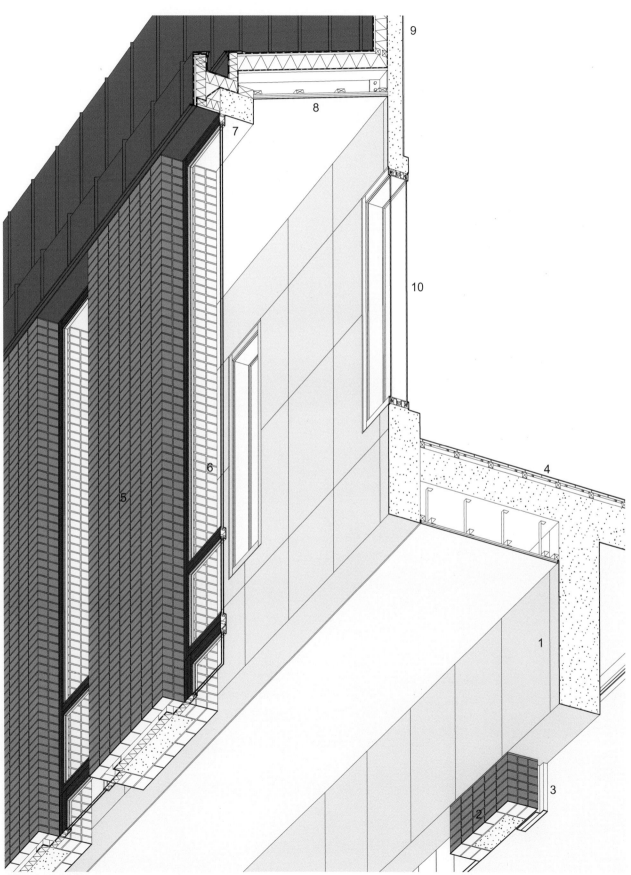

Cut-away section through main gallery and cloister

*Photo: Ioana Marinescu*

*Photo: Ioana Marinescu*

*Photo: Dewi Tannatt Lloyd*

*Photo: Ioana Marinescu*

*Photo: Sergison Bates Architects*

*Photo: Sergison Bates Architects*

# Ruthin Craft Centre, Denbighshire

Architect: Sergison Bates Architects
Structural Engineer: Greig Ling

Ruthin's new Centre for Applied Arts sits next to a roundabout between the town centre and an industrial zone of large sheds. It is a single storey building housing three galleries, six artist studios, education workshops, a tourist information gateway, a shop and a café. Most of the functions have independent entrances on to a central courtyard with a wide overhanging roof around the edge that forms an ambulatory.

The site was once a railway yard and has a 2-metre layer of gravel over its surface underlain by peat and clay. Penetrating the gravel layer would have introduced the need for piled foundations so the ground floor slab was cast as a 250 mm thick ribbed raft directly on the gravel.

The walls are load-bearing insulated concrete panels, cast flat on site and tilted up into position, which helps distribute the load evenly across the raft. The surface of the ground floor slab was power floated and coated locally with a de-bonding agent so the wall panels could be cast directly against it with 300 mm high timber upstand formwork.

A 150 mm inner structural leaf, or wythe, was cast first with a central layer of reinforcing mesh. A layer of rigid polystyrene insulation with protruding kevlar wall ties was pressed into the wet concrete surface. A 65 mm thick rust-coloured concrete outer wythe was then cast on top, the outer face of which was partially treated with a roller and scratched to give it a subtle vertical texture. The textured areas help break down the scale of the walls and introduce a hand-crafted quality poignant to the building's function. After 72 hours the panels were lifted up into the vertical position and packed level on steel shims.

Oak framed doors and windows have been set flush with the concrete walls preventing a reading of its thickness. The roof above has a timber structure with a steel beam at each ridge or valley cantilevering out beyond the walls to support the wide overhang around the courtyard. The geometry meant the softwood carcassing forming the overhang roof and soffit had to vary around the perimeter. The zinc roof rises and falls, echoing the form of the surrounding Clwydian hills.

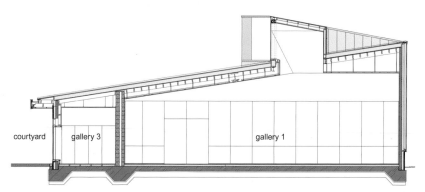

North–south section through galleries – 1:200

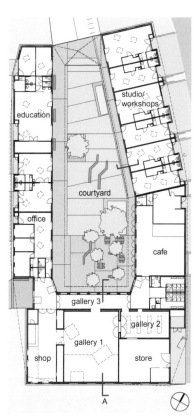

Ground floor plan – 1:800

Photograph of model

**Drawing labels:**

1. Ground floor
2.5 mm linoleum on levelling compound bonded to screed.
75 mm trowelled screed with mesh reinforcement.
50 mm rigid polystyrene insulation.
Liquid-applied DPM (damp proof membrane).
250 mm thick reinforced concrete slab.
Raft slab thickening to 800 mm at perimeter.

2. Typical wall panel
65 mm coloured concrete outer leaf tied to inner leaf with kevlar ties.
104 mm rigid polystyrene insulation.
150 mm structural reinforced concrete inner leaf.
Panels located on slab edge with stainless steel dowels, packed to correct level on steel shims and gaps packed with grout.

3. Slab edge at opening
Liquid applied DPM over slab edge.
50 mm extruded polystyrene perimeter insulation.
150 mm reinforced concrete inner leaf of panel.
Levelled in-situ concrete upstand in front of inner wall panel up to ground level.
Flexible liquid applied DPM over panel and upstand from slab up to finished floor level.

4. Timber spandrel panel
20 mm rebated oak board cladding.
Aluminium drip fixed to underside of bottom board.
130 × 50 mm softwood frame with 130 × 68 mm softwood cill member packed up off panel upstand and sealed with compressible sealant.
18 mm WBP plywood sheathing.
94 × 32 mm softwood studwork inner frame.
94 mm mineral wool insulation between studs.
18 mm plywood internal lining.

5. Timber shutter
130 × 50 mm softwood frame with 68 × 20 mm oak strip externally to form rebate for shutter.
100 × 20 mm rebated oak board cladding.
Aluminium drip fixed to underside of bottom board.
44 mm solid core.
Continuous weather seal to all sides of rebate.

6. Fixed window
130 × 32 mm vertical softwood mullions with 68 × 20 mm oak strip externally to form rebate for glazing.
Double-glazed sealed unit consisting of 4 mm outer pane, 16 mm argon filled cavity, 4 mm inner pane with low-e coating and anti-UV coating.
100 × 20 mm softwood internal glazing beads.

7. Door
130 × 50 mm softwood frame with 68 × 20 mm oak strip externally.
Double-glazed sealed unit consisting of 4 mm outer pane, 16 mm argon filled cavity, 4 mm inner pane with low-e coating and anti-UV coating.

83 × 18 mm oak door stop screwed to frame and pelleted to hide screws.
44 mm solid core door.
125 × 20 mm oak glazing beads to outer face of door.
22 × 14 mm softwood glazing beads internally.
Mill finish aluminium sheet kick plate adhesive fixed to outer face of door below glass.
Aluminium drip adhesive fixed to underside of bottom board.
100 × 15 mm proprietary threshold ramp and bottom seal.

8. Roof
Standing seam zinc sheet fixed on clips through insulation to plywood.
Breather membrane.
200 mm insulation.
Bituminous vapour barrier.
18 mm plywood deck.
250 × 50 mm softwood joists at 400 mm centres spanning between steel beams.
Steel beams spanning from ridge to eaves.
75 × 60 mm softwood battens fixed to underside of joists.
1200 × 600 × 15 mm wood wool panels screwed to battens.

9. Roof overhang
Standing seam zinc sheet fixed on clips to plywood.
Breather membrane.
18 mm plywood deck.
200 × 50 mm softwood counter-battens at 600 mm centres with firings fixed on top.
200 × 50 mm softwood joists at 600 mm centres spanning between steel eaves beam and concrete wall.
Steel eaves beam.
50 × 40 mm softwood battens fixed to underside of joists.
26 mm deep pressed zinc interlocking soffit panels secret-fixed to battens.

10. Fascia
50 × 40 mm softwood battens fixed to softwood blocking in web of steel eaves beam.
18 mm plywood fascia board.
Standing seam zinc sheet cladding fixed on clips to plywood.
Ventilation gap behind plywood with insect mesh over openings.

11. Gutter
Pressed zinc gutter supported on formed plywood and softwood battens.

12. Courtyard paving
150 mm concrete slab with jet washed finish to expose aggregate.
Two separating layers of 1200 mm gauge polythene.
Sand blinding on compacted hardcore.

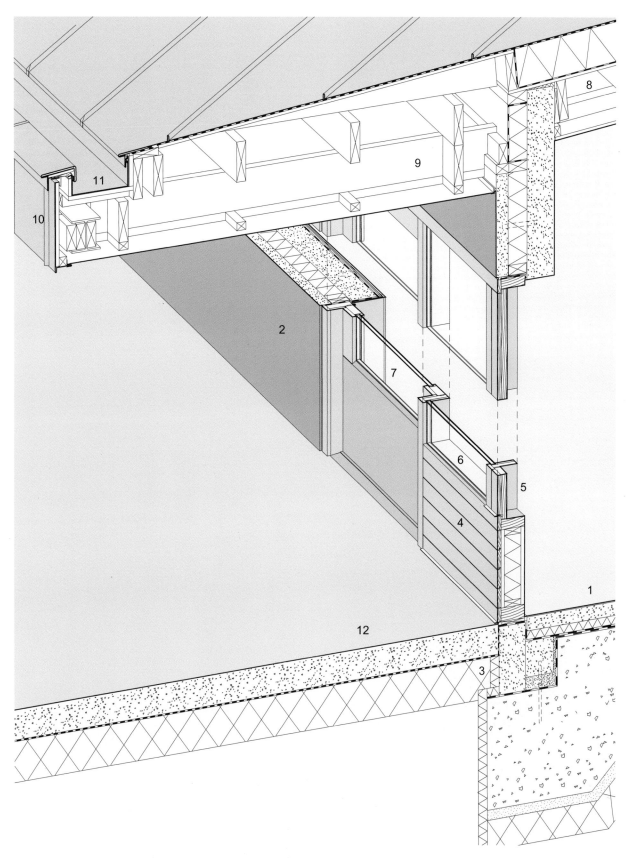

Cut-away section through roof and wall opening to courtyard

*Photo: Peter Cook/VIEW*

# Siobhan Davies Dance Centre
# Southwark, London

Architect: Sarah Wigglesworth Architects
Structural Engineer: Price & Myers
Design & Build Contractor: Design & Display Systems

*Photo: Sarah Wigglesworth Architects*

Five twisting ribbons of sky-blue GRP (glass reinforced plastic) make up the roof of a new dance studio for the Siobhan Davies Dance Company. The studio has been built on top of a London Board school building from 1898, which has been completely refurbished to make a new headquarters for the Company.

A steel structure has been built across the top of the two-storey building to provide an unobstructed 190 square metre space for rehearsal and performance. Pairs of steel portals span 11.5 metres across the space at 3.4 metre centres. One portal in the pair is a mirror image of the other about their centreline and they are bolted 500 mm apart. Steel purlins span between the portals defining the twisting shape of the roof.

The roof finish is a shell of GRP panels, made off-site by laying glass fibre sheets over a mould and coating them with resin. The final mould is itself made from GRP from an original bent plywood mould made up by joiners. A moulding process was suggested by the roof's complex two-directional curves and because each panel could be repeated several times. Ridges on the rear and a downstand on all sides mean the panels only require intermediate support at joint lines above the purlins. Once fixed in place the GRP panels were sprayed with insulating foam on the inside to deaden the noise of rainfall. Further acoustic insulation is provided by a 5 mm thick acoustic membrane laid over mineral wool. The roof soffit is finished in birch-faced plywood strips, cut in the workshop to a tapered profile and fixed to timber battens behind.

*Photo: Sarah Wigglesworth Architects*

Glazing is fixed in aluminium channels between the ribbons of the roof. Strips of fluorescent lighting are concealed above and below the rooflight windows to avoid a harsh transition from day to night. The billowing roof achieves the client's apparently opposing desires for an introspective space in which to dance under the sky.

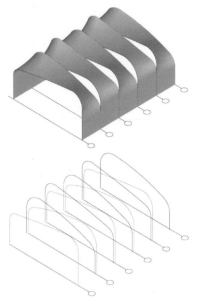

Diagrams showing roof setting
out – NTS

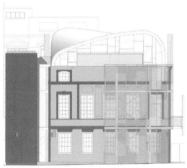

East elevation – 1:400

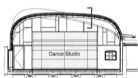

Dance studio section – 1:400

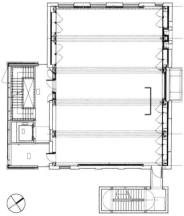

Dance studio plan – 1:400

**Drawing labels:**

**1. Primary steel structure**
Paired curved 254 × 146 × 87 kg universal
beam (UB) portals at 3365 mm centres bolted
500 mm apart.

**2. Purlins**
100 × 100 × 10 mm equal angle (EA) purlins
at varying centres spanning between primary
steels and bolted to 10 mm thick mild steel
cleats welded to UBs.

**3. Fixing cleats**
310 × 60 mm folded mild steel cleats bolted to
purlins to support roof panels.

**4. Roof panels**
3.5 m long × 2 m wide prefabricated GRP (glass
reinforced plastic) roof panels bolted through
edge downstands to fixing brackets and cleats
on purlins.
Joints between panels filled with silicone sealant.
Small drip channel cast into cill to channel
rainwater to roof edge and avoid staining of
leading edge.

**5. Fixing brackets**
Mild steel angle brackets bolted to lower UBs
to support roof panel cill, glazing cill channel
and performance lighting bar.
Mild steel angle brackets bolted to upper UBs
to support roof panel top edge, fascia and
glazing head channel.

**6. Fascia**
200 × 200 × 5 mm thick prefabricated GRP
fascia bolted through edge downstands to
fixing brackets.
Small drip channel cast into top of fascia to
channel rainwater to roof edge and avoid
staining of leading edge.

**7. Roof insulation build-up**
100 mm acoustic insulation spray applied to
rear of panels to deaden sound of rainfall.

5 mm thick Tecsound acoustic membrane with
joints lapped 200 mm.
100 mm mineral wool insulation.
3 mm hardboard.
Continuous vapour barrier.
50 × 50 mm softwood battens adhesive fixed to
purlin angles.

**8. Ceiling**
3660 mm long × 12 mm thick birch faced
plywood strips pre-cut to taper from 100 mm to
79 or 89 mm wide.
Each strip arrived on site with intermittent
blocks pinned and glued on the back. The next
piece was pinned and glued to the previous one
through these blocks.
Once the whole ceiling was fixed the ends of
the boards were cut to a neat line.

**9. Internal fascia**
12 mm thick birch faced plywood fascia pinned
and glued to softwood battens behind.

**10. Rooflight window**
50 × 50 mm aluminium channel bolted to fixing
brackets at top and bottom of rooflight opening.
Four double-glazed sealed units make up each
rooflight.
6.8 mm laminated acoustic glass inner pane
with acid etching on face 3 facing cavity.
Argon filled cavity.
6 mm toughened outer pane with low-e coating
on face 2 facing cavity.

**11. Performance lighting bar**
48.3 mm diameter curved galvanised steel
circular hollow section (CHS) with welded
lugs for bolting to steel roof beams via fixing
brackets.
Bar is sized to hang standard theatre lights.

**12. Lighting**
Fluorescent strip lights fixed in recesses above
and below rooflight window.

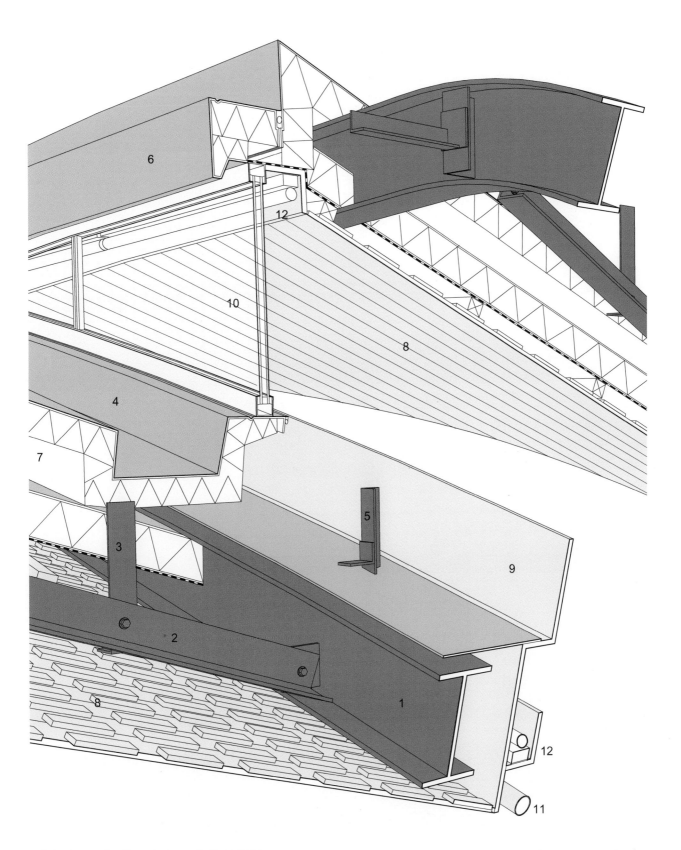

Cut-away section through dance studio rooflight

*Photo: Morley von Sternberg*

*Photo: Morley von Sternberg*

# Rich Mix,
# Bethnal Green, London

Architect: Penoyre & Prasad
Specialist Subcontractor: Taurus Littrow

A moving screen of louvres adds a dynamic new façade to an arts centre in a converted 1960s garment factory. Located on the vibrant and evolving fringe where the City of London peters out into the gritty streets of Bethnal Green the Rich Mix aims to be a point of exchange between the extraordinary mix of cultures in the area.

Recording studios, a performance space and three cinemas are all acoustically isolated from the existing concrete structure using 'box-in-box' construction. To ensure acoustic separation of each function a new concrete slab has been cast on neoprene isolators over the existing floor. Independent walls have been built off this slab separated from a conventional partition wall with an air gap to make a free-standing room. A new fourth floor and roof have been added using a steel structure with profiled aluminium cladding. The original roof slab has been strengthened with a reinforced concrete topping to carry the additional weight of the acoustic floor of the bar/performance space above.

*Photo: Penoyre & Prasad*

On the main street façade the louvre screen is suspended from steel brackets bolted to the new steel structure. The louvres are bolted to stainless steel rods that are restrained back through the existing precast panels to the concrete structure. Fixing locations for the brackets have been carefully positioned to avoid the weaker panel edges. Groups of twelve louvres can be remotely angled from inside each room so the changing external pattern is derived directly from the desires of the users.

The louvres themselves are made up from four anodised extruded aluminium pieces clipped to an extruded aluminium core. One of the underside pieces is anodised gold giving the façade a reflective shimmer when seen from below. The silver top surfaces can be angled to reflect light into the rooms or when the louvres are closed completely, images can be projected onto the façade.

*Photo: Morley von Sternberg*

53

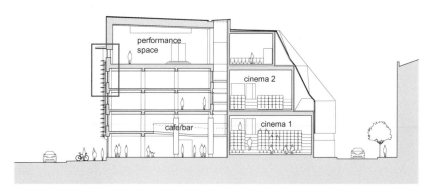

North–south section – 1:500

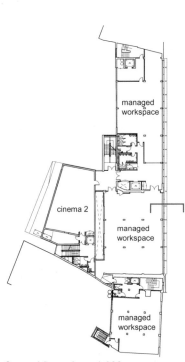

Second floor plan – 1:800

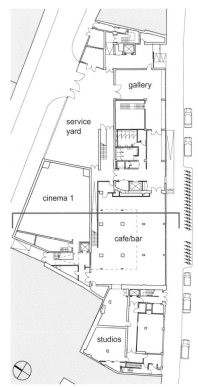

Ground floor plan – 1:800

**Drawing labels:**

1. Existing building structure
510 × 240 mm reinforced concrete columns at nominal 6.400 m centres along façade.
340 mm deep reinforced concrete beams spanning back to next row of columns.
310 mm wide × 360 mm deep reinforced concrete down-stand beam along façade.

2. Existing building external wall
1400 mm high × 100 mm thick precast concrete spandrel panels impregnated with carbon-arrest sealant and painted with black masonry paint.
40 mm air gap.
600 mm high × 150 mm thick reinforced concrete up-stand wall.

3. Existing fins
100 × 45 mm aluminium rectangular hollow section fins fixed to window mullions.
New coloured polyester powder coated (PPC) pressed aluminium sheath fixed to existing fins with self-tapping screws.

4. Cornice bracket
1400 mm long tapered 300 × 300 mm galvanised steel T-bracket bolted to internal stub bracket.
Galvanised steel internal stub-bracket bolted to new steelwork.
40 mm thick structural grade nylon thermal break spacer between T-bracket and internal stub-bracket.
3150 × 1230 mm galvanised steel grating brises-soleil spanning between T-brackets.

5. Fourth floor steelwork
305 × 305 mm steel universal columns at nominal 6.4 m centres bolted to existing fourth-floor concrete slab.

6. Fourth floor glazing
Continuous window with drained PPC aluminium curtain walling frame.
Double-glazed sealed units.
PPC pressed aluminium flashing cill to cover existing concrete coping.

7. Fascia and roof cladding
Profiled aluminium standing seam cladding.
200 mm thick mineral wool insulation compressed to 165 mm.
Liner tray.
PPC pressed aluminium flashing between fascia cladding and new glazing.

8. Fourth floor
Existing roof build-up removed.
Existing concrete scabbled and 75 mm reinforced concrete topping applied to reinforce existing slab.
Neoprene isolating battens.
18 mm plywood.
130 mm reinforced concrete slab with 40 mm granolithic screed ground off and sealed.
140 mm concrete blockwork inner wall built up of slab.

9. Louvre hanger
60 × 40 mm stainless steel box section drop rod suspended from steel tab on cornice bracket with adjustable stainless steel turnbuckle.

10. Stabilising brackets
Folded stainless steel flat bracket bolted with resin anchors into existing concrete upstand via 90 mm diameter zinc plated spacer tubes inserted in core drilled holes in precast panels.
100 × 50 mm stainless steel box section bolted to bracket and bolted to drop rod.

11. Louvres
570 × 74 × 3070 mm long aluminium louvres arranged in two banks of six operated together by one motor.
Louvre blades made up from four anodised extruded aluminium face plates clipped onto an extruded aluminium core.
30 × 12 mm silver anodised aluminium link arm connecting six louvres together.
Electric motor fixed to drop rod and link arms.
Armoured cable to control unit set into window cill board internally.

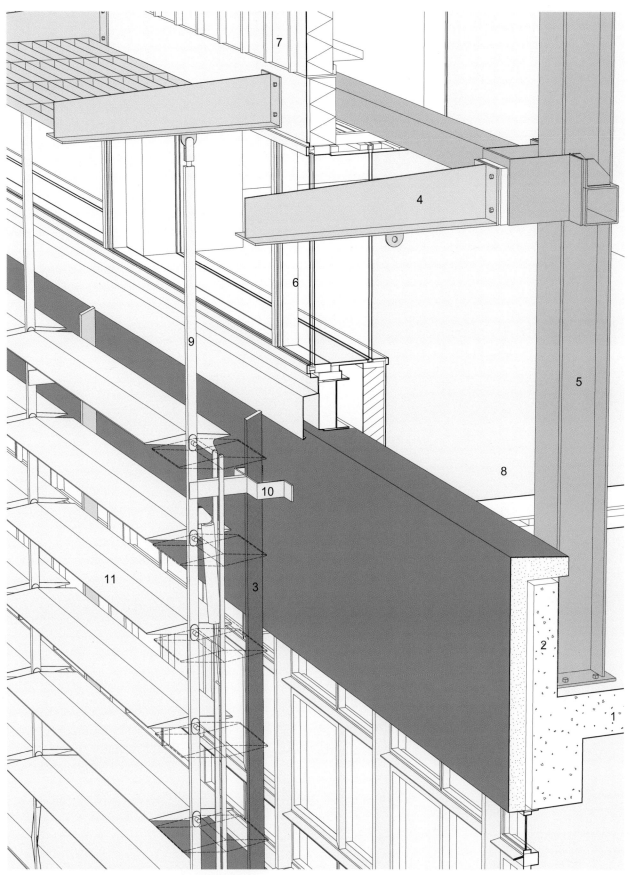

Cut-away section through south façade and louvres

# MIMA, Middlesbrough

Architect: Designed by Erick van Egeraat
Structural Engineer: Buro Happold

Middlesbrough's new Institute of Modern Art is a distinctive free-standing pavilion facing the town hall across the town's principal civic space Victoria Square. The main approach to the Institute is across the square, which was the subject of a redesign at the same time by Dutch landscape architects West 8.

Addressing the square is a four-storey glass enclosure that wraps around a white limestone wall to make a 15-metre high foyer space. Three different surface textures have been used to give the stone variation. Most are rough sawn while some are pitched and some are bush-hammered. The thickness of the individual pieces varies and the coursing is irregular to make the stone sizes appear random. Each stone piece is individually supported by dowels welded to galvanised steel brackets (stainless steel on the external walls), which fit into a proprietary channel system. The channels in turn are fixed to a steel structure behind.

In the foyer a full length gash slices the stone wall in two, marking the location of the main staircase. The top half is hung vertically from the roof on 150 × 75 mm steel channels. The lower part has a steel truss structure that sits on the ground at the bottom of the stair and spans 24 metres to a second truss cantilevering off the main steel frame just inside the line of the glazing. The truss incorporates the first, second and third floor edge beams to tie the whole structure together.

A self-supporting aluminium curtain wall encloses the foyer, its mullions tied back to primary oval section steel columns to resist wind loads with steel brackets that were site welded to make up for the difference in tolerance between the curtain wall and the structural steelwork. The oval columns support steel roof beams that cantilever out beyond the curtain wall. Irregularly spaced stainless steel wires tie the roof edge down to the ground to resist uplift, requiring precise adjustment of the tension so the wires remain taught under snow load but do not exert significant bending in the roof beams under standard loads. A dancing line of suspended light tubes signal the presence of the Institute at night to the town across the square.

East–west section through staircase – 1:600

Second floor plan – 1:900

Ground floor plan – 1:900

Drawing labels:

1. Steel columns
480 × 240 mm oval shaped hollow steel columns at 2130 mm centres.
Two coats of MIO (micaceous iron oxide) paint finish.

2. Curtain walling
125 × 60 mm PPC (polyester powder coated) proprietary aluminium mullions at 2130 mm centres.
90 × 230 × 12 mm Y-shaped steel lateral support plates at 3000 mm centres, site welded to oval columns to transfer wind load back to steel columns.
Two coats of MIO paint finish.
110 × 60 mm PPC proprietary aluminium transoms at 3000 mm centres.
Double-glazed sealed units with 8 mm toughened glass outer pane, 12 mm air gap, 10.8 mm laminated glass inner pane held in place with vertical proprietary curtain walling pressure plates. Black structural silicone horizontal joints.
Remotely operated louvre vent in roof void over curtain wall for natural ventilation.

3. Roof structure
356 × 171 mm UBs (universal beam) at 2130 mm centres cantilevering off oval columns to form roof overhang.
Three 203 × 133 mm UBs spanning between primary beams above stone curtain, above curtain walling and at roof edge.

4. Roof ties
20 mm diameter stainless steel cables at varying centres fixed to roof edge beam.
Bottom of cable fixed to stainless steel post-tensioning anchor fixed into concrete strip foundation.

5. Roof
Single ply membrane on 80 mm rigid insulation.
32 mm liner panel supported on purlins at 1000 mm centres set to roof profile with proprietary strut system.
Metal decking to span between primary structure as a working platform for roof installation.

6. Ceiling
1200 × 2130 mm galvanised expanded mesh panels fixed to 82 × 41 mm galvanised box sections at 1200 mm centres spanning between primary structural members.

7. Roof edge
Single ply membrane on 18 mm marine grade ply.
225 × 50 mm tapering structural timber supports with galvanised brackets to secondary beams.
200 × 300 × 6 mm painted steel edge trim.

8. Stone curtain upper section
Primary structure consisting of vertical
150 × 75 mm PFCs (parallel flange channel) at

2130 mm centres, horizontal 150 × 75 mm PFCs at 2860 mm centres and 203 × 203 mm UC (universal column) bottom cord.
Horizontal 142C13 galvanised steel light gauge sections with toes toward each other at 1000 mm centres.
Proprietary galvanised steel (stainless steel externally) stone support system with vertical toothed channels at 600 mm centres fixed to horizontal structure to accept adjustable dowel anchors.
1200 mm long × 40/50/60 mm thick × various heights Turkish limestone with nominal 3 mm open joints.
Three surface textures used – rough sawn, bush-hammered and pitched.

9. Stone curtain lower section
Primary truss with 250 × 150 mm RHS (rolled hollow section) top cord and 452 × 152 mm UB bottom cord.
Continuous 95 mm slot in stone, for continuous cold cathode light over stair.
Stone as above.

10. Balustrade
15 mm thick toughened glass balustrade.
100 × 12 mm continuous clamping plate fixed with M16 bolts at 500 mm centres to steel angle bolted to steel structure.

11. Handrail
20 × 60 mm polished stainless steel flat uprights with 60 mm continuous stainless steel flat top rail.
150 × 70 mm profiled black cherry handrail with recess in underside screwed to top rail.

12. Staircase
30 mm thick Italian sandstone stone treads and risers bedded on 3 mm thin bed adhesive.
Levelling screed applied to surface of in-situ concrete stair for a surface regularity of SR1.
1800 mm wide in-situ concrete staircase spanning between floor landings with intermediate support at landings.
12.5 mm plasterboard fixed to underside of stair on furring channels, with skim coat and paint finish.

13. Typical floor (upper floors) overall build-up 120 mm
3–5 mm liquid resin finish.
50 mm thick floating polymer modified fibre reinforced screed.
70 mm rigid insulation with underfloor heating.
130 mm concrete slab on galvanised steel deck spanning between steel beams.

14. Suspended ceiling
Proprietary suspended ceiling system.
12.5 mm plasterboard with skim coat and paint finish.

Cut-away section through foyer roof, stair and glazing

*Photo: Brisac Gonzales*

# Multi Purpose Hall
# Aurillac, France

Architect: Brisac Gonzales Architects

A ribbon of precast concrete panels inlaid with glass blocks wraps around a new hall known as Le Prisme in the Auvergne region of central France. Essentially a black box, the 4500 seat hall will be used for theatre, concerts, fairs and sports events. The strong band of back-lit panels breaks the lumpen mass of the hall in two horizontally giving it a dynamic form and an identity at a scale commensurate with its function.

Up to mid-height, the hall has a structure of in-situ concrete walls that are exposed internally. Above this, a precast system of T-shaped columns at 11 m centres and 250 mm thick reinforced concrete wall panels takes over. Roof trusses spanning the full 40 m width of the hall span onto each column. The trusses sit on elastomeric pads to isolate them acoustically from the walls. The roof itself acts as an acoustic damper. A standard insulated metal deck system is raised off the purlins on brackets with a second layer of mineral wool acoustic insulation beneath. The gap between the two is ventilated to prevent condensation and the junction with the walls is sealed.

Externally the upper half of the building is clad in a 9 metre-high band of precast glass reinforced concrete panels set out in long curves. Each 50 mm thick panel is reinforced in two directions with stainless steel rods to avoid future corrosion problems. The panels are inlaid with over 25,000 pyramidal glass blocks with a Fresnel lens surface, which both reflects and refracts light. The joints between the panels are sealed with rubber wiper seals to prevent light leakage. A structure of galvanised steel members supports the panels off the main concrete walls and forms a void in between for maintenance access. During the day, the sun glints off the white concrete and outer faces of the blocks while at night the façades transform into shimmering curtains of coloured light.

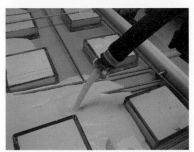

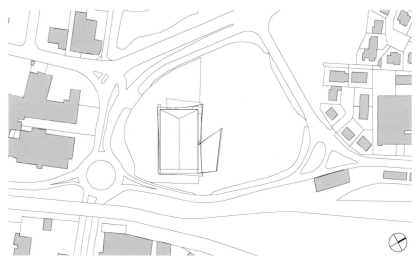

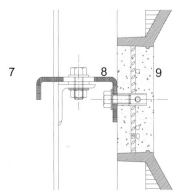

Detail section through typical concrete panel showing glass lens and fixing bracket – 1:5

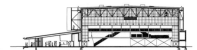

North–south section – 1:1500

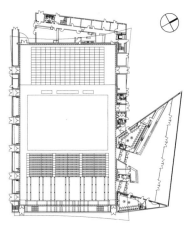

Ground floor plan – 1:1500

Drawing labels:

1. External wall
800 × 300mm T-shaped precast reinforced concrete columns at nominal 11m centres.
250mm thick precast reinforced concrete wall panels bolted to columns.
175mm void for acoustic attenuation with horizontal closers to prevent stack effect air movement in cavity.
100mm mineral wool thermal insulation.
Vapour barrier.
25mm black wood-fibre acoustic panel inner lining.

2. Roof trusses
Steel roof trusses at 11m centres tapered to form 3% fall to roof (3970mm high at centre of roof) made up from:
HEA 300 (290 × 300mm I-section) top chord.
HEA 200 (190 × 200mm I-section) diagonal braces.
IPE 180 (180 × 91mm I-section) vertical members generally.
HEA 260 (250 × 260mm I-section) vertical end member.
HEA 300 (290 × 300mm I-section) bottom chord.

3. Roof trusses bracket
Steel bracket bolted to precast concrete wall. Truss rests on and is bolted to 300 × 300mm elastomeric isolation pad which is bolted to the fixing bracket.

4. Roof
Multi-layer bituminous waterproof membrane.
100mm mineral wool insulation mechanically fixed to metal deck.
56mm deep galvanised steel deck supported on 200 × 50mm brackets off purlins.
Minimum 100mm ventilated air gap.
80mm thick mineral wool acoustic insulation panels on profiled galvanised steel tray.
Proprietary suspended ceiling system hung from tray with 600 × 600mm acoustic absorbent panels between purlins.
IPE 360 (360 × 170mm I-section) purlins at nominal 2.5m centres.

5. Roof edge
500 × 370mm folded galvanised steel gutter supported on 600 × 500mm galvanised steel

angle brackets bolted to precast wall at 1.5m centres.
Galvanised steel edge capping fixed to roof edge and overlapped into gutter.
End of acoustic panels wrapped in insulation.
Gap between acoustic panels and top of concrete wall sealed with expanding foam.

6. Outrigger structure
IPE 360 (360 × 170mm I-section) horizontal galvanised steel beams fixed back to concrete wall via horizontal galvanised steel struts with diagonal bracing.

7. Vertical rails
IPE 120 (120 × 64mm I-section) galvanised steel vertical rails at 1500mm centres bolted to horizontal out-rigger beams.

8. Brackets
230mm long 50 × 50mm galvanised steel angles with slotted holes welded to vertical rails.
110 × 50 × 6mm thick folded stainless steel brackets with slotted holes bolted to stainless steel sockets cast into cladding panels.
Brackets bolted to angles on vertical rails using M12 stainless steel bolts via 28 × 14mm slotted holes to allow alignment tolerance with neoprene isolation washers to prevent bimetallic corrosion.

9. Cladding panels
1490 × 1490 × 50mm thick precast glass-reinforced concrete cladding panels with four M12 stainless steel fixing sockets cast into rear.
160 × 160mm pyramidal cast glass blocks cast into concrete panel at 300mm centres.
6mm stainless steel reinforcement bars in both directions between glass blocks.
Two M12 sockets cast into top edge of panel for lifting into position.

10. Lighting
Wide angle projector luminaires mounted on concrete wall in two offset rows at top and bottom of façade.
Lamps have a fixed colour and each colour is on a separate circuit.

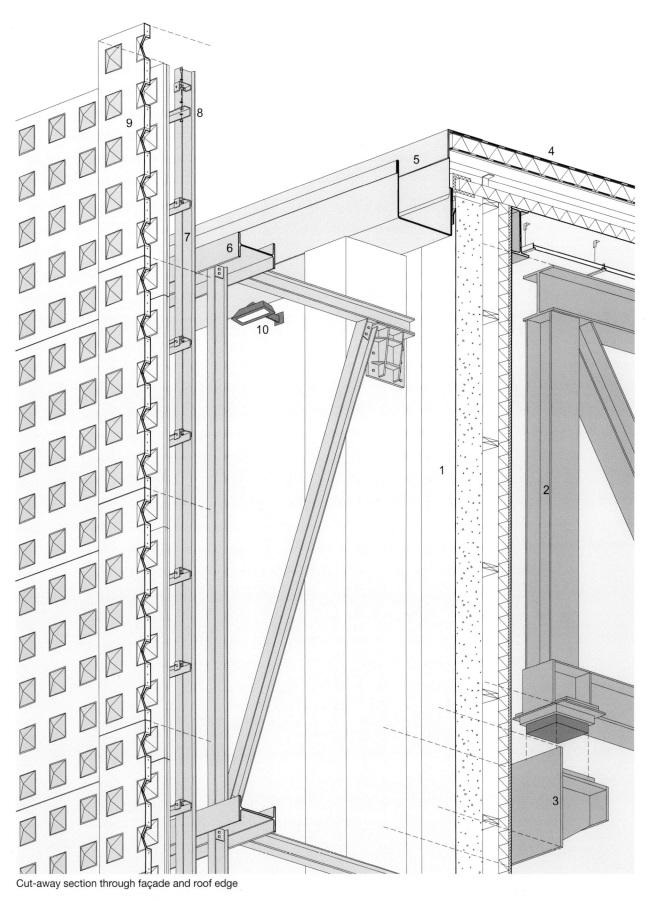

Cut-away section through façade and roof edge

*Photo: Niall McLaughlin Architects*

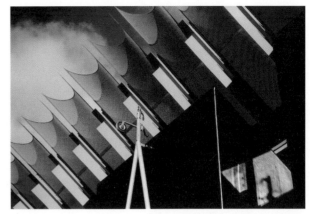

Photo: Niall McLaughlin Architects

Photo: Niall McLaughlin Architects

Photo: Niall McLaughlin Architects

Photo: Niall McLaughlin Architects

# ARC, Hull

Architect: Niall McLaughlin Architects
Structural Engineers: Price & Myers
M&E Engineers: XCO2 Conisbee

The ARC is an education resource intended to showcase building and environmental developments arising from regeneration activities in the Humber region. It is also a learning resource in itself, a building that stimulates debate, provides an exciting venue for events and is a dynamic landmark in Hull's city centre. It is intended to be dismantled and moved to different locations over a 20-year period, evolving as it goes to incorporate advances in construction and environmental technology. 'I'd like to think that in 20 years time it might not look remotely like this', says McLaughlin.

The building is engineered to be carbon neutral by generating the same amount of energy as it uses through renewable sources. An array of photovoltaic panels and wind turbines produce electricity and a wood pellet boiler supplies hot water to an underfloor heating system. Fresh air is drawn in at the eaves across an external gutter with water misters to provide evaporative cooling when necessary.

To enable the structure to be dismantled and reassembled, the foundations are a series of precast concrete padstones that sit on the ground. The floor is made from prefabricated steel framed 'cassette' units bolted together and filled with ballast to resist wind uplift. The roof is a lean-to structure of 24 steel beam rafters spanning from an eaves beam along the edge of the floor cassettes to a ladder truss at the ridge. Five steel framed 'caravans' containing offices, WCs and plant rest on their own concrete padstone foundations and support the ladder truss above.

Translucent GRP roof panels 13 m long are fixed to the steel rafters forming a low thermal conductivity waterproof skin. A reflective, shimmering surface of curved aluminium mesh is fixed to the underside of the rafters and to the outside of the GRP panels as solar shading. In one event images of the sea, filmed in real time, were projected onto the mesh screen outside, reminding passers-by of the city's maritime past.

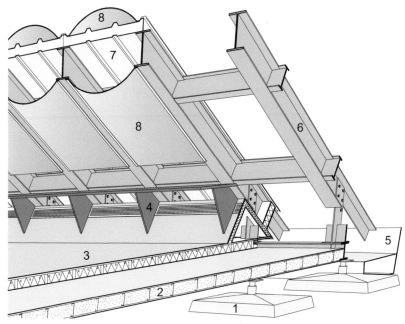

Cutaway section through roof eaves

Rendered view from south end

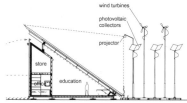

wind turbines
photovoltaic collectors
projector
store
office
education

Section – 1:500

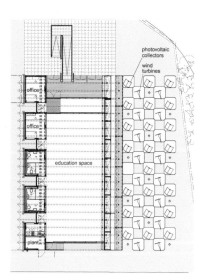

photovoltaic collectors
wind turbines
offices
offices
education space
plant

Site plan – 1:500

Drawing labels:

1. Padstone foundations
900 × 900 × 125mm thick concrete padstones at between 2.1m and 2.8m centres on compacted ground.
Adjustable height steel pedestal on each padstone to allow levelling of floor cassettes.

2. Floor cassettes
Prefabricated floor cassette with 152 × 76mm steel channel edge frame on three sides for bolting to adjacent cassettes.
203 × 203mm universal column eaves beam on roof eaves edge to support roof steels.
125 × 50mm light gauge steel channels spanning between edge steels.
12mm WBP plywood sheathing screwed to channels on top and bottom faces.
Voids filled with broken brick ballast to give weight to resist wind uplift.

3. Built-up floor
100mm thick rigid insulation laid between softwood studs.
Underfloor heating pipes.
18mm WBP plywood floor screwed to softwood studs.
2.5mm linoleum floor finish adhesive fixed and wrapping up vertical face of eaves upstand.

4. Desk
30mm MDF desk with fold-down top finished with high gloss 2-pack toughened cellulose paint fixed to eaves upstand.

5. Gutter
1000 × 250mm deep stainless steel troughs in 4m lengths bolted together to form gutter.
150mm wide aluminium ventilation grille with insect mesh set into plywood soffit over gutter.
Ultraviolet filter in eaves upstand treats incoming air to kill bacteria.

6. Steel roof structure
305 × 165mm × 40kg universal beam (UB) rafters at 1m centres bolted to 700 × 200mm steel connector plates bolted to eaves beam on floor cassettes.
Bottom flange and lower half of web cut off where beam protrudes through envelope at eaves.

Bottom flange cut off where beam protrudes through envelope at top.
305 × 102mm × 31kg UB purlins bolted between beams at minimum 1.8m centres.

7. Translucent roof panels
13m long × 1m wide × 80mm thick translucent profiled GRP panels joined with proprietary metal capping strips.

8. Mesh roof panels
1mm thick marine grade aluminium mesh with channel frames to long edges fixed above and below roof steels over full height of roof.
3mm neoprene isolation strips full length between aluminium and polycarbonate/steel.

9. Steel ladder beam
Steel ladder beam welded up from 90 × 50mm rectangular hollow section (RHS) top and bottom members and 90 × 50mm RHS verticals at nominal 600mm centres.
Roof steels bolted via cleats to top of ladder beam.

10. Glazing
Polyester powder coated aluminium glazing bars fixed to face of ladder beam and to 60 × 40mm RHS frames on sides of caravans.
Double-glazed sealed units with toughened outer pane, argon filled cavity and laminated inner pane.

11. Aluminium flashing
Polyester powder coated aluminium flashing with joints lapped and sealed with butyl sealant.

12. Caravans
Five 'caravans' sitting on concrete padstones supporting ladder beam above.
Each caravan has a steel carcass welded up from 60 × 60mm square hollow sections (SHS).
150 × 50mm softwood studwork screwed to steel carcass and infilled with mineral wool insulation.
12mm birch faced plywood internal finish with vapour barrier.
18mm WBP plywood stressed skin outer sheathing with blue pigmented fibreglass resin finish.

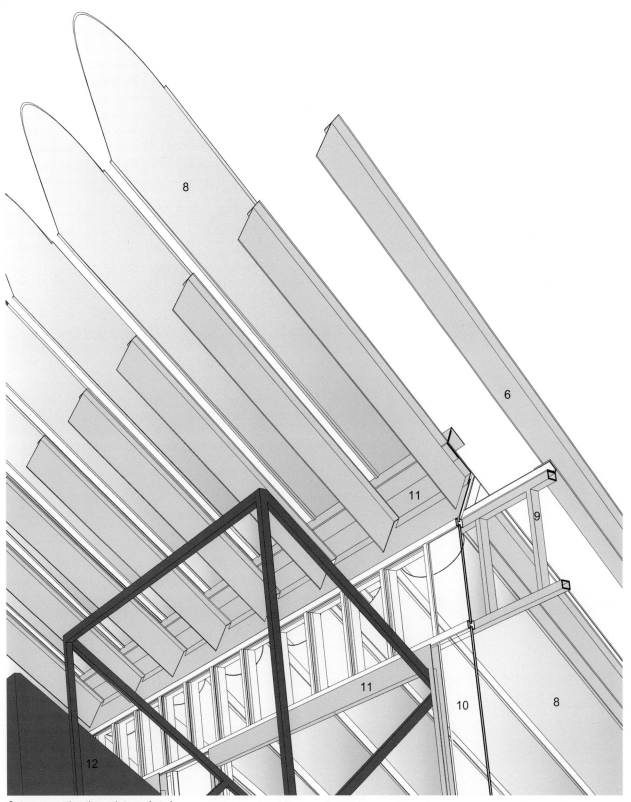

Cutaway section through top of roof

*Photo: Sutherland Hussey Architects*

# Resource Centre
# Grizedale Forrest Park, Cumbria

Architect: Sutherland Hussey Architects
Structural Engineer: Burgess Roughton

Grizedale Forrest Park is the headquarters of the Forestry Commission in the north-west of England. The Commission has a holistic vision for the 2500 hectare park which aims to create opportunities for visitors, local communities and businesses. In 2002, Sutherland Hussey won a competition to develop a masterplan for the whole estate, the first phase of which is a new Resource Centre that provides facilities for schools and community groups. The Centre consists of a new structure for the main classroom on the southern flank of an existing stone building that has been adapted for support spaces.

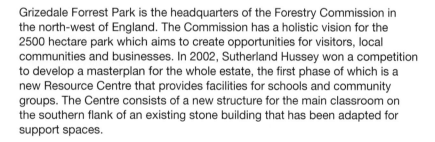

The classroom has a pitched roof rising to a 7.5 m high glazed façade commanding spectacular views down the dale. Six inverted Douglas fir trusses carry the roof. To stabilise them in transit, and while they were lifted into place, they were assembled in softwood cradles which were cut away on site. On the south façade the roof trusses are carried on a flitched timber truss that spans the whole width of the building between two flitched columns. Below the truss a deep bay window is formed with a steel structure hung off the truss at the top and cantilevered off a concrete blockwork plinth at the bottom. In order to avoid intermediate columns beneath the truss the side walls of the classroom have additional bracing at high level so the south façade is effectively open in structural terms.

Above the bay window oak framed glazing has been fixed to the face of the truss. The glazing has a screen of timber strips sandwiched between the panes of glass to limit solar gain. Above the façade truss a line of solid timber opening flaps provide ventilation to the space. The roof is clad with cedar shingles which wrap down the timber framed upper parts of the flank walls and project forward in a cowl to shade the south façade glazing. Rather than closing the ventilation gaps with mesh a continuous slot has been left open to allow a colony of bats resident in the roof of the existing building to roost in the new roof.

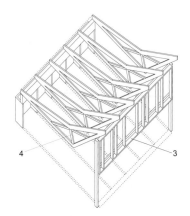

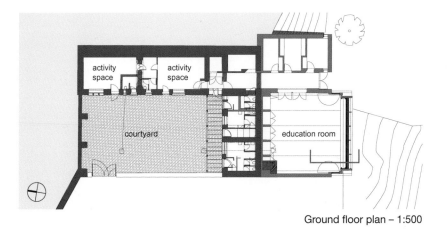

Ground floor plan – 1:500

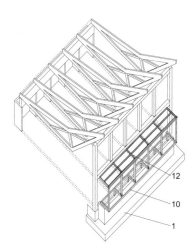

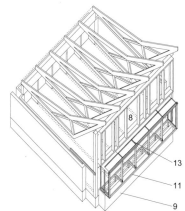

Diagrams showing structural build-up

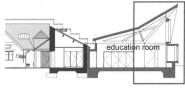

North–south section – 1:500

Drawing labels:

1. Foundation
1850 × 600mm reinforced concrete strip footing.
215mm dense concrete blockwork inner leaf supporting floor slab edge with bituminous tanking membrane applied to outer face.
215mm dense concrete blockwork outer leaf.
25mm cavity filled with lean-mix concrete up to DPC level.

2. Ground floor
129 × 22mm tongued and grooved white oak floorboards with oiled finish.
75mm sand/cement screed with mesh reinforcement.
75mm rigid insulation.
150mm reinforced concrete ground-bearing slab.
Bituminous tanking membrane.
Sand blinding on compacted hardcore.

3. Façade truss
C24 grade Douglas fir façade truss spanning 10m between 300 × 400mm C24 grade Douglas fir flitch columns at either end.
300 × 320mm top boom with central steel flitch plate.
300 × 320mm bottom boom with central steel flitch plate.
200 × 250mm vertical struts.
12mm diameter tensile rod cross bracing bolted to flitch plates at nodes.

4. Inverted roof truss
Six C24 grade Douglas fir roof trusses spanning from south façade truss to reinforced concrete upstand in north wall at 1990mm centres.
300 × 125mm top member.
175 × 125mm diagonals.
300 × 125mm bottom member.
150 × 125mm central post.
Timber members planed and sanded all round.
10mm stainless steel plate connectors between members fixed with countersunk bolts.

5. Roof
Triple lapped 400mm cedar shingles fixed to 38 × 19mm treated horizontal battens at 95mm centres.
38 × 25mm treated counter-battens aligned with purlins.
Breather membrane.

18mm plywood sarking board.
60mm rigid urethane insulation.
100 × 50mm treated softwood purlins.
50mm rigid urethane insulation between purlins.
Vapour barrier.
144 × 16mm tongued and grooved redwood soffit boards fixed to battens at 350mm centres fixed to purlins.
Vacuum treated with fire retardant.

6. Roof edge
131 × 106mm profiled cedar edge capping with 37 × 25mm rout in back face to slot over and protect top of shingles.
20mm ventilation gap below capping left open to allow access for bats.
Roof breather membrane dressed down and fixed to front of outrigger rafters.
270 × 19mm oak fascia board.
144 × 30mm American oak tongued and grooved soffit boards fixed to battens at 350mm centres suspended below rafters at an angle to allow any moisture to drain out.

7. High level vents
65 × 65mm oak window frame with 270 × 125mm cill.
Opening vent panels made from 50 × 38mm softwood frame with 18mm oak veneered exterior grade plywood outer sheathing and 12mm oak veneered plywood inner lining.
38 × 38mm oak strips screwed and glued to plywood panel from behind.

8. Upper windows
300 × 132mm oak head and cill supported off façade truss on continuous stainless steel Z-section at cill.
300 × 69mm oak mullions at varying centres.
30mm double-glazed sealed units with interstitial timber grid and self-cleaning coating.
External oak beads flush with face of mullion (sizes vary to allow installation from outside).

9. Plinth
140mm concrete blockwork inner leaf with bituminous tanking membrane applied to outer face.
25mm cavity filled with lean-mix concrete up to DPC level.
150mm Grizedale slate wall tied to 100mm concrete blockwork with stainless steel ties.

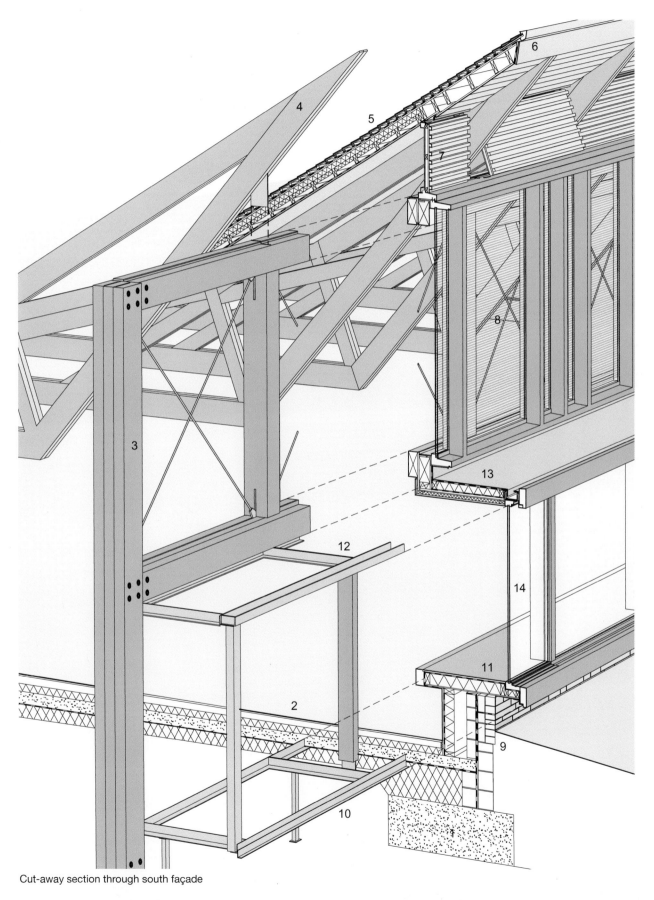

Cut-away section through south façade

10. Lower window cill structure
Galvanised steel frame made from
100 × 75 mm angles bolted to extended flitch
plate of bottom member of façade truss.

11. Lower window cill
18 mm oak veneered plywood inner lining.
Vapour barrier and cill DPC.
140 × 50 mm softwood studwork frame.
140 mm mineral wool insulation between studs.
18 mm oak veneered exterior grade plywood
deck fixed in steel angle frame.

12. Lower window roof structure
Galvanised steel frame made from
100 × 75 mm angles bolted to extended flitch
plate of bottom member of façade truss.
200 × 90 mm PFC (parallel flange channel)
gutter welded to outer face of frame.
Pressed metal gutter lining.

13. Lower window roof
Single ply roofing membrane.
Tapered rigid insulation.
Vapour barrier.
18 mm plywood deck fixed into steel angle
frame.
50 × 38 mm softwood frame with 38 mm
insulation in between studs.
18 mm oak veneered plywood inner lining.

14. Lower window
200 × 80 mm oak posts at 1990 mm centres
fixed to upper and lower structure via steel
brackets.
24 mm double-glazed sealed unit.
35 × 20 mm oak capping bead.
221 × 91 mm cedar fascia fixed to steel
structure at head, cill and sides of window with
mitred corner joints.

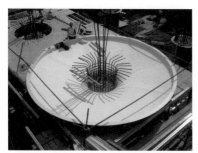

*Photo: Grimshaw*

*Photo: Edmund Sumner/VIEW*

*Photo: Grimshaw*

*Photo: Edmund Sumner/VIEW*

# Thermae Bath Spa
# Bath

Architect: Grimshaw Architects
Stone supply & installation: Bath Stone Group

A succession of baths have been built since Roman times to take advantage of the mineral-rich hot springs beneath the city of Bath, most significantly in the Georgian period when Bath was the most fashionable resort in England and from when much of the present day city survives. Following a bather's death from meningitis in 1978, however, the public baths closed. In 2006 a new spa complex opened enabling people once again to take the waters, albeit with much more stringent sanitary arrangements. The new spa is a cluster of new and refurbished buildings including the Hot Bath by John Wood the Younger and the Cross Bath by Thomas Baldwin and John Palmer.

The new building contains two bathing pools fed with water from the hot-springs. A rooftop pool sits on top of a Bath stone cube containing treatment facilities, held up on four mushroom columns emerging from a ground level pool. Plant is crammed into two basement levels surrounded by secant piled retaining walls. The mushroom columns were cast in-situ using glass reinforced plastic (GRP) formwork to give a smooth finish.

The roof-top pool is concrete with a hydrophobic and pore-blocking Ingredient to make it waterproof. A paint-on epoxy coating provides a further waterproof layer, although problems with it peeling off contributed to a 3-year delay on the project. The cube walls are stack-bonded Bath stone ashlar, cut from deep base strata in local mines. Steel and glass bridges span between the cube and the surrounding listed buildings. A glass skin wraps around the cube, suspended from the second floor slab on stainless steel tension rods and restrained against wind load by 300 × 200 mm rectangular hollow section (RHS) posts which also help prop the terrace above.

The treatment areas have small circular glass windows providing daylight and limited views out while maintaining complete privacy. They sit flush with the stone on the outside and are lined inside with GRP cones. Massage and steam rooms are enclosed with curved 15 mm toughened glass held by stainless steel clamping plates top and bottom. Precast white concrete benches conceal lighting that glows through the steam-filled rooms.

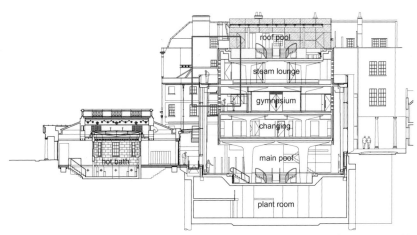

East–west section through new building and Hot Bath – 1:500

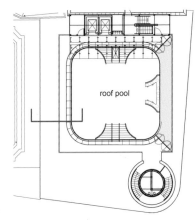

Roof plan – 1:500

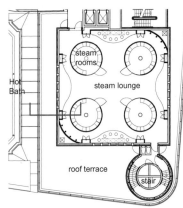

Second floor plan – 1:500

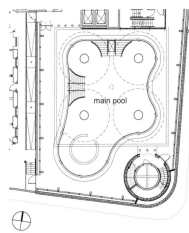

Ground floor plan – 1:500

Drawing labels:

1. Primary structure
Four reinforced concrete mushroom columns cast in-situ with fibreglass formwork.
Epoxy paint finish.

2. Roof-top pool
Epoxy based paint system in pool areas.
200 mm thick reinforced concrete slab with waterproof additive.

3. Pool edge
700 × 380 mm precast concrete edge units with integral drainage channels.
500 mm wide solid Vitrathene polyethylene grating with specially designed anti-slip grooves and curved profiles.

4. Roof
300 × 900 × 20 mm thick Kashmir white granite paving slabs with flamed finish and sealant coating.
50 mm thick extruded polystyrene insulation.
Minimum 90 mm thick proprietary quick-drying screed laid to fall.
Underfloor heating pipes to prevent ice forming in winter.
Solvent-free polyurethane-based waterproof membrane lapped up and sealed against precast edge units.
Drain outlet as secondary protection and to allow any failure in the primary waterproofing to be identified.
200 mm thick reinforced concrete slab with waterproof additive.

5. Roof level balustrade
Laminated glass balustrade comprising 12 mm thick toughened inner layer, 1.5 mm interlayer and 12 mm thick toughened outer layer with acid etch effect to internal face.
60 mm diameter satin finish stainless steel handrail.
200 × 150 × 15 mm galvanised mild steel (MS) angle bracket bolted to concrete.
150 × 150 × 15 mm galvanised MS clamping angle.

6. Stone wall
1063 × 502 × 75 mm thick Bath stone ashlar with 8 mm lime mortar joints recessed to a depth of 10 mm.

Stainless steel shelf angles at each floor level to support stone.
Proprietary grade 316 stainless steel adjustable dowel and anchor system to restrain each stone.
45 mm air gap.
55 mm water repellent rigid glass mineral wool insulation.
Asphaltic membrane liquid applied to face of concrete.
Vertical mineral wool cavity barriers as fire stops at centrelines of cube.
175 mm thick reinforced concrete wall.

7. Windows
325 mm diameter hole cast into concrete wall.
220 mm diameter hole cut in stone.
Conical glass reinforced plastic (GRP) reveal with preformed DPM cloak fitted around opening.
190 mm diameter × 26 mm thick sealed double-glazed lens unit bonded to stainless steel ring with dowel fixing to rear of stone cladding in sealant bed to seal against stone façade.
Grade 316 stainless steel circular collar and GRP cone dressed to interior textured render wall finish.

8. Second floor
20 mm thick Kashmir white granite stone paving slabs with flamed finish and sealant coating.
Screed with underfloor heating.
50 mm thick extruded polystyrene insulation.
200 mm thick reinforced concrete slab.

9. Bench
140 × 540 mm precast reinforced white concrete bench units with concealed peripheral low voltage led lighting.

10. Pod glazing
15 mm thick curved 2850 mm diameter toughened/laminated glass.
Grade 316 stainless steel bottom channel bolted to screed.
Stainless steel top channel bolted into recess in column head with galvanised steel channel secondary support structure above suspended ceilings.

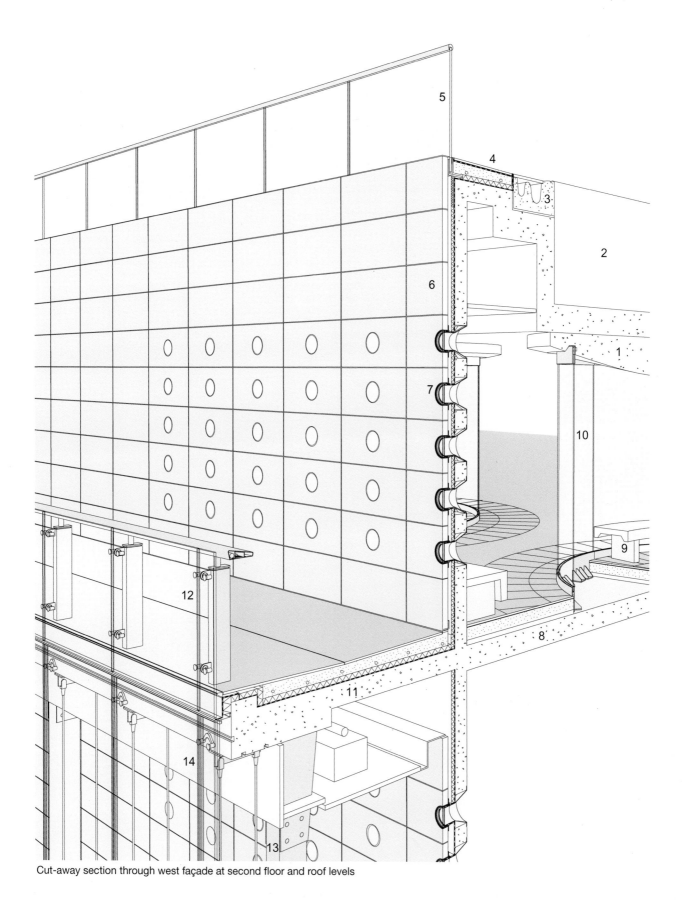

Cut-away section through west façade at second floor and roof levels

11. Terrace
300 mm wide random coursed 20 mm thick
Kashmir white granite paving slabs with flamed
finish and sealant coating.
50 mm thick extruded polystyrene insulation.
Minimum 90 mm thick proprietary quick-drying
screed laid to fall.
Underfloor heating pipes to prevent ice forming
in winter.
Proprietary single ply waterproof membrane
with welded joints lapped up and sealed
against anchored edge units.
Drain outlet with secondary inlet bonded to
membrane to collect water that has passed
through finished floor.
200 mm thick reinforced concrete slab.

12. Terrace balustrade
Laminated glass balustrade comprising 10 mm
thick toughened inner layer, 1.5 mm interlayer
and 8 mm thick toughened outer layer with acid
etch effect to internal face.
245 × 78 × 4 mm gauge folded stainless steel
handrail with mild steel louvre to underside.
Cold cathode lighting tube.
160 × 80 × 8 mm rectangular hollow section
(RHS) mullions at 1.5 m centres.
48 mm diameter stainless steel tube welded to
10 mm plate screwed to top of mullion.

Glass bolted to 98 × 70 × 8 mm half-round
lugs welded to mullions.

13. Secondary steel structure
300 × 200 mm galvanised steel posts at 4.5 m
centres to assist in supporting terrace above
and provide wind bracing to glazing.
Post bolted to 203 × 102 mm preformed
welded and galvanised MS bracket at head
bolted into slab.

14. Glazing
Outer pane comprises 6 mm heat-soaked glass,
1.5 mm PVB interlayer, 6 mm heat-soaked
glass.
16 mm air gap.
Inner pane comprising 8 mm toughened glass,
1.5 mm PVB interlayer, 10 mm toughened glass.
Vertical aluminium carrier frame bolted to
54 × 50 mm aluminium mullion with two
40 × 12 mm aluminium stiffeners.
12 mm diameter stainless steel tensionable
rods bolted via steel bracket to slab to support
glazing below.
Glazed units supported by proprietary cast
stainless steel spider fixings.
12 mm wide black silicon seal joints to
prefabricated sealed glazed units (maximum
size 3558 × 1770 mm).

*Photo: Tim Griffith*

*Photo: Denton Corker Marshall*

*Photo: Denton Corker Marshall*

*Photo: Denton Corker Marshall*

*Photo: Tim Griffith*

# Civil Justice Centre
# Manchester

Architect: Denton Corker Marshall
Structural, Mechanical & Electrical Engineer: Mott MacDonald

Manchester's new Civil Justice Centre contains 47 court rooms, 75 consultation rooms and is the Headquarters for the Ministry of Justice in the Northwest. The fiendishly complicated separate circulation requirements of a courthouse are resolved by dividing the floors into four strips in plan, an atrium on the west façade, then public circulation, then the courtrooms and finally the judges offices on the east façade. These divisions are expressed by changes of material and set-backs in plan and section. The 16-storey steel framed building is naturally ventilated with air taken in through wind scoops in the side of the atrium.

At the north and south ends courtrooms project out beyond the main building frame. Double columns at the end of the main frame provide seatings for 12 metre high prefabricated trusses which were craned into position and held with temporary bracing until the floors could be cast. Tension forces at the top of the trusses and compression forces at the bottom are distributed back to the building's concrete core through composite steel deck concrete floors.

Double-skinned façades on all three sides of the projecting volumes provide both acoustic isolation and environmental control. The inner skin is supported via a secondary structure of steel ladder beams bolted to the primary structure at each floor level. Insulated aluminium framed infill panels span between the steel beams. The steel and aluminium frames are clad with coloured 3 mm aluminium sheets on the outside and galvanised steel sheets on the inside.

The outer skin is laminated glass hung from galvanised steel beams bolted back to the secondary structure at the top. Stainless steel tension rods are bolted to galvanised steel struts at the bottom bolted back to the secondary structure. An intermediate stainless steel strut at mid-height braces the glazing against wind loads. A random pattern of colours on the inner skin interacts with reflections of the sky to give an ephemeral depth to the façade.

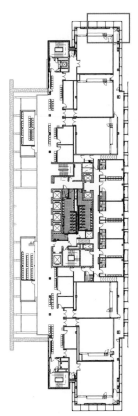

Level 7 floor plan – Scale 1:1000

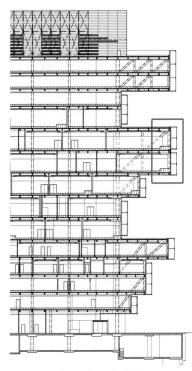

North–south section – 1:1000

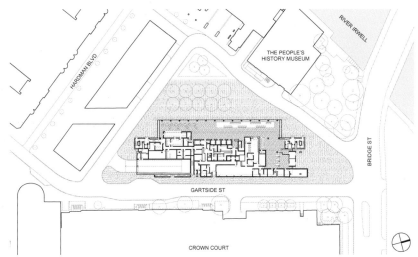

Site location plan – 1:2000

Drawing labels:

1. Structural steel frame
356 × 406 mm × 287 kg UC (universal column) column.
457 × 191 mm × 67 kg UB (universal beam) edge beams.
457 × 191 mm × 74 kg UB floor and roof beams at 2840 mm centres.
All steelwork clad with 30 mm 'Class 0' fire encasement board to provide 2 hour fire resistance.

2. Roof
600 × 600 × 50 mm concrete pavers as ballast on 15 mm plastic spacer supports.
Geotextile membrane.
160 mm extruded polystyrene insulation.
7 mm rubber-modified bitumen waterproof membrane applied to concrete and up vertical face of angle with termination bar at top.
145 mm thick reinforced concrete slab on profiled galvanised steel deck.
400 × 100 × 2 mm galvanised steel angle screw-fixed to concrete to form upstand.
Concealed grid MF suspended plasterboard ceiling.

3. Floor
Proprietary raised access floor system consisting of 600 × 600 × 32 mm chipboard core with galvanised steel shell on galvanised steel adjustable pedestals to create 375 mm service zone.
145 mm thick reinforced concrete slab on profiled galvanised steel deck.
3 mm thick aluminium soffit panels with 120 mm mineral wool insulation fixed to aluminium secondary support system bolted to primary steelwork.

4. Secondary structure
100 × 100 × 7 mm SHS (square hollow section) ladder frames bolted to galvanised steel brackets bolted to primary steel beams and concrete roof slab.
120 mm mineral wool insulation between members. Breather membrane on outer face.
80 × 60 × 5 mm aluminium channel brackets bolted to steel members at maximum 600 mm centres via thermal break spacers to support cladding.

5. Infill panels
194 mm deep interlocking thermally broken aluminium mullion and transom profiles bolted to secondary structure.
3 mm galvanised steel sheet inner lining secret-fixed to panel frames via angles bolted to rear of sheets.

6. Cladding
PPC 3 mm aluminium sheets secret-fixed to panel frames via aluminium Z-profiles bolted to rear of sheets.

7. Window
194 mm deep thermally broken aluminium window frame.
Double-glazed sealed unit consisting of 12.8 mm laminated inner pane with low-E coating, 16 mm air gap and 8 mm toughened outer pane.

8. Outer skin upper support
120 × 120 × 10 mm SHS cantilevered support beam bolted to secondary structure.
100 × 50 × 6.3 mm RHS (rectangular hollow section) bolted between beams at mid-span.
12 mm diameter stainless steel tension rods bolted to 60 × 12 mm stainless steel plate bracket bolted to end plates of support beams.
Folded PPC (polyester powder coated) 3 mm aluminium sheet roof screwed to brackets on steel structure.

9. Outer skin lower strut
80 × 60 × 7 mm galvanised RHS struts bolted to secondary structure.
80 × 60 × 7 mm galvanised RHS bolted between struts at mid-span.

10. Outer skin central strut
50 × 5 mm CHS (circular hollow section) brushed stainless steel strut bolted to 10 mm stainless steel plate bolted to aluminium infill panel frame.
Brushed stainless steel cross-bracket consisting of 520 mm long 80 × 25 mm horizontal member welded to 520 mm long 80 × 12 mm vertical member welded to CHS.
80 × 25 mm horizontal member is continuous over first two glass panels at corners in both directions for stiffness.

11. Outer skin glazing
24.8 mm or 25.5 mm laminated glass mechanically fixed with 120 × 70 × 10 mm brushed stainless steel clamping plates.
165 × 110 mm extruded aluminium angle frames bolted to support beams at top and to struts at bottom of glazing.

12. Floor of façade void
30 mm deep galvanised steel grating with 80 × 6 mm edges bolted to lower struts.
132 × 125 mm recessed aluminium up-lighter recess flush with grating.
PPC 3 mm aluminium sheet soffit secret-fixed to steel struts via aluminium Z-profiles bolted to rear of sheets.

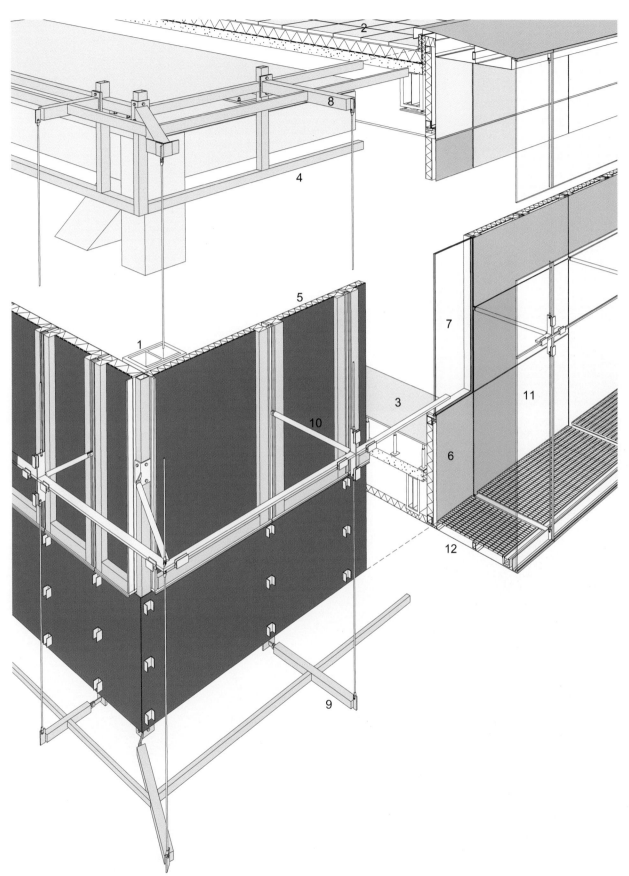

Cut-away section through projecting courtroom on north elevation

Photo: Michael Moran

*Photo: Michael Moran*

# Sean O'Casey Community Centre Dublin

Architect: O'Donnell + Tuomey
Structural Engineer: Casey O'Rourke

Set in a neighbourhood of two-storey brick terraced houses, the corrugated concrete walls and circular windows of the Sean O'Casey Community Centre are a distinctive new landmark in the Dublin district of East Wall. The building houses four main facilities – a crèche, day care facilities for the elderly, a 153-seat theatre and a sports hall sharing a single entrance. The different elements of the brief are arranged around four courtyards that provide the necessary separation between activities while also allowing oblique visual links between them.

Corrugated concrete walls with circular cut-out windows define the outer shell of the Centre. The walls are load-bearing and were cast in-situ using corrugated galvanised steel sheets screwed to the plywood face of the formwork. Circular voids were formed by fixing plywood drums to the formwork. The window frames are unsealed iroko that is already fading to grey to match the concrete. To control shrinkage cracking the walls were poured in a number of sections so one section would have a few days to dry out before the next section was poured. Day joints are concealed in flat strips, which also serve to break the walls up into carefully proportioned corrugated panels.

The roofs are also in-situ concrete with the smooth soffit exposed on its underside. The joints were all set out and the surface was laboriously rubbed down by hand once the phenolic faced birch plywood formwork was removed. Numerous trials and samples of the concrete mix were carried out on site. The concrete walls and steel columns are built off reinforced concrete strip foundations. Rather than using piled foundations a cheaper alternative was used of improving the ground using vibrated stone columns.

Internally the four courtyards are surrounded by full height glazed screens made from 250 × 75 mm iroko members. Around the courtyards the roof is supported on 114 mm diameter steel columns cast directly into the roof slab. The columns are at close enough centres that the concrete can form a beam between them. A head plate with shear studs welded to it ties into the reinforcement to resist punching shear.

*Photo: O'Donnell + Tuomey*

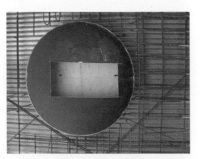

*Photo: O'Donnell + Tuomey*

*Photo: O'Donnell + Tuomey*

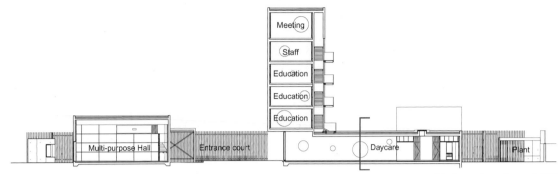

East–west section – 1:500

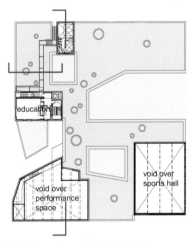

First floor plan – Scale 1:1000

Ground floor plan – Scale 1:1000

Drawing labels:

1. Foundations
1200 × 400mm reinforced concrete strip footing below external wall on 50mm sand blinding.
900 × 300mm reinforced concrete strip footing below steel columns on 50mm sand blinding.
Vibrated stone columns at varying centres to improve ground below footings.
Ground floor slab thickens at edges to 400 × 400mm at courtyard perimeter.

2. Ground floor
55mm brick pavers with two coats clear sealant.
100mm screed with underfloor heating pipes cast in.
25mm service void formed between edge of screed and wall using 18mm WBP plywood formwork.
75mm rigid urethane insulation.
DPM (damp proof membrane) laid over slab and finished 150mm above finished floor level in cast-in groove in concrete upstand.
265mm thick reinforced concrete slab, thickening to 400 × 400mm at courtyard perimeter.
50mm blinding and 200mm compacted hardcore.

3. External concrete wall
500mm high × 250mm wide reinforced concrete kicker with hydrophilic strip on top.
300mm thick reinforced concrete wall cast in-situ with corrugated surface and class C finish externally.
Internal breather membrane lapped over and bonded to DPM base.
100 × 75mm vertical softwood studs at 400mm centres.
100mm high density insulation between studs.
Vapour barrier.
75 × 25mm softwood battens forming 25mm service void.
15mm skimmed plasterboard internal lining with painted finish.

4. Concrete formwork
1220 × 3810 × 0.4mm corrugated galvanised steel sheets nailed to plywood and holes sealed.
Sheets overlapped by 1½; corrugations to ensure consistent finish.

5. External window
Ex 150 × 75mm iroko window frame screwed to concrete via galvanised steel angle brackets.

Bituminous DPC fixed to frame, dressed over internal breather membrane and bonded to concrete.
Breathable mastic seal externally.
15mm skimmed plasterboard internal lining fixed to 50mm softwood studwork to form window reveal.

6. Steel structure
114 × 6mm galvanised steel CHS (circular hollow section) columns at 2.5m centres to courtyard perimeter with painted finish.
275 × 275 × 15mm baseplate welded to CHS and bolted to concrete footing.
Column cased in 50mm mass concrete up to slab level as corrosion protection.
400 × 200 × 20mm thick steel plate welded to top of CHS and cast into roof slab 75mm above underside.
Ten 19mm diameter × 120mm high shear studs welded to top side of plate to tie column head into reinforcement of slab and resist punching shear.

7. Roof
Two layer polymer modified bitumen waterproof membrane with mineral chips on exposed surfaces.
Tapered PIR (polyisocyanurate) insulation varying from 110 to 270mm thick to form 1:80 fall.
1.2mm foil cored reinforced vapour barrier.
300mm fair-faced reinforced concrete roof slab left exposed internally with Class C patterned finish.
Plywood formwork with joints and fixings set out to correspond with plan arrangement.

8. Rooflight
375mm high × 75mm wide reinforced concrete upstand.
25mm PIR insulation around upstand.
75 × 50mm softwood kerb screwed to concrete upstand.
Top layer of polymer modified bitumen waterproof membrane dressed up vertical face and under rooflight frame.
700/1400 or 2100mm diameter circular extruded aluminium frame screwed to kerb to ensure 1:100 fall.
Walk-on double-glazed sealed unit consisting of 21.5mm toughened laminated outer pane,

*Photo: Anthony Coleman*

*Photo: Anthony Coleman*

*Photo: Anthony Coleman*

*Photo: Cottrell & Vermeulen
Architecture*

*Photo: Cottrell & Vermeulen
Architecture*

# Bellingham Gateway Building
# Lewisham, London

Architect: Cottrell & Vermeulen Architecture
Structural Engineer: Engineers HRW

The Gateway Building is a place where children and young people can take part in sport and leisure activities while meeting other people their own age in safe surroundings. Housed beneath an asymmetric pitched roof that snakes along the edge of a playing field, the building contains a nursery for 0–2 year-olds, an activity room and a café. The leisure facilities, funded by Sport England are intended to introduce young people from deprived backgrounds to activities they may not otherwise get the chance to try.

The structural frame is made up of a series of steel portals built off a concrete raft foundation with a perimeter ring beam. The frame is stiffened with 175 mm deep softwood purlins and noggins braced with a plywood deck. Working on a very low budget the architects have made something special out of very basic materials.

Different types of cladding and rooflights allow light in and out off the building in a playful way without breaking the roof profile. On the north and west sides corrugated cement fibre cladding is used near ground level where it is susceptible to vandalism painted with an anti-graffiti coating. Translucent glass reinforced plastic (GRP) sheets cover the rest of the roof and walls with insulation, a breather membrane and a ventilation gap behind. On the east side sedum covers part of the roof so that the surface of the park seems to wrap up and engage with the building. The plants are held in place on the 25 degree pitch by a woven geotextile 'blanket'.

Above the entrance porch the insulation and plywood sheathing have been left out so that light can shine right through the roof and illuminate the lobby below. The lobby ceiling externally and the sliding folding gates are made from the same translucent GRP, backlit to emphasise the entrance. Elsewhere on the west elevation the plywood behind the GRP cladding has been painted in bright colours so that at night the building seems to glow from within.

Steel portal frame structure

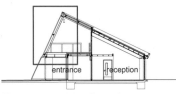

East-west section through
entrance – Scale 1:400

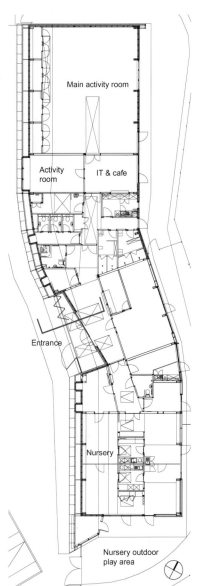

Ground floor plan – Scale 1:400

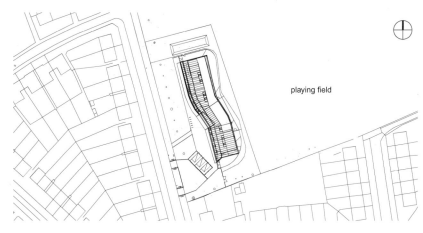

playing field

Site location plan – 1:2000

Drawing labels:

1. Steel frame generally
Seventeen steel portals at between 3.15 m
and 3.75 m centres made up from welded
356 × 171 mm universal beams (UB) bolted
down to concrete slab.

2. Steel frame over entrance
356 × 171 mm UB ridge beam.
356 × 171 mm UB eaves beam over entrance.
203 × 133 × 30 UB tie beam over central spine
wall.
152 × 152 mm universal column (UC)
secondary steels to support timber purlins.

3. West elevation low-level cladding
175 × 38 mm treated softwood purlins at
600 mm centres.
Corrugated cement-fibre sheet cladding
fixed at 65 degree angle with self-tapping
screws.
Clear anti-vandal permeable paint finish.
Independent timber framed wall behind made
up from 150 × 38 mm softwood studwork.
100 mm polyisocyanurate (PIR) insulation
between studs.
12 mm sheathing ply and breather membrane
externally.
Vapour barrier.
Plasterboard lining internally in nursery and
office areas.
15 mm gypsum bonded wood particle board in
activity rooms, café, corridor and reception.

4. West elevation high-level cladding
Corrugated translucent glass reinforced plastic
(GRP) external cladding fixed to SW battens
through plywood with self-tapping screws at
1800 mm centres.
9 mm hardwood facing plywood pre-decorated
with weathershield paint where colour required,
the rest of the plywood pre-decorated with
wood stain.
50 × 50 mm horizontal softwood battens at
nominal 600 centres.
Breather membrane.
150 × 50 mm vertical battens at 1250 mm
centres fixed with stainless steel brackets.
100 mm PIR insulation with 50 mm ventilation
gap above.
Vapour control layer.
18 mm plywood deck.
175 × 38 mm softwood purlins at 600 mm
centres.

5. GRP cladding to entrance area
Corrugated translucent GRP external cladding
fixed to softwood purlins with self-tapping
screws.
175 × 50 mm softwood purlins at 2.27 m
centres fixed to steel frame.

6. Aluminium flashing
Folded 2 mm mill finish aluminium flashing used
to roof ridge area.
Polyester powder coated (PPC) aluminium
corner flashing and window surrounds.

7. East elevation green roof
Sedum blanket held in place by retention strips.
5 mm root-resistant layer.
4 mm bitumen and high-tensile woven glass
fibre waterproof layer.
100 mm PIR insulation boards.
Vapour barrier.
18 mm plywood decking.
175 × 38 mm softwood purlins at 600 mm
centres.

8. Gutter
240 × 160 mm folded PPC aluminium gutter
over entrance fixed to steel with self-tapping
screws.

9. Entrance external soffit
Corrugated translucent GRP ceiling lining fixed
to 50 × 50 mm softwood battens above with
self-tapping screws.

10. Entrance lobby ceiling
Corrugated translucent GRP ceiling lining
fixed to 125 × 50 mm timber battens above
with self-tapping screws.
6 mm perforated hardboard.
100 mm PIR insulation.

11. Entrance gates
2330 mm high folding-sliding steel framed gates
with corrugated translucent GRP in-fill panels.
Steel frame made up from 50 × 50 mm
galvanised steel angles.
Track bolted to steel beam above.

12. Entrance doors
PPC aluminium door frames with double-glazed
sealed units.

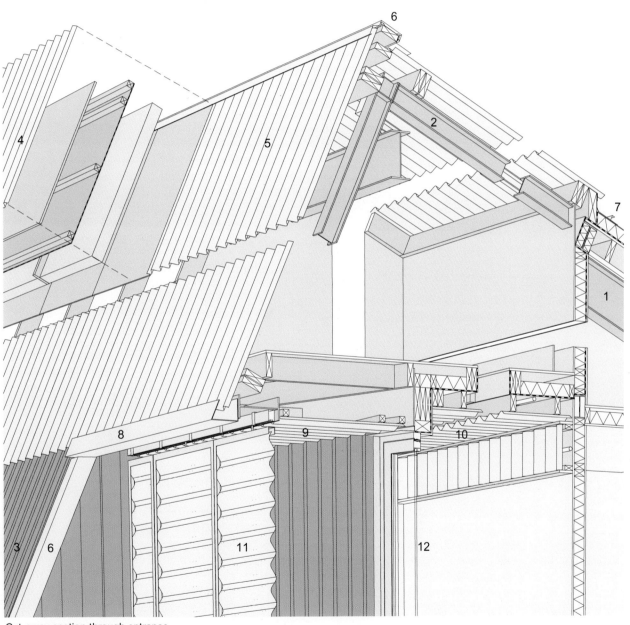

Cut-away section through entrance

Photo: Fluid

Photo: Fluid

Photo: Fluid

Photo: Morley von Sternberg

# Maryland Early Years Centre
# Stratford, London

Architect: Fluid
Structural Engineer: Conisbee
Prefabricated Panels: Framework CDM

Maryland Early Years Centre in east London was built in an incredibly short 5-month period using a prefabricated timber panel superstructure. The single-storey Centre houses a daycare room for 2–5-year-olds, a staff training room and a classroom which is shared with the next-door primary school.

Deep concrete trench footings pass through 1.5 m of fill to bear on a sand and gravel layer below. Basements from a previous row of terraced houses that were discovered during the works had to be filled with concrete in places to ensure a firm base. A 200 mm thick ground floor slab spans between the footings with a 140 mm perimeter upstand to raise the timber wall panels off the ground.

The walls and roof were prefabricated and brought to site in panels. The wall panels consist of 140 mm softwood studs with insulation between, breathable wood-fibre board external sheathing and an OSB (oriented strand board) inner lining. A 360 mm deep laminated softwood beam runs around the perimeter of the building at roof level and across the top of the central wall tying all the panels together. The roof panels consist of 350 mm deep composite timber beams conjoined with a plywood top deck. They sit on the wall panels and fix laterally into the tie beam.

On the south side a steel framed canopy shelters an enclosed outdoor play space. The canopy has a translucent polycarbonate roof and the soffit is made up of larch strips with 10 mm gaps between so some light can pass through it.

Externally the walls are clad with GRP (glass-fibre reinforced plastic), a material normally used for roofing, chosen so that its translucency would reveal something of the construction beneath. The GRP is wrapped around the corners in a curve, reinforcing the horizontality of the building and softening its edges. The bright orange and lime-green façades provide a splash of much needed colour in a rather run-down setting.

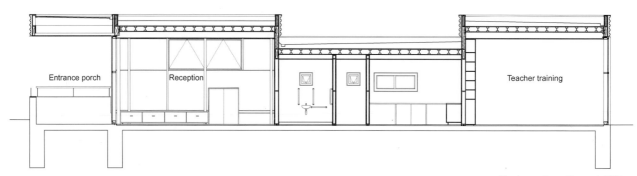

East–west section – 1:150

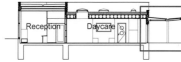

North–south section – Scale 1:400

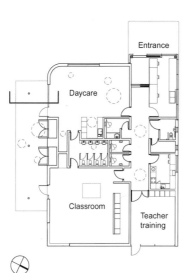

Ground floor plan – Scale 1:400

Drawing labels:

1. Foundations
C35 mass concrete trench fill foundations to 1.5 m depth into gravel.

2. External landscaping
Artificial grass laid on 9 mm shock-absorbing pad.
130 mm trowelled concrete base laid to fall away from building.
150 mm granular sub-base.
100 mm concrete blinding.

3. Ground floor
3 mm vinyl floor finish.
22 mm tongued and grooved particle board flooring.
72 mm extruded polystyrene insulation with integral underfloor heating pipes.
200 mm thick mesh reinforced C35 concrete slab spanning between trench footings.
1200 mm gauge polythene damp proof membrane.
100 mm well rolled sand blinding.

4. Ground floor slab edge
140 × 90 mm concrete upstand.
Bituminous DPM (damp proof membrane) lapped over polythene DPM below slab and over blinding externally.
Bituminous DPM bonded to vertical face of slab edge.
Liquid applied bituminous DPM applied to top and bottom joints to form continuous waterproof layer.
3 mm bituminous protection board.
25 mm extruded polystyrene insulation internally at floor edge.

5. Typical wall
51 mm translucent sinusoidal GRP (glass reinforced plastic) with polyester film fixed back to purlins with lacquered self-drilling fasteners located in valleys of sinusoidal GRP.
50 mm cavity and vertical galvanised steel Z-profile purlins.
Prefabricated wall cassettes made up from 140 × 38 mm softwood timber studs at 600 mm centres with mineral wool insulation.
22 mm thick wood-fibre board external sheathing.
18 mm oriented strand board and vapour control layer internally.
12.5 mm plasterboard with plaster skim finish internally.

6. Window
100 × 50 mm aluminium box frame with 50 × 50 mm aluminium framed tilt and turn window opening lights.
Double-glazed sealed units made up from 4 mm toughened inner pane, 16 mm argon filled cavity, 4 mm toughened outer pane with soft low E coating.

7. Window head
90 × 360 mm laminated softwood beam over opening.
22 mm thick wood-fibre board sheathing.

135 × 30 mm mill finish pressed aluminium external flashing fixed to beam.
Plasterboard returned internally at head and jambs with skim coat and paint finish.

8. Tie beam
90 × 360 mm laminated softwood tie beam bolted across top of all cassettes around building perimeter and across central spine wall.

9. Roof
EPDM waterproof membrane.
150 mm extruded polystyrene insulation laid to falls.
Polythene vapour control membrane.
350 mm deep prefabricated roof cassettes made up from 350 mm deep engineered timber beams with 18 mm WBP plywood deck.
18 mm plywood soffit.
1200 × 600 mm high density glass wool acoustic ceiling panels on ceiling grid suspended from cassette soffit on isolating wires.

10. Parapet
Prefabricated upstand wall cassettes made up from 140 × 38 mm softwood studwork.
22 mm wood-fibre board to external face of cassette.
9 mm OSB sheathing to internal face.
EPDM waterproof membrane dressed up and over upstand.
285 × 50 mm mill finish aluminium coping.

11. Canopy steel structure
168 mm diameter CHS (circular hollow section) columns at 5530 mm centres.
150 × 75 mm steel UEA (unequal angle) bolted through plywood sheathing to timber beam.
Paired 100 × 100 mm SHS (square hollow section) cranked beams bolted to UEA and either side of CHS.
200 × 100 mm RHS (rectangular hollow section) bolted between SHS beams below gutter.
125 × 65 mm PFC (parallel flange channel) welded to ends of SHS beams along canopy edges.

12. Canopy gutter
300 × 75 × 1.5 mm pressed aluminium box gutter fixed to 75 × 38 mm softwood battens on both sides.
76 mm diameter aluminium rainwater pipes inserted inside CHS columns.
300 × 150 mm cut-out near base of columns for rainwater pipe outlet.

13. Canopy roof
10 mm thick translucent polycarbonate sheets clamped into proprietary aluminium patent glazing bars at 655 mm centres.
Glazing bars screwed to 75 × 38 mm softwood battens at 975 mm centres.
100 × 50 mm C24 softwood joists at 655 mm centres spanning between steel members.
50 × 38 mm treated softwood battens fixed to undersides of joists.
50 × 25 mm larch slats screwed to battens at 60 mm centres.
300 mm deep mill finish pressed aluminium flashing to all three edges of canopy.

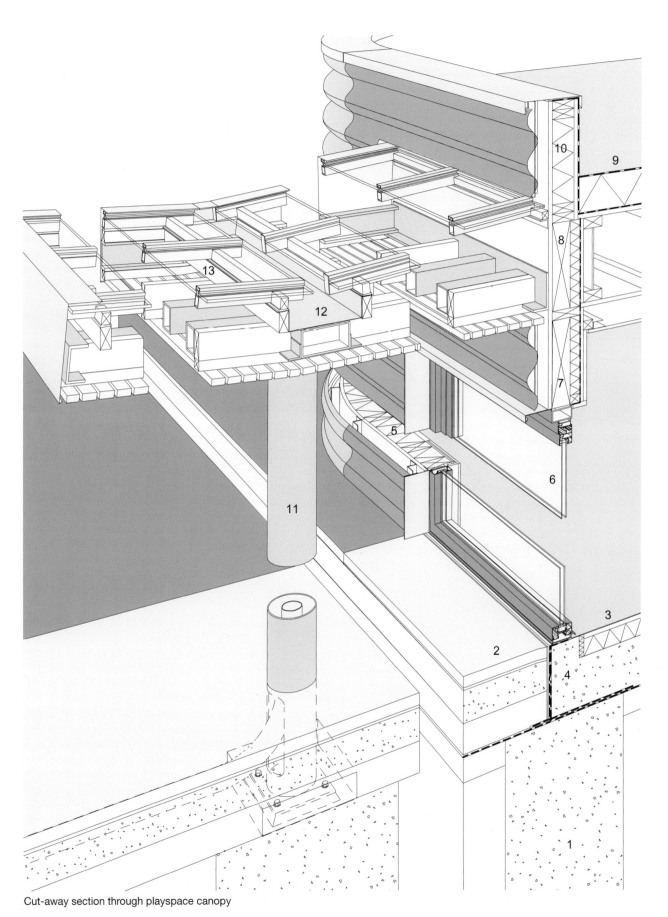

Cut-away section through playspace canopy

# Emmaus School
# Wybourn, Sheffield

### Architect: DSDHA
### Structural Engineer: Price & Myers

Draped across a hillside above Sheffield city centre, the Wybourn Estate has a dramatic landscape setting with panoramic views across to the Peak District. In 2005 the Council adopted a masterplan intended to counter the social problems that have blighted the area since the decline of local industries in the 1970s and 1980s. One of the first tangible products of the plan is the Emmaus Primary School that replaces and unites a Roman Catholic and a Church of England faith school that were suffering from declining numbers of pupils.

The foundation is a concrete raft to bridge across a fault line in the rock that runs diagonally under the building. The frame is steel with precast concrete plank floors and roof for speed and economy. The project was procured under a two-stage tender process allowing the contractor a lot of input on construction decisions.

Rooflights have been used extensively to give a high quality of light on a tiny budget. Two two-storey blocks containing classrooms, administration and a hall are oriented at a splayed angle to one another to make a central circulation space with a long rooflight over the staircase. At the entrance a precast concrete bridge spans from a retaining wall outside onto the building's steel frame. Precast elements have also been used for the long ramp down the north elevation and retaining walls for ease of maintenance and a predictable high quality finish. The entrance façade is a standard aluminium curtain walling system. Inside, the entrance bridge looks down on a double height 'sacred space' through a glazed wall, framed in hardwood to give a half-hour fire rating.

Published in 2003, Building Bulletin 93 set strict acoustic standards for the first time for new schools. A degree of experimentation was involved in detailing walls, floors and ceilings that would comply with the regulations and be economical and practical to build. In the circulation space large acoustic absorbent ceiling boards with taped and filled joints have been used in preference to a typical suspended ceiling grid. All classroom walls are made from two independent double-boarded metal studwork frames separated by mineral wool. At the façade the isolation is continued with two separate curtain wall mullions with an insulated aluminium panel between them.

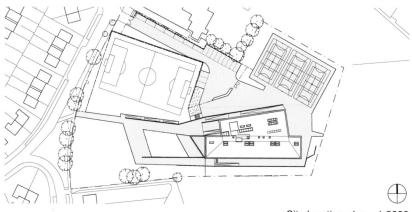

Site location plan – 1:2000

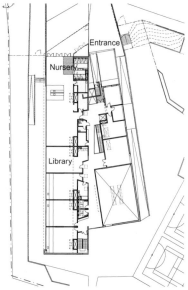

Upper level plan – Scale 1:1000

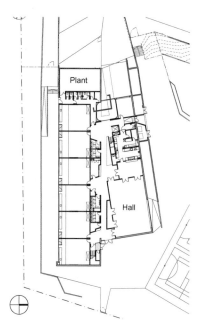

Lower level plan – Scale 1:1000

North–south section – Scale 1:1000

Drawing labels:

1. Primary structure
Steel frame.
Precast concrete planks spanning between steel beams.

2. First floor
10 mm carpet floor finish.
25 mm tongued and grooved particle board floor.
35 mm rigid polystyrene insulation with underfloor heating pipes.
5 mm impact absorbing layer turned up at edges.
50 mm sand-cement screed.
150 mm precast concrete planks.
Acoustic suspended ceiling panels.

3. Entrance bridge
20 mm thick coir mat flush with adjacent floor finish.
12 mm plywood base.
35 mm rigid acoustic insulation.
Acoustic isolating membrane.
75 × 75 mm mild steel angle at entrance threshold.
50 mm sand-cement screed.
150 mm thick precast concrete floor slab.

4. Typical external wall
20 mm sand-cement render external finish with stainless steel angle stop beads.
100 mm concrete blockwork.
100 mm full-fill mineral wool insulation.
100 mm concrete blockwork.
12.5 mm plasterboard fixed to blockwork on dabs with taped joints and painted finish internally.

5. Internal acoustic wall
Two layers 12.5 mm plasterboard with painted finish.
80 × 40 mm galvanised steel inner stud frame with deflection head detail at top.
30 mm mineral wool insulation suspended in cavity between studs.
80 × 40 mm galvanised steel outer stud frame independent from inner frame with deflection head detail at top.
Two layers 12.5 mm plasterboard with painted finish.

6. Internal/external wall junction
35 mm insulation and damp proof membrane between blockwork and metal studs.

Black painted softwood packer between curtain wall frame and internal wall.

7. Roof
20 mm mastic asphalt with solar reflective treatment.
Separating membrane.
100 mm fully bonded PIS (polyisocyanurate) insulation.
Liquid applied bituminous vapour control layer.
Minimum 35 mm thick sand-cement screed laid to 1:70 fall.
200 mm precast concrete slabs spanning between primary steel members.
75 × 50 mm softwood battens.
Suspended ceiling panels perforated for acoustic absorbency.

8. Parapet
525 mm wide PPC (polyester powder coated) pressed aluminium coping fixed on clips to plywood.
PPC pressed aluminium flashing forming 170 mm high × 50 mm deep recess.
18 mm WBP plywood base for flashings on softwood studwork fixed to steel frame.
200 × 90 mm PFC (parallel flange channel) bolted between stub posts.
200 mm insulation retained to studwork with galvanised wire mesh.
Vapour barrier.
170 mm insulation behind anodised aluminium curtain wall panel.

9. Rooflight upstand
20 mm mastic asphalt on separating layer.
18 mm WBP plywood external sheathing.
150 × 50 mm softwood studwork frame.
150 mm insulation between studs.
Vapour barrier.
12.5 mm plasterboard internal lining with paint finish.

10. Rooflight
PPC aluminium frame screwed to 50 × 50 mm softwood sub-frame.
Double-glazed sealed units with 6.4 mm inner pane, 10 mm cavity, 6 mm toughened outer pane.

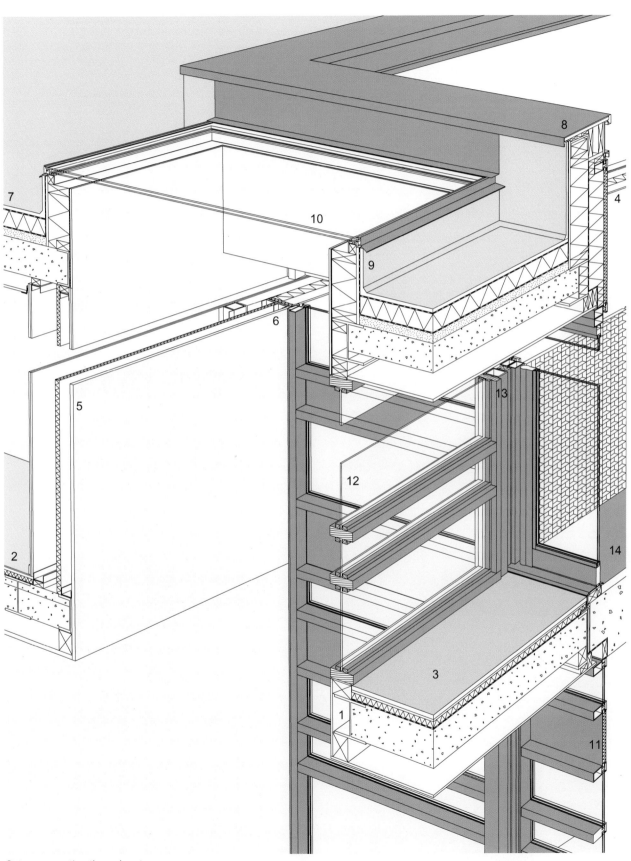

Cut-away section through entrance

11. External glazed wall
130 × 50 mm aluminium curtain walling box
frame with anodised finish.
Double-glazed sealed units with 6 mm inner
pane, 10 mm cavity, 6 mm outer pane.
Opaque panels made up from PPC pressed
aluminium front and rear sheets with thermally
isolating spacers and rigid insulation between.

12. Internal glazed screen
150 × 50 mm hardwood frame with paint finish
to provide 30 minutes fire resistance.
Laminated fire resistant single glazing.
32 × 20 mm hardwood glazing beads screw
fixed on both sides of glass.

13. Curtain wall/glazed screen junction
100 × 100 mm SHS (square hollow section)
steel post.

50 × 50 mm solid softwood blocking with
12 mm painted MDF faces.
Intumescent perimeter seals to give 30 minutes'
fire resistance.

14. Entrance ramp
9 m long × 1920 mm wide × 375 mm thick
precast concrete slab spanning between
steel frame and retaining wall in
landscaping.
100 × 100 mm galvanised steel angle cast into
end of concrete slab bears on 300 × 100 mm
PFC beam spanning between 100 × 100 mm
SHS posts at entrance.
50 mm asphalt surface finish.
1100 mm high balustrade made up from
1200 mm wide × 1530 mm high galvanised
steel grating panels bolted to edge of ramp.

Photo: Hélène Binet

Photo: Eric Parry Architects

# Bedford School Music School
# Bedford

Architect: Eric Parry Architects
Structural Engineer: Adams Kara Taylor
Acoustic Consultant: Paul Gillieron Acoustic Design

The red brick grandeur of Bedford School's main building and chapel date from the early twentieth century, a time when attitudes to education were very different from today. In the twenty-first century, the school has made a concerted effort to redress this image with two buildings by Eric Parry which are more intimate and specific to their place, a new library (see *Architecture in Detail*, Vol. 1) and a Music School. The Music School consists of three distinct elements, a teaching block, a practice block and a recital hall arranged around a common 'street' space. The recital hall addresses the playing fields with a distinctly modern interpretation of a portico. Inside, it has a flat floor and stackable seating for up to 200 audience members and performers.

Due to the proximity of mature trees and the clay soil piled foundations were used with concrete ground beams. Blockwork cavity walls separate the different rooms where acoustic isolation is required. The steel frame of the recital hall was erected in prefabricated sections with 4 mm bead-blasted stainless steel sheet cladding already fixed in place. Large areas of full-height glazing in stainless steel frames alternate with the solid stainless steel panels around three sides of the six metre high room to maximise natural lighting. Stainless steel solar shading blinds can be lowered outside the glass to reduce direct solar gain and glare. The $5 \times 4$ mm horizontal fins have a profile that only allows direct sun penetration at an angle of less than 20 degrees.

Photo: Eric Parry Architects

An occupied reverberation time of 1.5 seconds for mid frequencies has been achieved by maximising reflective surfaces. When occupancy levels are low, banks of 45 mm thick MDF doors can be opened to reveal acoustic boxes lined with absorbent insulation that reduces the reverberation time. Overhead four large radiant heating panels double as acoustic reflectors. Fresh air is supplied through grilles at seated head height in the three external walls and extracted at a high level on the internal wall. The noise from the ventilation system is kept to a very low level of NR20 by supplying the air via a plenum below the floor at low velocity. Outside, the grass banks up towards the façade making a rostrum for musicians to play summer concerts under the overhanging canopy.

Photo: Eric Parry Architects

Ground floor plan – Scale 1:600

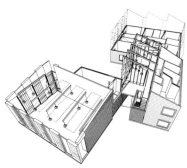

Isometric view from west end

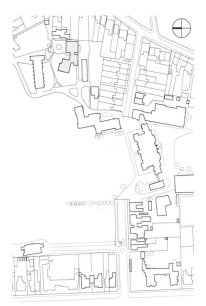

Site location plan – 1:5000

East–west section – Scale 1:600

Drawing labels:

1. Foundations
600 × 500mm reinforced concrete ground beam.
500mm diameter reinforced concrete piles.
200mm wide × 1070mm high reinforced concrete upstand retaining wall.
100mm thick × 725mm wide reinforced concrete toe to form base of plenum.
50mm extruded polystyrene insulation around ring beam and toe.

2. Plenum
815 × 700mm plenum for air supply to recital room.
100mm wide dense concrete blockwork wall to form inside edge.
Floor and walls of plenum painted with bituminous waterproof membrane.
50mm extruded polystyrene insulation around walls and floor of plenum.
Perforated metal wearing surface to floor.

3. Ground floor
15mm thick engineered oak laminate timber sprung floor fixed with clips.
75mm thick sand/cement screed.
50mm thick high density expanded polystyrene insulation.
200mm thick precast concrete planks spanning between reinforced concrete and blockwork walls.
Void beneath floor ventilated by telescopic vents.

4. Structural frame
Load-bearing ladder-frames made up from two 203 × 102mm × 23kg universal beam (UB) columns at 1495mm or 1443mm centres, horizontal 100 × 50mm parallel flange channel (PFC) members at 1690mm centres and 100 × 50mm PFC diagonal cross-braces.
All steelwork delivered to site with two-coat zinc phosphate paint system and pre-clad with stainless steel.

5. Ground floor slab edge
50mm high 4mm stainless steel recessed skirting fixed down to concrete upstand at base of solid panels.
Sleeved 100mm wide vent slot supply air from plenum between columns rising to wall grilles.
DPC bonded to stainless steel window frame and dressed down over face of concrete upstand wall.
125mm wide gravel strip between building and grass.

6. External wall cladding
4mm thick × 5500mm high × 1740mm wide bead-blasted stainless-steel panel with laser-cut vertical abutments bolted to supporting structure in rigid joints.
Stainless steel pressed section subframe for stiffening pre-drilled for fixing back to mild steel frame with isolating spacers to prevent bi-metallic corrosion.
Pre-drilled midpoint noggins fixing cladding back to pre-drilled mild steel angle cross-bracing at 850mm centres approx.
Puddle welded pressed stainless steel corner stiffening angles stop short at top and bottom by 20mm to sleeve over inboard skirting U-section.
12mm plywood backing to stainless steel panel up to 1500mm height to prevent 'barrelling' impact noise.

7. External wall internal linings
Water repellent insulation between columns.
Vapour barrier.
1250 × 200mm low-velocity supply ventilation/heating air duct with 1100 × 300mm grilles.
69 × 44mm softwood studwork framing.
25mm thick MDF panels with routed grooves to line up with door divisions above secret-fixed to studwork.
Three-coat shop finish paint system to MDF internal lining.

8. Acoustic boxes
Five 3585mm high × 331mm wide × 44mm thick pivot-hung MDF doors.
Stainless steel bar on ratchet mechanism fixed to bottom lip of doors so all doors open and close together.
Black fabric lining over acoustic insulation inside boxes.

9. Glazing
Fixing plate welded across flanges of UB columns at 1800mm vertical centres.
Glazing angle frame made from
125 × 65 × 8mm stainless steel folded plate welded at corners and bolted to plates on UBs with isolating membrane to prevent bi-metallic corrosion.
50 × 50 × 6mm stainless steel angle glazing bead fixed to frame with countersunk bolts.
1800 × 5500mm double-glazed sealed unit formed from 12mm clear toughened inner pane, 16mm cavity, 12.8mm laminated Pilkington 'K' glass outer pane.

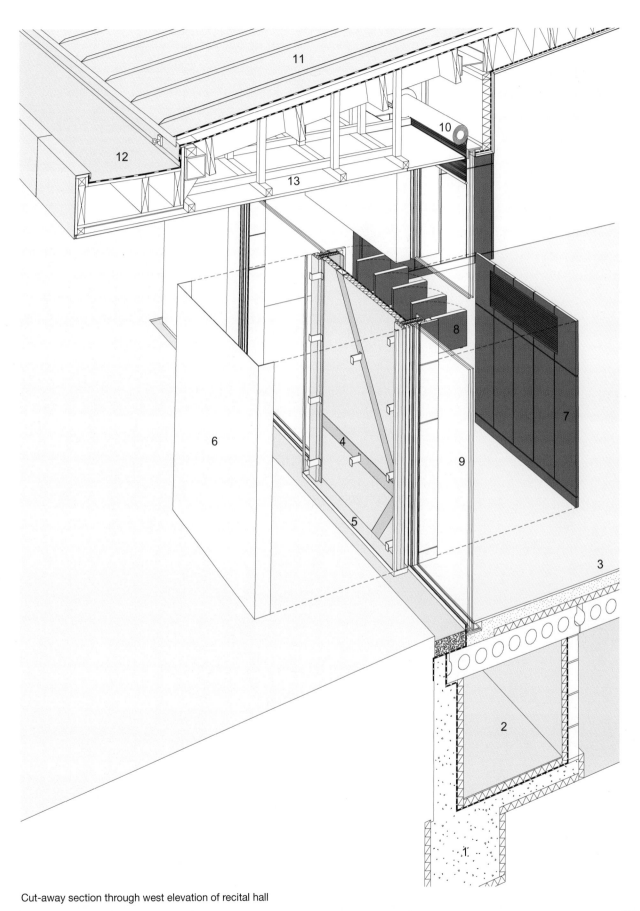

Cut-away section through west elevation of recital hall

10. Roller shutter
External deployable solar shading on rolling mechanism fixed at head to steel frame.
Vertical guides screwed to 150 mm long × 50 × 5 mm stainless steel flats welded to glazing angle frame at 1340 mm centres.

11. Roof
0.7 mm gauge zinc-alloy standing seam roof finish.
8 mm acoustic underlay and breather membrane.
WBP plywood deck.
305 × 165 mm UB roof beams at 3400 mm centres.
250 × 50 mm C24 softwood joists at 600 mm centres notched into roof beams.
250 mm mineral wool insulation between joists.
Vapour barrier.
Two layers 12.5 mm plasterboard with 3 mm skim coat.

12. Gutter
1 mm thick zinc-coated aluminium coping and 400 mm high fascia fixed over upstand and in shadow gap under.
Single-ply waterproof membrane.
18 mm WBP plywood deck laid to 1:100 minimum fall.
150 × 150 × 8 mm square hollow section (SHS) gutter support beam bolted between primary roof beams.
788 × 383 mm × 10 mm thick gutter steel support brackets bolted to gutter support beam at 800 mm centres.
Eye bolts for clip-on safety system fixed to 90 × 90 × 5 mm steel SHS stubs welded to 15 mm thick plates bolted to gutter support beam.

13. Soffit
1 mm thick zinc-coated aluminium panels fixed to studwork behind.
Removable panels to soffit to allow maintenance access to sunshade roller shutters.

*Photo: Anthony Weller*

# Sanger Building, Bryanston School Dorset

Architect: Hopkins Architects Ltd
Structural Engineer: Buro Happold

The Sanger Building contains classrooms, laboratories and a 120-seat lecture theatre for science and maths teaching at Bryanston, a school for 13–18-year-olds in Dorset. Red hand-made bricks with precast concrete details relate the horseshoe shaped block to the vast Richard Norman Shaw house dating from 1897 at the centre of the school estate. The outside elevation is an insulated cavity wall with a half-brick thick (102.5 mm) outer leaf laid in stretcher bond. The inner elevation addresses a landscaped courtyard. Here the brick wall is laid in English bond and is fully load-bearing. Regular openings are formed with solid brick flat arches spanning 1810 mm between 890 mm wide piers, which are occupied by Douglas fir framed windows.

To carry the weight of the three-storey elevation the courtyard wall needs to be one and a half bricks thick. In the lower storey the loadings are near the limit of the bearing capacity of the bricks, while in the top storey the piers do not have sufficient mass to resist wind loads, so reinforcement rods were inserted in a void in the centre of the piers and concrete poured around them to make a wind post that also serves to hold down the lightweight roof. The floor slabs nominally span between the courtyard and park elevations but Building Regulations require a degree of redundancy to avoid disproportionate collapse so the slabs also bear on the cross walls. On the courtyard elevations, the floor slabs are isolated from the walls with strips of insulation to prevent load being transferred into the arches. At each pier a pocket was left in the brick and the slab cast into the pier to ensure a rigid connection.

Were the piers to be insulated, and a true load-bearing English bond external wall maintained, the piers would become excessively thick and the floor slabs would still have to penetrate the insulation and cavity to bear on the external wall. The detail illustrates the difficulties in achieving current standards of thermal performance with monolithic construction.

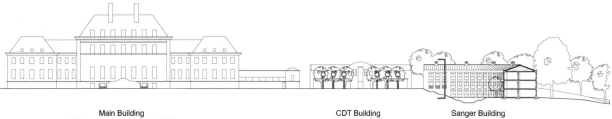

Main Building
(Richard Norman Shaw – 1897)

CDT Building
(CZWG – 1998)

Sanger Building
(Hopkins – 2007)

North–south section through site – Scale 1:1500

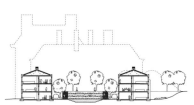

East–west section – 1:1500

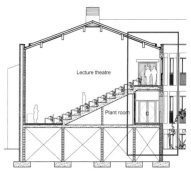

First floor plan – 1:1000

Section through lecture theatre and
external walkway – 1:400

Drawing labels:

1. External walls
328 mm thick load-bearing handmade brick
(compressive strength 25 N/mm$^2$) wall laid in
English bond.
Lime mortar mixed 1:1:6 (1 part Portland
cement, 1 part hydrated lime and 6 parts sand).

2. Brick arch
328 mm wide × 440 mm high arch built from
pre-formed special tapered bricks with 20 mm
camber and spanning 1810 mm.

3. Boss
Precast concrete capping built into external
course of brickwork to indicate bearing of floor
slab behind.
Floor slab cast into brick pier.

4. Colonnade floor
400 × 400 × 65 mm concrete pavers on 15 mm
sand bed.
Damp proof membrane.
Rigid insulation tapered from 50 mm to fall to
outside.
250 mm reinforced concrete slab.

5. Plant room floor
130 mm wearing screed in plant room.
Damp proof membrane.
250 mm reinforced concrete slab.
215 mm walls supporting slab formed from
215 × 102.5 × 65 mm blocks laid flat.

6. Balustrade
1700 × 1100 mm painted steel balustrade
bolted to brickwork piers on both sides.
Balustrade made up from 45 mm diameter
handrail, 18 mm diameter rods, 60 × 15 mm flat
uprights, top and bottom flat rails.

7. Second floor openings
Douglas fir window panels consisting of
Douglas fir framed opening windows and
insulated spandrel panel below.
Double-glazed sealed units consisting of two
panes of 6 mm glass with 12 mm air gap.
75 × 50 mm softwood studwork frame with
mineral wool insulation between studs.
Vapour barrier fixed to inner face of studs.
Internal and external solid panels made up from
50 × 25 mm hardwood Douglas fir frames with
69 × 19 mm tongued and grooved board infill.

8. Lecture theatre floor
Carpet floor finish.
Minimum 200 mm thick precast concrete
elements to form rake for seating with
850 × 392 mm steps.

203 × 133 mm UB (universal beam) at back of
rake supported on SHS posts in plant room
wall.

9. Second floor
Carpet floor finish.
75 mm sand/cement screed.
25 mm insulation.
250 mm reinforced concrete slab.
15 mm calcium silicate board soffit.

10. Plant room wall
125 × 125 mm concrete upstand at base.
5.1 m high 120 × 120 × 10 mm SHS (square
hollow section) posts at 2.3 m centres.
120 × 45 mm softwood studs at 715 mm
centres vertically and 1300 mm centres
horizontally.
15 mm plasterboard internal lining to provide 1
hour fire rating.
Mineral wool insulation between studs.
15 mm WBP plywood external sheathing
painted dark green.
106 × 25 mm solid larch louvre blades fixed to
110 × 45 mm notched vertical larch battens at
a 45 degree angle.
130 × 25 mm larch external skirting.
Localised cut-outs in partition where
necessary for ducts from plant equipment with
intumescent grille behind louvres to maintain
fire protection.

11. Roof
Zinc alloy standing seam roof finish.
Fibre mat underlay to create air gap preventing
moisture build-up and corrosion.
120 mm polyurethane insulation boards with
integral softwood strips to allow fixing of zinc
clips.
Vapour barrier.
Two layers 18 mm plywood deck.
100 × 100 mm softwood joists.
495 × 165 mm glulam timber beams at
2055 mm centres spanning 9.4 m from gable
end wall to cross wall.
Plywood soffit panels.
Alternate rows of panels have slots with black
fabric and 30 mm mineral fibre insulation behind
to absorb sound.

12. Gutter
Precast concrete coping fixed down to
brickwork with stainless steel dowels.
Lead flashing dressed down over gutter lining.
Single ply PVC membrane gutter lining.
Vapour barrier.
Two layers 18 mm plywood gutter deck.

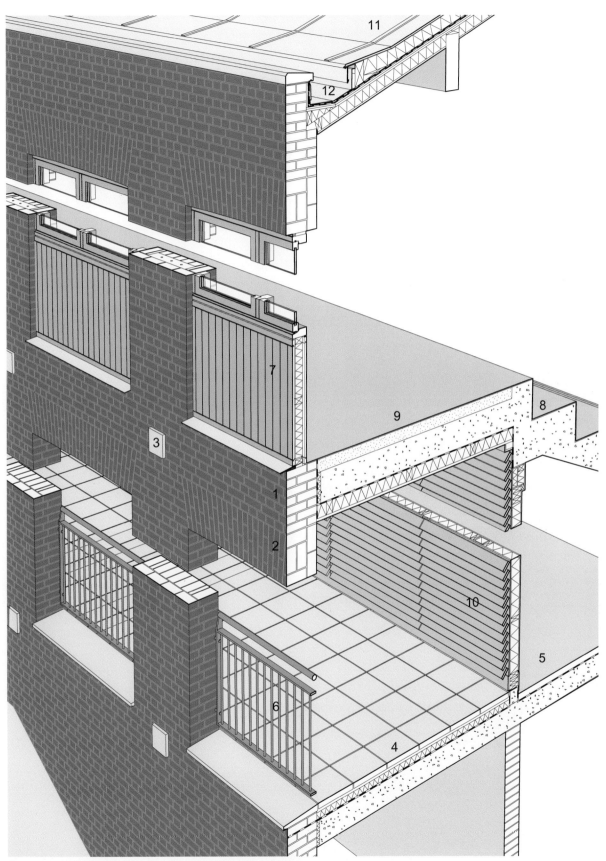

Cut-away section through colonnade and rear of lecture theatre

*Photo: Amos Goldreich*

*Photo: Amos Goldreich*

*Photo: Amos Goldreich*

# Scitec, Oundle School
# Northamptonshire

Architect: Feilden Clegg Bradley
Structural Engineer: Jane Wernick Associates

Scitec is Oundle School's new science and technology centre, a development intended to provide a unifying focus to the disparate school facilities, currently scattered about the town. Phase 1, completed in the summer of 2007, consists of 16 laboratories over two floors accessed from a top-lit gallery space. It has a structure of concrete walls and slabs on a raft foundation, all cast in-situ. The next phases include art and design studios, a library and a lecture theatre, which will all be accessed off a central mall parallel and open to the laboratory circulation space.

Externally the walls are clad in 100mm thick ashlar blocks of Clipsham limestone laid with thin 3mm joints. The stone walls are divided into three lifts with stainless steel shelf angles at first floor and roof levels. The stones in the bottom row of each lift have a stepped profile to sit on the shelf angle and allow a 3mm joint so the horizontal movement joints look like all the other joints. At the base of the wall the stone bears on a concrete nib set just below ground level.

At the west end of the gallery, a stair winds up around a central concrete column that widens into a wall at roof level. Each stone tread appears to cantilever off the concrete wall but in fact merely rests on the tread below, carrying the vertical load down to a concrete landing at the bottom. The treads are not built into the concrete walls but are each attached by two stainless steel dowels that resist the tread's tendency to twist and transfer the resulting torsion into the wall. The stone treads have been rebated on the underside so that they interlock, ensuring they cannot twist relative to one another.

To allow the first floor landing to be set away from the walls its outer edge is hung from the roof on two stainless steel rods. The handrail and balustrades are fixed to steel uprights that cantilever from the ends of the stone treads. Each material has been used deliberately to exploit its primary characteristics. The staircase is intended as a teaching tool where forces of compression, tension, bending, torsion and shear can be clearly explained.

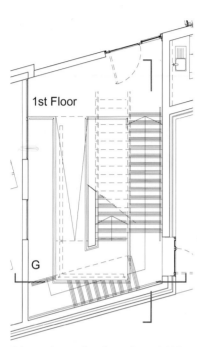

West staircase first floor plan – 1:125

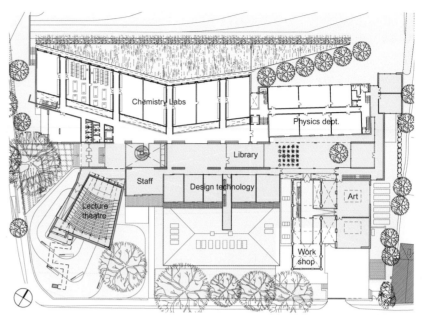

First floor plan – 1:1250

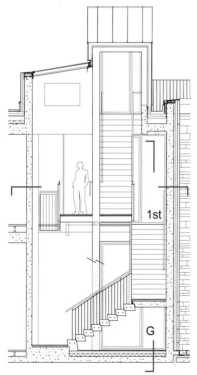

West staircase north–south
section – 1:125

Drawing labels:

1. Ground floor
50 mm concrete paving slabs.
85 mm screed.
Polythene vapour barrier.
90 mm extruded polystyrene insulation acting
as raised floor for services routes.
200 mm thick reinforced concrete raft
thickening to 400 mm at edges.
Bituminous tanking membrane.
Sand blinding on compacted hardcore.

2. External wall below ground level
100 mm extruded polystyrene insulation.
Liquid applied bituminous tanking membrane.
250 mm thick in-situ concrete internal walls.
Translucent sealed finish.

3. Wall detail at ground level
Continuous 220 × 200 mm reinforced concrete
nib to support outer leaf.
Liquid applied bituminous damp proof
membrane dressed down over tanking below.
Heavy duty protection board.
Engineering brick external leaf below ground
level.
Bituminous damp proof course minimum
150 mm above external ground level fixed with
tape and mechanical fixing.

4. External wall
100 mm thick load-bearing Clipsham limestone
in variable courses and random lengths.
Stone bedded on 3 mm mortar joints and
dowelled onto stainless steel cavity ties fixed
back to concrete wall.
Stainless steel shelf angle supporting stone at
first floor level.
120 mm cavity with 100 mm mineral wool
insulation.
Liquid applied bituminous damp proof
membrane.

250 mm thick in-situ concrete internal walls.
Translucent sealed finish.

5. External window
125 × 50 mm aluminium box section frame
bolted back to concrete with intermittent steel
angle brackets.
Double-glazed sealed unit.
285 × 26 mm veneered MDF internal lining
fixed to concrete wall with 10 mm shadow gap
in between.
Internal venetian blind fixed into recess in oak
head lining.

6. Internal wall
200 mm thick in-situ concrete internal walls.
Translucent sealed finish.

7. Window between stair and laboratory
125 × 55 mm box section frame bolted into
concrete.
Double-glazed sealed unit.
Window to provide acoustic separation and
1 hour fire resistance.
60 × 20 mm pressed aluminium channel to
accommodate tolerance between wall
and frame.

8. Central column
1000 × 250 mm reinforced concrete column
between ground floor and first floor landing
supporting spine wall above.

9. Landings
200 mm thick reinforced concrete landings cast
in-situ.
30 mm thick stone finish to top and edge
bedded on 20 mm flexible adhesive bed.
Continuous aluminium strip at perimeter of
landings secret-fixed to concrete to cover
mortar bed.

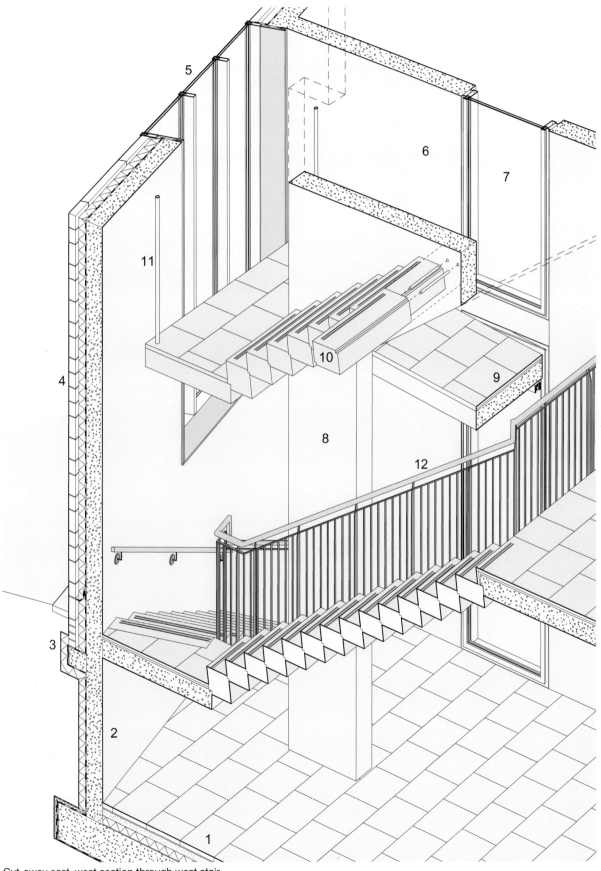

Cut-away east–west section through west stair

10. Stair
1100 mm long × 389 × 228 mm profiled stone treads between first and second floors.
1200 mm long × 354 × 208 mm profiled stone treads between ground and first floors.
Two 450 mm long × 25 mm diameter stainless steel dowels resin bonded into holes in wall and tread.

11. Hangers
Two 25 mm stainless steel hanger rods to support first floor landing from roof slab above. Hanger rod passes through landing via stainless steel sleeve cast into pre-drilled 28 mm diameter hole in slab.
3 mm neoprene pad on 12 mm thick × 75 mm diameter stainless steel plate on underside of slab fastened with stainless steel nut on threaded end of rod.
Gap between rod and sleeve and joint with stone filled with resin.

12. Balustrade
Painted steel balustrade.
75 × 12 mm profiled flat uprights at 900 mm centres fixed into ends of stone treads with resin anchor bolts.
10 × 25 mm flat horizontal and vertical members forming intermediate balustrade panel bolted to uprights.
47 mm diameter waxed oak balustrade drilled and glued to 10 mm stainless steel rods seam welded to top rail.

*Photo: Morley von Sternberg*

*Photo: Morley von Sternberg*

*Photo: Porphyrios Associates*

*Photo: Porphyrios Associates*

# Ann's Court, Selwyn College Cambridge

Architects: Porphyrios Associates
Structural Engineer: Hannah Reed

In 1996 Porphyrios Associates won an invited competition for a major building programme at Selwyn College. Ann's Court, the first phase to be complete, houses the College's administration offices, a basement archive and 44 new study-bedrooms. The building has load-bearing masonry cavity walls supporting pre-cast concrete plank floors and a timber roof. At ground floor an arcade of six stone arches shelter a covered walkway which, in phase 2 will be extended around the quadrangle lawn.

A watertight basement has been made for the archive using secant piling, a technique where concrete piles are poured at centres just under twice their diameter. Before they have fully gone off the intermediate spaces are drilled out, cutting into the piles on either side. Softer concrete is then poured into the new holes forming a continuous waterproof wall. The area inside the piles was dug out and an in-situ concrete facing cast against the inner faces to prevent degradation of the soft concrete. A drained cavity and concrete blockwork inner leaf provide belt-and-braces protection against water ingress.

French Farge limestone has been used to make the arcade columns and voussoirs, simply bonded with lime mortar in the traditional way. The stone could happily take the vertical load but the two end piers are not wide enough to resist outward thrust from the arches so a reinforced concrete beam has been cast just below first floor level to tie the arches together. The voussoirs act as permanent formwork for the concrete beam, tied into it with stainless steel dowels.

The outer leaf of the main walls is one brick thick. Flat arches over the windows at ground and second floors were prefabricated by bonding special shaped bricks to a concrete lintel to look like a traditional brick arch with a 10 mm camber. Ann's Court is a true load-bearing masonry building unafraid to use modern methods where tight tolerances are required or traditional techniques cannot be proven satisfactory by calculation.

*Photo: Morley von Sternberg*

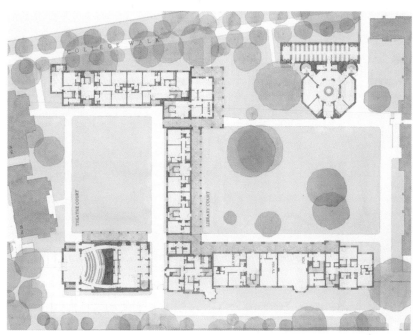

Site location plan – 1:1200

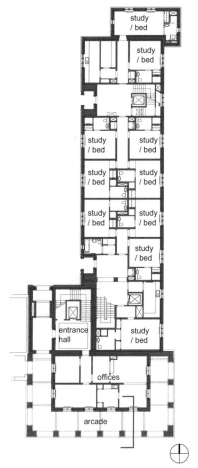

Ground floor plan – 1:500

Drawing labels:

1. Foundations
600mm diameter concrete piles at 3040mm
centres below each arcade column.
1200 × 500mm reinforced concrete ground beam.

2. Arcade floor
50mm thick York stone paving.
30mm mortar bed.
70mm thick screed.
350mm thick reinforced concrete slab.
80mm thick York stone edge step.

3. Load bearing masonry walls
215mm thick Coleford Saxon Multi brick outer
leaf (265mm below ground floor cill).
25mm cavity.
75mm rigid polystyrene insulation.
215mm thick concrete blockwork inner leaf.
13mm plaster.
200 × 32mm profiled softwood skirting.

4. Arcade columns
655 × 655mm solid Farge limestone columns
made up of 450mm high blocks with no dowels.

5. Arcade arch
Nine 720 × 325mm Farge limestone voussoirs
built off column capitals with mortar joints to
form arch.
Temporary timber formwork propped on
scaffolding to support stones until each arch is
complete.
Two 20mm diameter stainless steel dowels
glued into each stone to provide key with
concrete beam above.

6. Concrete beam
450mm thick reinforced concrete poured
over arches to form continuous beam tying

arches together and resisting outward thrust
at ends.
Polythene sheet between stone and concrete to
prevent staining of stone.
730mm high × 225mm thick reinforced
concrete up-stand above first floor level.

7. First floor
180mm deep proprietary suspended floor
system with adjustable steel pedestals and
600 × 600mm particle board floor panels.
200mm thick precast concrete planks bearing
on concrete beam.
75mm mineral wool insulation.
50 × 50mm softwood battens.
Two layers calcium silicate board ceiling with
paint finish.
40 × 40mm softwood moulding around
perimeter.

8. Brickwork below cill
102mm thick Coleford Saxon Multi brick outer
leaf restrained to concrete with stainless steel
wall ties.

9. Stone band
535 × 440mm profiled Ketton stone cill
course.

10. Typical window
Hardwood window.
Precast concrete boot lintel at head in inner
leaf.
Flat arches in outer leaf prefabricated from
bricks bonded to concrete lintel.
25mm thick softwood cill.
Recess in head lining internally for roller blind.

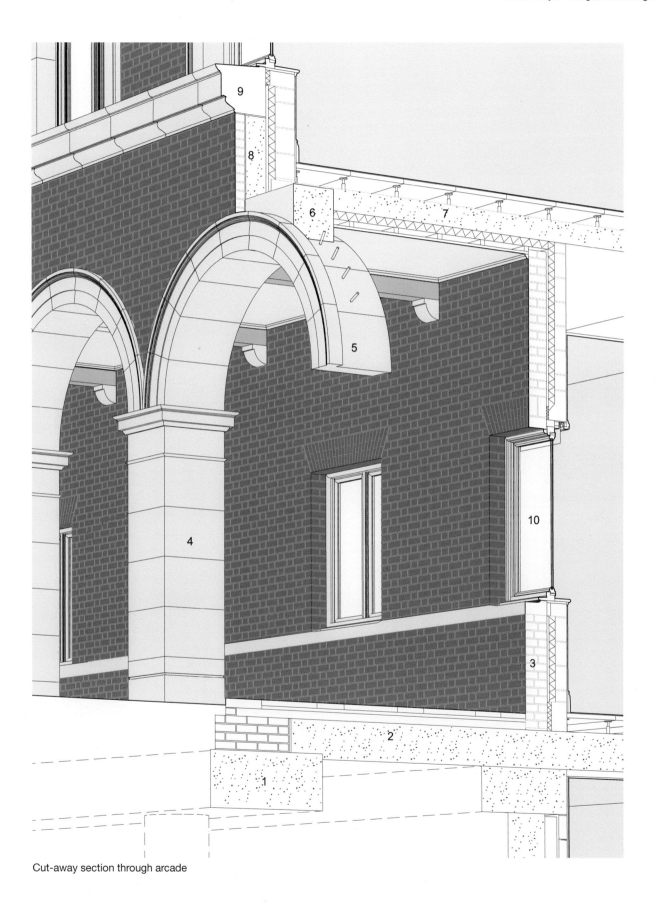

Cut-away section through arcade

*Photo: 5th Studio*

*Photo: 5th Studio*

*Photo: David Stewart*

*Photo: David Stewart*

# Wolfson Building
# Trinity College, Cambridge

Architect: 5th Studio
Structural Engineer: Cameron Taylor
Glazing Installer: F. A. Firman

Two new glass seminar rooms have been hung beneath the cave-like undercrofts of the Wolfson Building, a 90-bedroom student hall of residence for Trinity College hidden amongst the courtyards of central Cambridge. Designed by the Architects Co-Partnership's and completed in 1972, the Wolfson Building exhibits a primitive palette of rough in-situ concrete and exposed brickwork in a wilfully monastic interpretation of college life. 5th Studio's refurbishment has raised the quality of the accommodation to reflect the more demanding expectations of the university's current students and conference clients.

On one side the hanging room's steel floor structure is bolted into the existing second floor concrete slab. The other side is suspended from the third floor on a single $50 \times 50$ mm steel box section hanger. Two larger box section posts support the façade glazing and transfer wind loads back to the concrete structure. The north façade is completely glazed with two sealed units, the largest of which measures $3.7 \times 2.6$ m. The only road access to the site is via a ramp shared with a supermarket below the building so manoeuvring the panes into place involved several operations using hoists to negotiate the changes in level. To prevent flexial deflection of the glass the units were moved in purpose-made timber cradles.

The building's exposed concrete slabs and un-insulated brick cavity walls are uneven so the space had to be carefully surveyed before the steel was ordered. Once in place, the steel was surveyed before the glass was ordered. Stainless steel channels were bonded to the rear of the large glass units with structural silicone so they could be secret-fixed back to steelwork and in places where access to the fixings from behind is restricted the glass is fixed with planar glazing bolts. The back face of the glass is painted black in places to conceal the floor or wall build-up behind. Two sections of laminated glass floor allow views up into the hanging room from the entrance below. The underside of the floor is clad in black laminated glass bringing natural light and reflections of the adjacent gardens into the once dark circulation core.

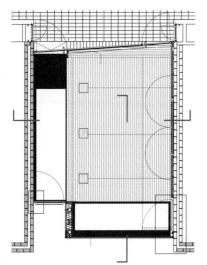

North hanging room Level 2
plan – 1:125

Level 2 floor plan – 1:600

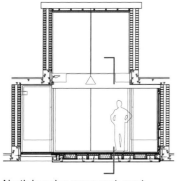

North hanging room east–west
section – 1:125

Site location diagram

Drawing labels:

1. Existing building fabric
185 mm thick reinforced concrete floor slabs
with 475 × 235 mm upstand beams at edges.
300 mm thick cavity walls with brick inner leaf,
90 mm cavity and brick outer leaf.

2. Corner steelwork
1000 × 350 × 20 mm head plate bolted
into existing second floor slab with twelve
expanding anchor fixings.
600 × 150 × 15 mm bearing plate welded to top
of head plate to sit on top of concrete upstand
beam and relieve shear force on bolt fixings.
50 × 50 × 6.3 mm SHS (square hollow section)
hanger welded to head plate via 10 mm flat plates.
Two 100 × 100 × 5 mm SHS windposts welded
to head plate via 10 mm flat plates.
120 × 100 mm T-section welded to bottom of
hanger and windposts for attachment to floor
beam below.

3. Structural steel floor
203 × 203 mm UC (universal column) floor
beam with 900 × 100 × 10 mm flat welded to
top to connect to hanger above.
Three 152 × 152 mm UC joists bolted to floor
beam and to existing second floor.
150 × 100 mm RHS (rectangular hollow section)
edge beam bolted to floor beam and to existing
second floor.

4. Large fixed window
Two double-glazed sealed units fixed to steel
cleats welded to steelwork or brackets bolted
to existing walls and soffits.
Glass fixed using both proprietary countersunk
black headed M8 bolts and stainless steel
channels factory bonded to glass with
structural silicone and bolted to steel cleats.
Sealed units made up from 12 mm toughened
outer pane and 18 mm thick clear toughened
laminated inner pane.

Outer leaf partially printed black on rear face to
conceal floor, wall and ceiling build up.

5. Glass floor
Clear laminated glass floor made up from two
thermally toughened glass layers and one heat
strengthened layer bearing onto neoprene strips
and packers.
Joints pointed with silicone sealant.
Edges printed black to conceal supporting
structure and floor build up.

6. Solid floor
22 mm thick oak boards secret-nailed and
glued to 18 mm plywood sheathing.
Vapour barrier.
150 × 50 mm softwood joists located in webs
of steel joists.
150 mm mineral wool insulation.
12 mm calcium-silicate board fixed below
steelwork to provide fire protection.

7. Soffit glazing
Black laminated glass made up from 6 mm float
upper leaf and 12 mm thermally toughened lower
leaf bolted to brackets off primary structure.

8. Vertical black glass
Black laminated glass made up from 6 mm float
upper leaf and 12 mm thermally toughened lower
leaf bolted to brackets off steel windposts.

9. Solid panel
175 × 50 mm softwood stud frame.
Mineral wool insulation between studs.
Polythene vapour barrier.
22 mm thick oak boards secret-nailed and
glued to 18 mm ply substrate.

10. Window
Inward opening steel framed door and frame
with micaceous iron oxide paint finish.
1450 × 1055 mm toughened glass balustrade
bolted to steel angle below cill of door.

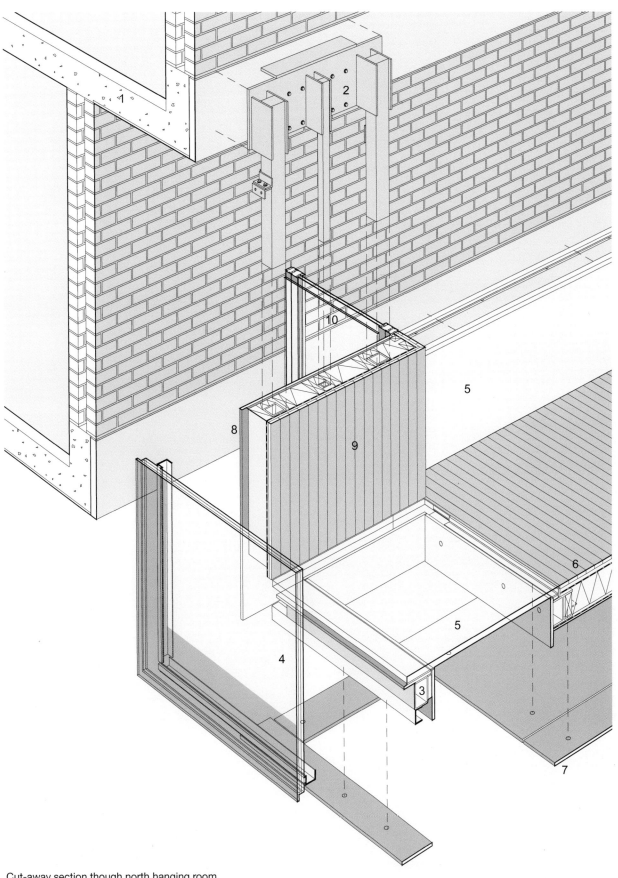

Cut-away section though north hanging room

Photo: Hufton & Crow

Photo: Hufton & Crow

Photo: Hufton & Crow

# Information Commons
# University of Sheffield

Architect: RMJM
Structural Engineer: Ramboll Whitby Bird

Information Commons is a 24-hour facility providing 1350 study places, a reference and loan library, a café and staff offices in a 11 500 square metre building near Sheffield city centre. The building is intended as the gateway to the campus, forging a strong relationship with the public realm and nearby transport links.

Photo: RMJM

An innovative system called Cobiax, a hybrid precast/in-situ concrete slab using recycled plastic void formers, has been used to form the floor slabs. 1.8 m wide pre-cast soffit panels incorporating 225 mm diameter hollow plastic balls were craned in and supported in place on a temporary scaffold. Held in place by a steel reinforcement cage, the balls replace concrete that would be structurally redundant, reducing the weight of the finished slab by up to 35%. Once positioned a top layer of in-situ concrete is poured to form a two-way spanning flat slab. Typically Cobiax uses 15–20% less reinforcement than a traditional flat slab and as the floor is lighter, wider spans can be achieved with fewer columns. Services are contained in a raised floor void so much of the concrete structure can be left exposed. The contractor estimates that a time reduction of 20% was achieved over traditional methods of building a flat slab.

Where extra strength is required around the column heads the void formers were omitted. Additional reinforcement is provided to resist punching shear by an array of shear links, C-shaped steel bars that tie the top and bottom layers of reinforcement together. The precast panels have a 12 mm chamfer on all edges and are tightly butt jointed except on column lines where a 50 mm wide recess has been left for tolerance. To disguise the different colour of the in-situ concrete the gap was plugged with a foam strip during pouring to make a 35 mm shadow gap.

Where a floor slab meets the atrium or one of several double-height spaces it has been covered by a precast concrete edge beam. As there are twelve different profiles of edge beam the budget did not stretch to steel shuttering. As an alternative, perspex was used to line a timber mould for the faces to be exposed and an exceptionally high quality finish was achieved.

Photo: RMJM

East–west section – 1:1200

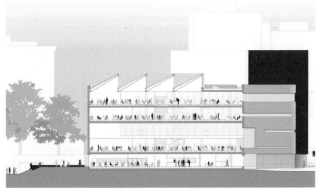

North–south section – 1:1200

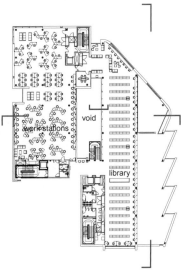

Second floor plan – 1:1200

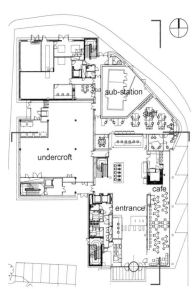

Ground floor plan – 1:1200

Drawing labels:

1. Typical column
450 mm diameter circular in-situ concrete column.

2. Structural floor
1800 mm wide × 70 mm thick precast concrete slab with fair face exposed on underside supported on temporary formwork.
Reinforcement mesh cast into precast slab with minimum 20 mm cover.
Precast panels typically butt jointed except on column lines.
12 mm chamfer on all four edges of each panel to form shadow gaps.
Reinforcement trusses cast into precast slab at 590 mm centres.
225 mm diameter HDPE (high density polyethylene) void former balls made from 70% recycled plastic.
Void formers held in place with steel cage cast into precast slab.
T2 mesh laid over void formers on site.
270 mm thick in-situ concrete topping with minimum 20 mm cover over void formers and reinforcement.
Level finish to top surface.

3. Joint on column line
50 mm gap between precast floor panels.
35 mm recess formed by temporary rigid foam strip between panels during pouring of in-situ topping.

4. Column junction
Void formers omitted around column heads for extra strength to resist punching shear.

300 mm high steel shear links cast into precast slab around column to strengthen floor locally.

5. Edge beam
660 mm high × varying width precast concrete edge beam.

6. Balustrade
180 × 40 mm solid beech cill.
10 mm shadow gap painted out to match beech.
18 mm beech veneered MDF perforated acoustic panel.
25 mm mineral wool insulation.
100 × 50 mm light gauge steel channel frame bolted to concrete edge beam.
12.5 mm plasterboard internal lining on proprietary steel rails.

7. Raised floor
600 × 600 × 25 mm proprietary floor panels.
Proprietary steel pedestals to create 375 mm floor void for services.

8. Air supply units
600 × 200 mm aluminium grilles set into special floor panel.
Terminal zone air supply unit fixed to floor panel with integral fan to control air supply locally.

9. Lighting
Light fittings lined up with joints in precast floor panels above.
Electrical wiring fed through 50 mm diameter hole drilled through panel joint from floor void above.

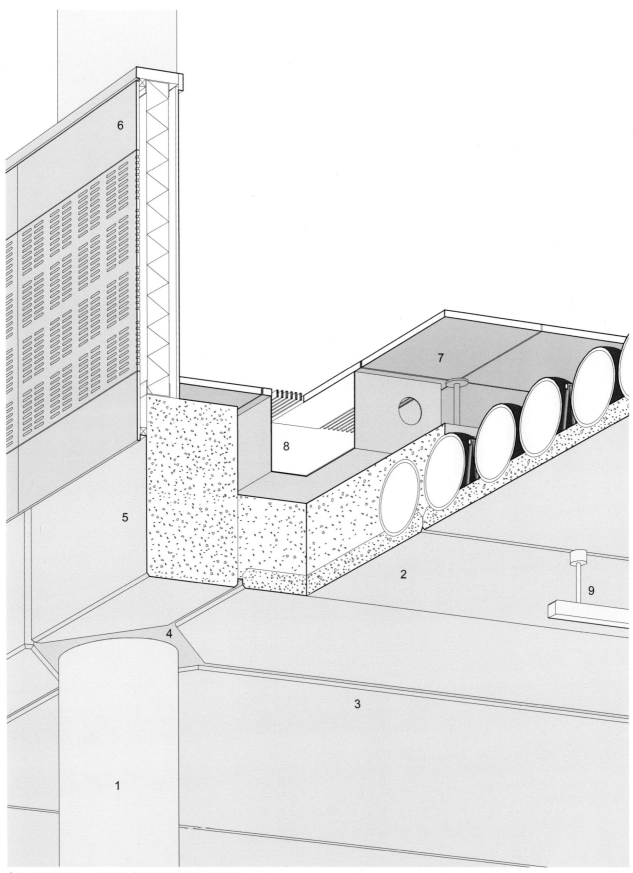

Cut-away section through floor slab edge at atrium

*Photo: Nick Kane*

# St John's Therapy Centre
# Wandsworth, London

Architect: Buschow Henley Architects
Structural Engineer: Price & Myers

St John's is a community healthcare building constructed under the LIFT (Local Improvement Finance Trust) scheme, a public-private partnership to design, build and operate community health buildings and local authority services. It combines two GP practices with services that have traditionally been provided in hospitals but do not require a patient to stay overnight, such as mental health, podiatry and physiotherapy clinics.

The primary frame consists of concrete columns and floor slabs. Where walls are required the frame has been infilled with a secondary structure of light-gauge steel channels. The building is clad in timber veneered panels made from wood fibre and paper bonded with phenolic resin and compressed at high pressure.

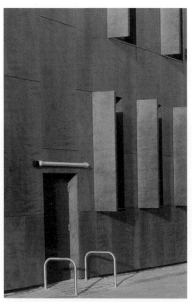

*Photo: Buschow Henley Ltd*

The windows have been detailed to respond to varying light, privacy and acoustic requirements of the different elevations. On the south side several windows project 100 mm beyond the face of the cladding. These are supported off the steel structure on aluminium angles and have bronze anodised aluminium curtain walling frames. Insulated flashings prevent a cold bridge around the edges of the frame. All other windows are timber, recessed flush with the inside face of the wall and clad externally with aluminium for ease of maintenance. On the east and west elevations, fins project on the south side of the windows to provide both solar shading and acoustic protection from traffic noise. The fins have a 6 mm steel plate core welded to a square hollow section (SHS) post that spans between the concrete floor slabs.

A galvanised steel balcony cantilevers off the concrete floor slab on the north elevation, made up in 2.4 m lengths for ease of transportation. The balustrade is made from 20 mm square steel bars except for the verticals at the end of each 2.4 m length which are 10 mm thick so that when two adjacent sections are joined the balustrade appears as one continuous run.

*Photo: Nick Kane*

Larger elements of the programme have been located at the front of the building and the many cellular consulting rooms towards the rear. This arrangement allows the front elevation to be more loosely composed with fewer, big openings that give the Centre a strong civic presence. The shiny lustre of the panels brings to mind a smaller, tactile object like a chestnut.

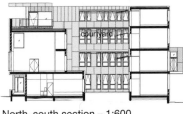

North–south section – 1:600

East–west section – 1:600

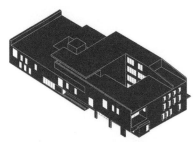

Axonometric view from south–east

First floor plan – 1:600

Drawing labels:

1. Structural frame
500 × 200mm in-situ reinforced concrete columns.

2. Typical floor
Rubber flooring on levelling screed.
300mm thick reinforced concrete floor slab spanning between columns.
Painted exposed concrete soffit.

3. External wall infill structure
225mm light gauge galvanised steel channel studs spanning from floor to ceiling.
225mm light gauge galvanised steel channel top and bottom tracks fixed to floor and ceiling.

4. Typical external cladding
10mm thick timber veneered panels made from wood fibre and paper bonded with phenolic resin and compressed at high pressure.
Panels screw-fixed to continuous vertical aluminium angle rainscreen cladding rails.
T-section cladding rails screwed to aluminium brackets screwed to sheathing at 900mm centres vertically and 600mm centres horizontally.
50mm rigid phenolic insulation.
Breather membrane.
10mm cement particle board sheathing fixed to steel channels.

5. Internal lining
Vapour barrier.
Two layers 12.5mm plasterboard taped and jointed with paint finish.
80 × 15mm softwood architraves around windows.

6. Typical opening window
Laminated softwood window frame with polyester powder coated (PPC) aluminium cladding and beads.
Double-glazed sealed unit consisting of 4mm toughened inner pane, 16mm air gap and 4mm toughened outer pane.
Damp-proof membrane (DPM) fixed to rear of window frame and dressed around cement particle board lining to lap over breather membrane.
10mm cement particle board sheathing screwed to steel structure at head and jambs.
50mm rigid PIS insulation in steel channel at jambs and head.
10mm thick timber veneered panel window reveals screwed to steel structure.

7. Vertical fins
60 × 60mm galvanised rectangular hollow section (RHS) post with 80 × 60mm unequal angle brackets welded top and bottom bolted to slab via 10mm nylon spacers for thermal isolation.
2425 × 715 × 6mm thick galvanised steel plate welded to RHS post.

2600mm high × 10mm thick timber veneered panels screwed to both sides of steel plate.
70 × 70mm satin anodised aluminium T-section sandwiched between panels to stiffen and protect edges of panels.

8. Projecting windows on south elevation
Bronze anodised aluminium window frames made up from 125 × 50mm curtain walling box sections.
Bronze anodised aluminium flashing with 25mm extruded polystyrene insulation screwed to window frame.
Double-glazed sealed unit consisting of 4mm toughened inner pane, 16mm air gap and 4mm toughened outer pane.
DPM bonded to outside of frame and dressed over cement particle board lining to lap over breather membrane.
Plasterboard internal reveals.
White painted MDF cill board.

9. Soffit
10mm thick timber veneered soffit panels screwed to aluminium rails.
100mm air gap.
50 × 50mm aluminium angle rails fixed to concrete slab via 50 × 50mm aluminium angle hangers at 600mm centres.
75mm rigid phenolic insulation.
Breather membrane.

10. Balcony structure
Galvanised steel balcony structure made up in 2400mm lengths with semi-gloss top coat paint finish.
1810mm long × 350mm deep × 90mm wide tapered steel angle brackets.

11. Balustrade
Galvanised steel balustrade made up in 2400mm lengths with semi-gloss top coat paint finish.
20 × 20mm square-section solid steel horizontal member welded to 20 × 20mm solid vertical members at 120mm centres continuously welded to 250 × 18mm bottom front plate.
Front plate bolted to 100 × 75mm galvanised steel angle.

12. Balcony decking
70 × 70mm galvanised steel angles back-to-back in 2400mm lengths bolted to angle brackets.
65 × 45mm black stained preservative treated softwood battens on softwood packers bolted to angles.
125 × 22mm black stained timber boards with 6mm gaps.

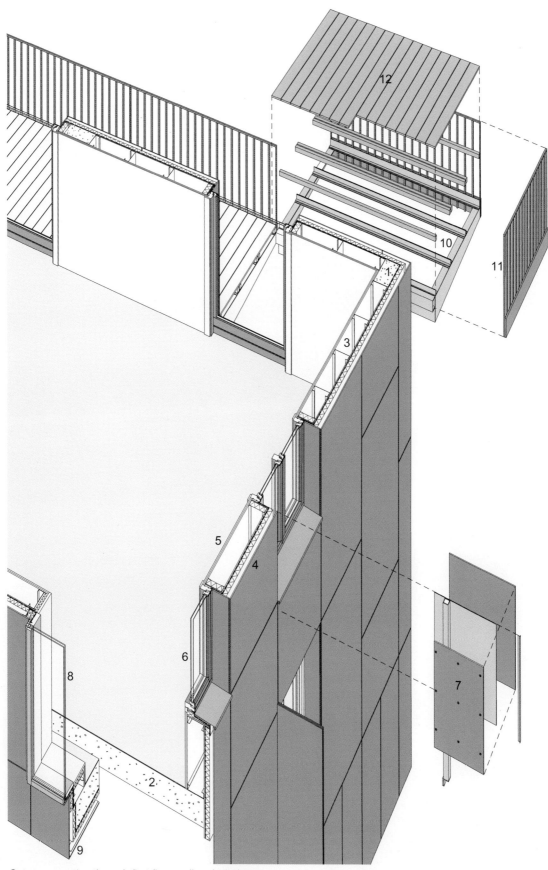

Cut-away section through first floor wall and windows

*Photo: Hélène Binet*

*Photo: Hélène Binet*

*Photo: Hélène Binet*

*Photo: Hélène Binet*

# Christchurch Tower, City of London

Architects: Boyarsky Murphy
Structural Engineer: Greig Ling

An abandoned church tower in the City of London has been put to new use as a private house. Designed by Christopher Wren in 1677, Christchurch was bombed in the Second World War and only the tower survived. Twelve levels of floors and platforms have been inserted into the 50 metre-high tower connected by a helter-skelter of stairs and ladders.

Some repair work had already been carried out to the structure in the 1950s when the damaged steeple was taken down and rebuilt off a new concrete ring beam and an inner skin of Fletton brickwork was used to strengthen the stone ashlar. The original staircase built into the stonework in one corner of the tower has been enclosed with fire doors allowing a second circulation route to rise more freely through the house. The walls are 3 metres thick at the base but narrow higher up so the floor areas increase towards the top. The ninth floor is devoted to a living room with a spiral stair up to a library above. Glass is difficult to form to the 570 mm radius of the spiral staircase so an acrylic balustrade was made by heating the flat sheet and dropping it into a curved mould. The acrylic appears completely clear unlike glass that usually has a green tinge.

Where the tower narrows a retractable ladder takes the place of the stair. An 85 × 95 mm aluminium box fixed to the central post of the spiral stair contains a fold out ladder that leads up to another glass platform and then to a lookout terrace in the steeple. The glass platform has a steel frame held just off the double-curving stone walls by ferrule spacers around the resin-anchor bolts that hold it up.

The stonework has been JOS cleaned, a chemical-free process where a small amount of water and a fine abrasive powder are sprayed in a gentle swirling vortex to remove dirt without damaging the stone. A 'Hawksmoor detail' has been used for the window cills, so called by English Heritage because it was developed for St George's, the church he designed in Bloomsbury. New lead flashings have been laid over plywood to protect rather than repair the stone beneath and the lead dressed over the edge in the traditional manner without a projecting drip.

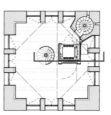

9 – living room

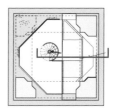

10 – library

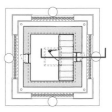

11 – mezzanine

Floor plans – 1:250

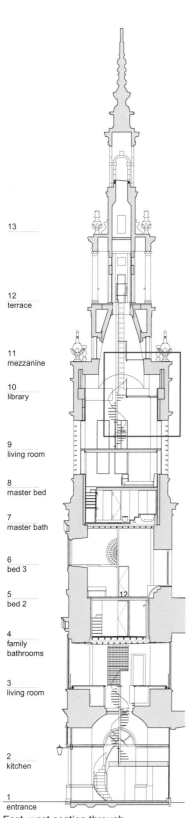

13

12
terrace

11
mezzanine

10
library

9
living room

8
master bed

7
master bath

6
bed 3

5
bed 2

4
family
bathrooms

3
living room

2
kitchen

1
entrance

East–west section through
tower – 1:250

**Drawing labels:**

1. Existing walls below level 10
Fletton solid bonded brickwork walls of varying thickness.
Portland stone ashlar external facing.
75 × 25 mm softwood battens.
12.5 mm plasterboard with skim coat and white emulsion paint finish.

2. Ring beam
710 mm deep concrete ring beam to support steeple above.
1260 deep × 200 mm wide concrete upstand above ring beam.
12.5 mm plasterboard with skim coat and white emulsion paint finish.

3. Existing walls above level 10
Portland stone ashlar JOS cleaned internally and left exposed.

4. Flashing
New code 4 lead flashing to parapet with 'Hawksmoor detail'.

5. Window
Steel W20 window frame openable for cleaning and ventilation from outside only.
6-12-6 double-glazed sealed unit with non-reflective glass.
177 × 35 mm solid oak internal cill.
New code 4 lead external cill.

6. Louvres
New 900 mm wide × 195 × 40 mm Portland stone louvres bedded in existing grooves in stone window surrounds.

7. Level 10 landing
160 × 80 mm rectangular hollow section (RHS) steel beams bolted into brickwork at both ends via 200 × 200 × 12 mm plates with four M16 expanding anchor fixings.
125 × 75 × 8 mm unequal angle (UA) bolted to brickwork with M16 expanding anchors at 300 mm centres to support outside edges of landing.
44 mm thick composite oak floor fixed to steelwork below at 300 mm centres.

8. Level 11 landing
Prefabricated steel landing structure consisting of 100 × 60 × 6.3 mm gauge RHS leading edge beam and 100 × 50 mm parallel flange channels (PFC) to other three edges bolted to stone walls with resin anchored M20 threaded bars embedded min. 300 mm into stone.
40 mm diameter stainless steel ferrule spacers between steel frame and walls.
Neoprene/silicone pads between steel and glass.
32 mm laminated clear glass floor made up from 18 mm toughened upper pane, pvb interlayer and 12 mm toughened lower pane.
Glass panels decorated on top face with all-over bead-blast finish and protective coating.

9. Balustrade
1100 mm high × 12 mm thick toughened clear glass balustrade.
Polyester powder-coated (PPC) 160 × 12 mm mild steel clamping plate bolted at 500 mm centres with countersunk bolts to steel landing structure.
Hard fibre isolation washers between steel and glass.

10. Staircase
114.3 mm diameter stainless steel central pole.
Polished stainless steel brackets welded to central tube.
570 mm radius × 40 mm thick solid oak treads screwed to brackets from below.
12 mm thick curved acrylic balustrade bolted to ends of treads with neoprene isolating washers.
35 mm diameter stainless steel handrail.

11. Ladder
114.3 mm diameter stainless steel circular hollow section post welded to top of stair post.
6.25 m high proprietary extruded anodised aluminium pull-out ladder with 525 mm wide rungs and integral handrail.
120 × 95 mm fixing brackets bolted to post at 1.5 m centres.
Safety system channel bolted to vertical.

12. Shelving
40 mm thick oak veneered shelving with solid oak lipping.

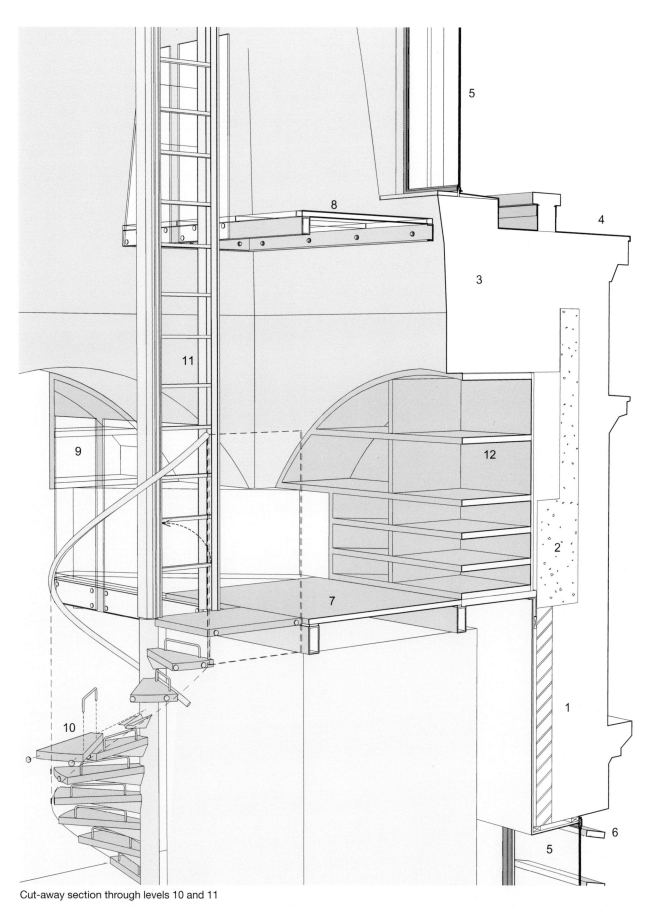

Cut-away section through levels 10 and 11

Photo: Tom Ebdon

Photo: Steve Ambrose

Photo: Steve Ambrose

Photo: Steve Ambrose

# Halligan House
# St Albans

Architect: Simon Conder Associates
Structural Engineer: Built Engineers

A restricted budget has encouraged expedient use of inexpensive materials to make a new house in a sub-urban street in St Albans. When the building plot was sold off from the neighbouring house in 1965, a covenant was put in place restricting the building height to a single storey with a flat roof. The four-bedroom house is over 20 metres deep and extends the full width of the plot so light is brought in through courtyards and high-level clerestories over the kitchen and living room. A corridor bisects the house from front to back with the bedrooms on one side and the living spaces on the other. There are two studies for the parents who both work from home part of the time.

Load-bearing blockwork walls have been built off concrete strip footings, almost 40% of which remain from a previous house by John Winter that stood on the site. The ground floor is beam and block, spanning between the strip footings and topped with a floating concrete slab. A colour hardener has been worked into the surface of the concrete to form a resilient wearing surface. A power float could not reach the edges of the rooms so all the floors were hand-trowelled for an even finish.

All the areas of glazing are framed with softwood posts that also support the raised clerestory roofs. Each softwood post has a hardwood strip routed and glued into its external face over which is screwed a pressed stainless steel profile. Double-glazed sealed units were bonded to the stainless steel plates in-situ using structural silicone. Where a timber post supports a roof joist the two were mitred and glued together with a biscuit joint. Softwood ribs were screwed and glued to the plywood roof deck so it could span further, enabling the spacing of the joists to match the 900mm spacing of the vertical posts.

The external walls are clad in insulated render. A 3.2m-high screen made from iroko forms a trellis up which plants can grow, concealing the front of the house. The posts are bolted to stainless steel base plates on concrete pads. The iroko strips span across the gate and garage doors, filtering the view into the entrance space and hinting at the sequence of rooms and courtyards that lies beyond.

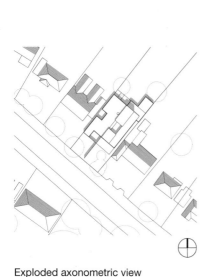

Exploded axonometric view

Ground floor plan – 1:300

Drawing labels:

1. Foundations
450 mm wide × nominal 150 mm deep mass concrete strip foundations.
275 mm wide 7 kN concrete foundation block wall.

2. Ground floor
155 mm deep precast concrete beams at 510 mm centres spanning between ground beams.
440 × 215 × 100 mm medium density concrete blocks laid between beams grouted with sand/cement slurry.
Three coats cold liquid-applied bituminous DPM (damp proof membrane).
Rigid urethane insulation boards.
Polythene sheet separating layer.
72 mm thick floating C35 concrete slab with 10 mm aggregate.
Under-floor heating pipes cast into concrete.
Coloured metallic dry-shake hardener sprinkled and trowelled into surface of concrete to form wearing surface.

3. Ground floor slab edge
Epoxy bonding adhesive applied to top of foundation blocks and 145 mm wide in-situ concrete plinth cast on top.
Three coats bituminous DPM applied to face of plinth.
75 mm extruded polystyrene insulation.
50 × 3 mm aluminium plate screwed to glazing frame as render stop bead.
Acrylic render external finish.

4. Glazing frame
145 × 72 mm C24 strength European redwood posts at 900 mm centres.
145 × 72 mm C24 strength European redwood transom.
70 × 25 mm hardwood strips glued into grooves in external face of posts and transoms.
72 × 35 mm pressed stainless steel top hat sections screwed to hardwood strips.

5. Glazing
Double-glazed sealed units comprising 8 mm clear toughened glass outer, 16 mm air filled cavity, 8.8 mm 'K' laminated low-e glass inner.
Outer leaf projects beyond spacer on all sides to cover stainless steel.
Clerestory glazing same units but inner leaf sand blasted.

6. Vent panel
Two 1060 mm high × 340 mm wide vent panels made from 44 mm solid core door blanks with hardwood lips and seals to all sides.
Two friction stay hinges rebated into side frames and two mortice latches operated by snib turns.
Aluminium drip flashing at head.

7. Roof
145 × 72 mm C24 strength European redwood joists at 900 mm centres.
15 mm WBP birch plywood fixed to top of joists.
9.5 mm plasterboard ceiling fixed to plywood between joists with plaster skim and painted finish.

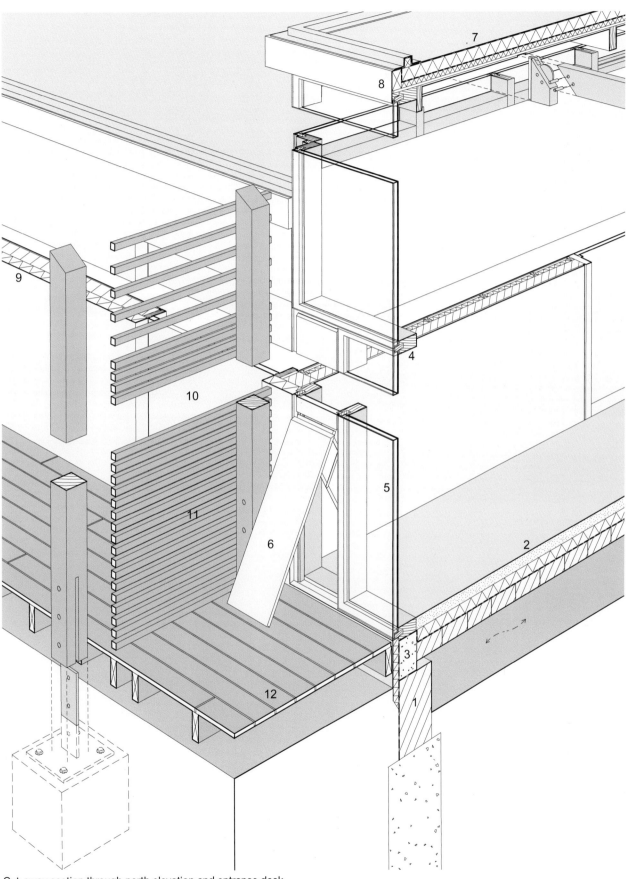

Cut-away section through north elevation and entrance deck

30 × 30 mm C24 strength ribs glued and
screwed to plywood at 400 mm centres to
stiffen roof deck.
30 mm rigid urethane insulation board between
ribs.
Polythene vapour control layer.
75 mm rigid urethane insulation board.
Fully adhered reinforced PVC waterproof
membrane with polyester fleece backing.

8. Roof edge detail
145 × 72 mm C24 strength European redwood
transom at head of glazing.
45 degree mitre at junctions of joists and posts
fixed with circular 15 mm WBP ply biscuits and
four dowels.
145 × 44 mm European redwood pelmet.
100 × 50 mm treated softwood edge strip fixed
to plywood deck around roof perimeter.
50 × 50 mm treated softwood batten fixed to
edge strip around roof perimeter to control
rainwater run-off.
100 × 165 mm PPC (polyester powder coated)
aluminium flashing with mitred corners fixed
to softwood edge strip and hot-air welded to
waterproof membrane.

9. Typical wall construction
Acrylic render external finish.
100 mm expanded polystyrene insulation
bonded to blockwork.
140 mm wide 7 kN concrete blockwork
load-bearing wall.
13 mm plaster internal finish.

10. Front door
140 × 100 mm concrete lintel.
152 × 58 mm hardwood frame with continuous
groove to accept flange of plaster stop bead.
235 × 72 mm hardwood threshold with
continuous drip groove to underside.
2100 mm high × 1200 mm wide × 44 mm thick
solid core softwood door leaf with hardwood lips
and seals to all sides mounted on floor pivot.

11. Fence
450 × 450 × 400 mm deep concrete pads at
1350 mm centres.
140 × 140 mm iroko posts with heads cut to
30° angle fixed to stainless steel base plates
bolted to pads.
38 × 38 mm iroko horizontal slats at 65 mm
vertical centres to door head level and at
130 mm centres above with three staggered
stainless steel screw fixings at each post.

12. Decking
140 × 25 mm iroko decking with 10 mm gaps
between planks with joints staggered and
centred over joists fixed with two stainless steel
screw fixings at each joist.
150 × 50 mm Tanalith E treated softwood joists
at 750 mm centres.
150 × 50 mm continuous Tanalith E treated
softwood wall mounted ledger spaced off
render face.
140 × 140 mm iroko post terminating directly
under decking with rear of head notched
to take continuous double joist comprising
144 × 44 mm iroko facing to continuous
150 × 50 mm treated softwood inner joist.

*Photo: Cristobal Palmer*

*Photo: Cristobal Palmer*

# Herringbone Houses
# Wandsworth, London

Architect: Alison Brooks Architects
Structural Engineer: Price & Myers

*Photo: Alison Brooks Architects*

Two houses in a leafy south London suburb are clad with hardwood in a herringbone pattern that gives them a distinctive identity from the surrounding Edwardian villas. The houses are approached down a 45 m-long driveway along the side of a bowls club, their squat forms rising above a fence to survey the bowling green. Each house is composed around a dramatic two-storey central hallway with a rooflight above so light is brought down deep into the plan. The stair is offset to one side so that from the front door you see straight through to the back garden with the sky above. From many points on the ground floor the surrounding mature trees and gardens are visible in two or three directions at once, giving the sense of the house as the centre of a landscape of internal and external spaces.

Each house has a steel frame on a concrete basement structure. The floors are precast concrete planks with screed and underfloor heating. The external walls consist of two studwork frames between the primary steel members, one supporting the inner plasterboard lining and the other supporting the external sheathing and cladding. Above and below the large sliding windows the steel beams have been over-sized to support them and provide head restraint as this was deemed cheaper than constructing more complicated secondary steelwork off the primary structure.

*Photo: Alison Brooks Architects*

The cladding is Ipe, one of the hardest, most durable tropical hardwoods. Site cutting of the timber was minimised by using 800 mm lengths, pre-cut with angled ends. The boards have been laid in alternating horizontal rows at an angle of 22.5 degrees fixed with countersunk stainless steel screws to horizontal softwood battens which, in turn, were fixed to vertical battens to provide a continuous air gap for ventilation behind the timber. Each board is fixed with a single screw at either end rather than the normal two and the holes were drilled prior to delivery to site to reduce on-site labour. Finally, each screw hole was laboriously capped with an ipe plug and sanded off flush. At the corners a thin L-shaped strip of ipe covers the end grain without disturbing the sweep of the herringbone bands around the houses. Light reflects off the timber turning the whole building into a magnificent composition of shimmering silver and copper brown.

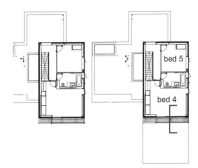

Second floor plan – 1:500

First floor plan – 1:500

Section AA – 1:500

Section BB – 1:500

Section CC – 1:500

Ground floor plan – 1:500

Drawing labels:

1. Primary steel frame
UC (universal column) columns with cross bracing.
RHS (rectangular hollow section) or UC beams.

2. Typical wall
65 × 19 mm profiled ipe boards, pre-cut in
800 mm lengths and pre-drilled, fixed with two
countersunk stainless steel screws at a 22.5°
angle to vertical in herringbone pattern.
50 × 25 mm treated softwood horizontal battens
at 800 mm centres.
50 × 25 mm treated softwood vertical battens at
600 mm centres.
Breather membrane.
50 × 50 mm treated softwood battens at 600 mm
centres with rigid insulation in between.
18 mm plywood sheathing.
20 mm rigid insulation.
195 mm thick studwork made up from
100 × 50 mm softwood studs at 600 mm centres
on external face and 70 × 50 mm softwood studs
at 600 mm centres on internal face.
Vapour barrier.
12.5 mm plasterboard with skim coat and
15 × 40 mm aluminium angle skirting.

3. Upper floor
150 × 20 mm floating hardwood flooring.
30 mm acoustic absorbent insulation.
65 mm screed with underfloor hot water heating pipes.
150 mm deep precast hollow core concrete
planks spanning between steel angles welded to
sides of beams as necessary.
Proprietary suspended ceiling system.
12.5 mm plasterboard with skim coat.

4. Balcony floor
150 × 19 mm ipe boards fixed with countersunk
stainless steel screws to hardwood battens.
Single ply PVC waterproof membrane with single
piece welded scupper outlet in back corner to
rainwater pipe concealed behind cladding.
Tapered rigid insulation at 1 in 80 fall to concealed
gutter at rear.
150 mm deep precast hollow core concrete
planks spanning between steel angles welded to
sides of beams as necessary.

5. Balcony flank wall
50 × 25 mm treated softwood carcassing to form
tapered balcony flank wall.
Straight wall at opposite end incorporates mild
steel ladder frame made up from 50 × 50 mm

SHS (square hollow section) edge members and
100 × 50 mm RHS horizontal members for stiffness.
65 × 19 mm profiled ipe boards, pre-cut in
800 mm lengths and pre-drilled, fixed with two
countersunk stainless steel screws at a 22.5°
angle to vertical in herringbone pattern.
50 × 50 mm ipe angle cover strip at corner.

6. Balustrade
16 mm clear toughened glass cantilevered
balustrade.
Steel plate bracket and clamping plate to secure
balustrade back to primary steel frame at base.

7. Roof
Single ply PVC waterproof membrane.
120 mm tapered rigid insulation.
90 mm sand-cement structural topping.
Bituminous vapour barrier.
150 mm deep precast hollow core concrete
planks spanning between steel angles welded to
sides of beams as necessary.
Proprietary suspended ceiling system.
12.5 mm plasterboard lining with skim coat and
painted finish.

8. Roof perimeter upstand
185 × 75 mm softwood studwork upstand built
up of roof edge beam.
18 mm WBP plywood sheathing.

9. Balcony roof
Single ply PVC waterproof membrane.
18 mm WBP plywood on softwood carcassing.
Painted steel angle members bolted back to roof
edge beam to support balcony roof.
100 × 70 mm treated softwood battens at 800 mm
centres at 36° from horizontal to form soffit.
65 × 19 mm profiled ipe board soffit, pre-drilled
and fixed with two countersunk stainless steel
screws in herringbone pattern.

10. Window
Satin anodised aluminium sliding window frame
supported off primary steel floor beam on back-
to-back steel angle brackets and restrained to
roof beam at head.
Aluminium flashing at window head fixed behind
breather membrane.
Double-glazed sealed units.

11. Window support steelwork
Certain primary steel members oversized above
and below windows to support and restrain
window frames.

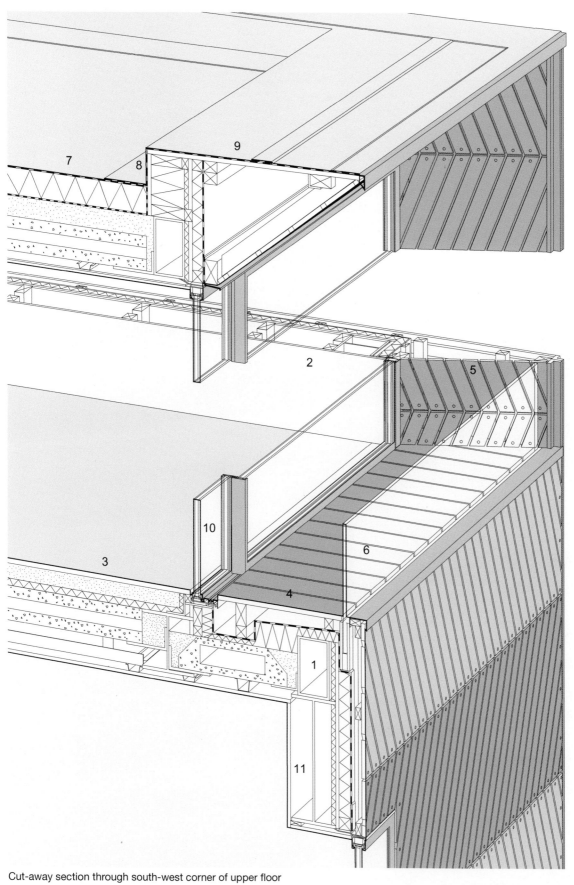

Cut-away section through south-west corner of upper floor

Photo: Denis Jones

Photo: Denis Jones

Photo: Gaunt Francis Architects

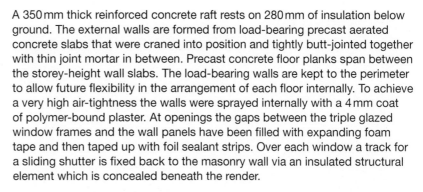

Photo: Peter White

Photo: Peter White

# GreenHouse, BRE, Watford

Architect: Gaunt Francis Architects
Structural, Environmental and Services Engineer: Arup

A prototype house at the BRE Innovation Park in Watford was the first home built by a major house-builder to achieve level 6 under the Code for Sustainable Homes. The Barratt GreenHouse was the winner in a popular vote in the British Homes Awards' Home for the Future Competition in 2007. The competition demanded a house with excellent sustainability credentials and design qualities but crucially one that could be built by a mainstream volume house-builder. It has a highly insulated concrete structure to provide thermal mass and incorporates measures such as rainwater harvesting, solar-thermal water heating and an air-source heat pump to reduce its impact on the environment.

A 350 mm thick reinforced concrete raft rests on 280 mm of insulation below ground. The external walls are formed from load-bearing precast aerated concrete slabs that were craned into position and tightly butt-jointed together with thin joint mortar in between. Precast concrete floor planks span between the storey-height wall slabs. The load-bearing walls are kept to the perimeter to allow future flexibility in the arrangement of each floor internally. To achieve a very high air-tightness the walls were sprayed internally with a 4 mm coat of polymer-bound plaster. At openings the gaps between the triple glazed window frames and the wall panels have been filled with expanding foam tape and then taped up with foil sealant strips. Over each window a track for a sliding shutter is fixed back to the masonry wall via an insulated structural element which is concealed beneath the render.

The roof and triangular gables were prefabricated and delivered to site as cassettes with insulation already in place. Part of the roof has a sedum blanket finish and the rest is clad in photo-voltaic and solar-thermal panels over a single-ply waterproof membrane. There was not enough roof area to achieve Code 6 requirement for energy generation with the efficiency of solar panels available at the time so additional panels are located behind the house. Also, rather bizarrely, two arrays of solar-thermal panels are fixed on a wall close beneath the eaves so as to be partially in the shadow of the roof. The house is being rigorously tested but there is still a way to go before the practicalities and costs of achieving Code 6 are realistic for the mass-housing market.

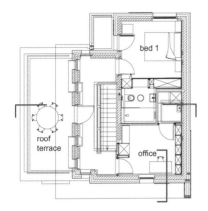

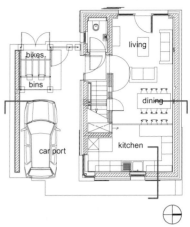

Second, first and ground floor plans – 1:200

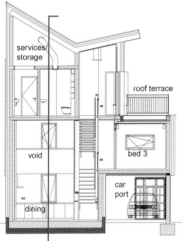

North–south section – 1:200

East–west section – Not to scale

Drawing labels:

1. Foundation and ground floor
18 mm tongued and grooved timber floorboards.
53 mm void formed with 45 × 45 mm softwood
battens with foam isolating strips bonded to
concrete floor at 400 mm centres.
350 mm reinforced concrete ground floor slab
and raft foundation.
500 mm gauge polyethylene vapour barrier.
80 mm extruded polystyrene thermal insulation.
1200 mm gauge radon gas barrier consisting of
polyethylene outer layers and aluminium foil core.
200 mm extruded polystyrene thermal insulation.
50 mm sand blinding.
100 mm mass concrete.
150 mm compacted hardcore.

2. External wall
Insulated render system consisting of
reinforced polymer render on 180 mm phenolic
foam insulation boards mechanically fixed to
concrete panels.
600 × 200 mm storey-height load-bearing
prefabricated aerated concrete panels with
thin-joint mortar.
4 mm spray applied polymer bound internal
coating to panels to seal joints.
25 mm vertical softwood battens.
12.5 mm plasterboard dry lining with plaster
skim finish.
Shadow gap beads at top and bottom.
90 × 15 mm softwood skirting.

3. Slab edge
Insulated render system consisting of
reinforced polymer render on 170 mm extruded
polystyrene insulation boards mechanically
fixed to concrete.
Radon gas barrier dressed up face of concrete
and mechanically fixed using render starter track.
Sealant strip between render starter track and
render below.

4. Upper floor
18 mm tongued and grooved timber floorboards.
53 mm void formed with 45 × 45 mm softwood
battens with foam isolating strips bonded to
concrete floor at 400 mm centres.
150 mm thick precast concrete planks spanning
between blockwork walls.
20 mm plaster finish to ceilings.

5. Typical window
Triple-glazed laminated softwood opening window.
20 mm expanding foam strips on all sides
between frame and blockwork.
Foil strip bonded between frame and blockwork
internally to seal joints.
100 × 75 × 8 mm steel angle brackets.
220 × 30 mm softwood external window
surround fixed back to blockwork on
100 × 75 × 8 mm steel angle brackets.

6. Shutter
Sliding shutters hung on extruded aluminium track.
Top track mechanically fixed to insulated fixing
element.
Bottom guide track screwed to front of
window cill.

7. External gable wall
Insulated render system consisting of reinforced
polymer render on 180 mm phenolic foam
insulation boards mechanically fixed to spandrel
panel.
Prefabricated spandrel panel consisting of
95 × 50 mm softwood studwork frame with
13 mm plywood inner and outer linings.

8. Sedum roof
Sedum roof blanket and waterproof system.
Prefabricated roof panel system consisting of:
22 mm bitumen impregnated sheathing board
made from sawdust and recycled paper.
55 × 50 mm softwood battens at 500 mm
centres with PIS (polyisocyanurate) insulation
between.
245 × 50 mm softwood rafters with PIS
insulation between.
12.5 mm OSB (oriented strand board) inner
sheathing.
Vapour barrier on inner face.

9. Roof verge
300 mm wide pebble perimeter strip around
sedum roof.
270 × 140 mm timber upstand.
Pre-patinated copper capping fixed to upstand
on copper clips.
525 mm deep pre-patinated copper cladding to
verge on isolating membrane.
Pre-patinated copper-clad soffit board.
50 mm shadow gap with black plastic board
lining between soffit and rendered wall.

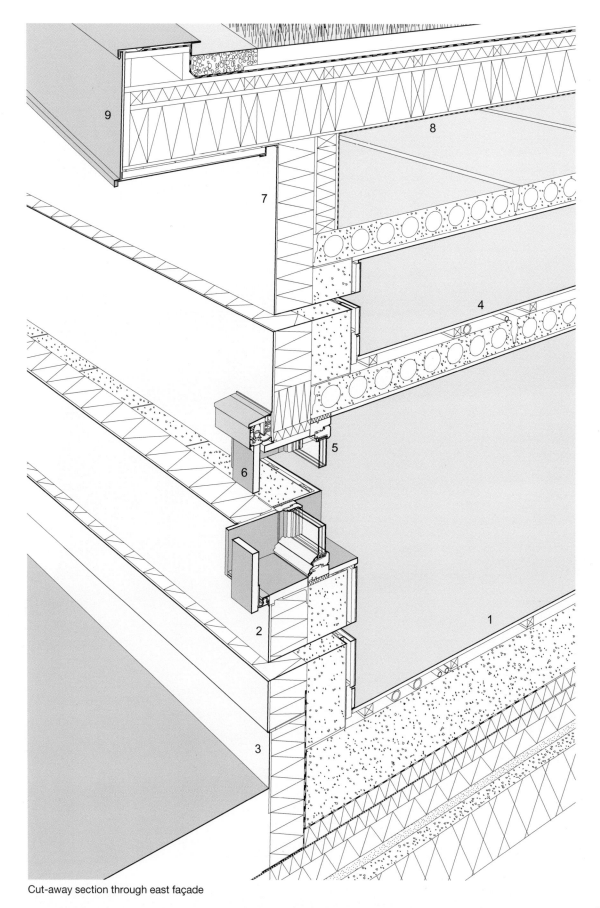

Cut-away section through east façade

Photo: bere:architects

Photo: bere:architects

# Focus House, Finsbury Park, London

Architect: bere:architects
Structural Engineer: Techniker

Photo: Jefferson Smith

Focus House incorporates low embodied energy materials and low lifetime energy consumption to minimise its carbon footprint. It is also a highly inventive home architecturally on a tight, infill site in north London. Only 2.8 m wide at the entrance, the house widens to 7 m at the back where it opens on to a small garden. The shell was constructed from prefabricated, cross-laminated, solid timber panels manufactured in Austria. The panels are made precisely to size with service chases, window and door openings factory-cut. Its thermal mass helps control temperature variations inside and the timber effectively stores 42.4 tonnes of carbon, easily offsetting the 3 tonnes emitted from its transportation.

Dark grey zinc-titanium cladding on all the external surfaces unites the volumes. The metal sheets are clipped to metal plates spiked directly into cellular glass insulation, so there are no thermal bridges across the insulation layer. The insulation is cut to falls and is 500 mm deep at its thick edge. The roofs fall to the south edge where the zinc is folded to form a continuous gutter that runs down the vertical faces in place of rainwater pipes. The ventilation gap behind the zinc was eliminated because the insulation is completely waterproof and vapour impermeable and the zinc has a special anti-corrosion coating on the back. The outer face of the insulation was covered with a torch-on felt. Loosely woven spun nylon matting beneath the zinc traps a layer of air and separates it from the insulation allowing for expansion and providing some acoustic insulation.

Photo: Jefferson Smith

Fresh air is supplied to the whole house with a mechanical ventilation system using a 95% efficient heat exchanger to warm incoming air with waste heat from the bathroom extracts. More than half the annual water heating energy will come from a solar installation high up on the south elevation, supplemented by a gas-fired boiler. Total carbon storage benefits of the Focus House amount to a total $CO_2$ extraction of 30 tonnes. This is calculated by total emissions of 3.11 tonnes for the concrete slab and foundations including piles (70% GGBS) and 5.24 tonnes for the zinc cladding, which has the lowest embodied carbon of any metal, set against $CO_2$ extraction of 39 tonnes for the wood structure.

Second floor plan – 1:300

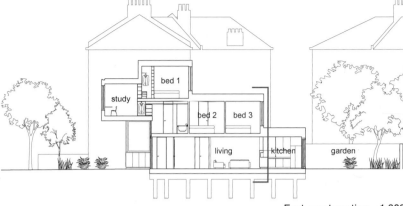

East–west section – 1:300

First floor plan – 1:300

Drawing labels:

1. Foundations
600 × 450 mm reinforced concrete ground beam with waterproof additive.
200 mm thick reinforced concrete slab with waterproof additive spanning between ground beams.
100 mm extruded polystyrene insulation below slab on 50 mm sand blinding.

2. Ground floor
180 × 21 mm European oak engineered timber floorboards with grey oiled finish.
Low temperature hot water underfloor heating pipes with metal radiation plates suspended between battens.
50 × 50 mm treated softwood battens at 300 mm centres.
50 mm rigid insulation between battens.
Polythene vapour barrier.
200 mm thick reinforced concrete slab with waterproof additive spanning between ground beams.
100 mm extruded polystyrene insulation below slab on 50 mm sand blinding.

3. Slab edge
200 × 150 mm concrete upstand around slab perimeter.
Bituminous liquid-applied waterproofing membrane to side and top of upstand.
100 mm rigid polystyrene insulation.
40 mm thick precast concrete paving slabs fixed back to upstand on stainless steel brackets.

4. Typical wall
Zinc alloy sheet cladding with angled double standing seams folded over clips spiked into insulation.
Bituminous felt waterproof layer.

Liquid applied bituminous sealant to fill any gaps in insulation.
140 mm foamglass insulation bonded to solid timber panel with bituminous adhesive.
128 mm (94 mm on upper floor) solid cross-laminated timber wall panel notched over and fixed to softwood batten wall plate fixed to concrete upstand.
Plasterboard fixed to inside face of timber panel with skim coat and paint finish.

5. Gutter
180 × 80 mm deep pre-formed folded zinc alloy sheet gutter folded over clips spiked into insulation.
Bituminous felt waterproof membrane.
Foamglass insulation around gutter.

6. Typical window
Proprietary softwood framed double-glazed high-performance window.
Softwood sub-frame fixed to structural timber panel.
Preformed-zinc alloy cill slotted into route in bottom of window frame.

7. Roof
Zinc alloy sheet cladding folded over clips spiked into insulation.
10 mm spun nylon open-weave matting to allow ventilation, expansion and acoustic isolation.
Bituminous felt waterproof layer.
Liquid applied bituminous sealant to fill any gaps in insulation.
Tapered Foamglass insulation varying from 500 mm maximum to 140 mm minimum thickness.
146 mm solid cross-laminated timber panel structural deck sealed internally with coloured natural wax.

Ground floor plan – 1:300

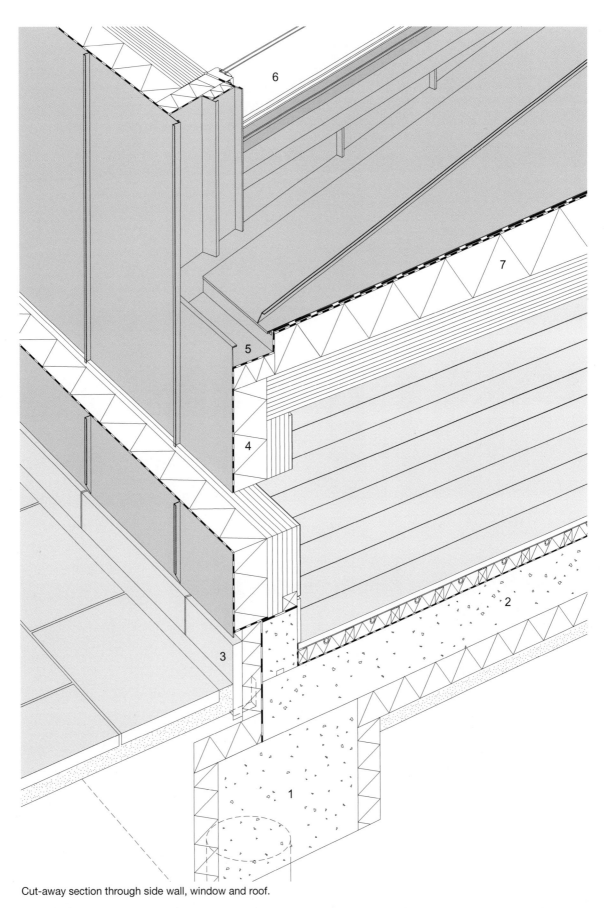

Cut-away section through side wall, window and roof.

*Photo: Prewett Bizley Architects*

*Photo: Prewett Bizley Architects*

*Photo: Astrid Kogler*

# 80% House, De Beauvoir Town London

## Architect: Prewett Bizley Architects

De Beauvoir Town is a tranquil conservation area of Victorian villas and terraces due north of the City in Hackney. This 'extreme' refurbishment of a typical terraced house is aimed at reducing its carbon emissions by 80% in line with the Government's pledge to cut greenhouse gas emissions by that amount by 2050.

*Photo: Prewett Bizley Architects*

The house has been extended by 2 metres to the rear at the lower two levels to create a kitchen/dining room at lower ground and a generous living space at upper ground level. A rooftop extension provides a third bedroom. The extra space offsets the area lost to extra insulation and provides a layout more appropriate to current patterns of inhabitation.

The two most important measures in reducing energy loss are high levels of insulation and air tightness. At the front a new, independent insulated wall has been built inside the existing brickwork. The existing joists were cut back and re-supported on a steel beam spanning between the party walls to remove the cold bridge. New timber sash windows have been installed incorporating micro-double-glazed units with 20 mm astragals to match the original windows.

The rear elevation has been rebuilt using the same stock bricks but as a 400 mm thick cavity wall with full-fill insulation and basalt-fibre wall ties to reduce cold bridging. The windows are triple glazed. Steel has been used to frame the large openings of the rear extension and concrete slabs at first and second floor provide thermal mass.

An excellent air tightness level of $1.1\,m^3/hr/m^2$ @ 50 Pa has been achieved by lining the existing walls with OSB and taping all joints. Fresh air is supplied by a MVHR (mechanical ventilation heat recovery) system which uses a heat exchanger to transfer heat from the extract air to the fresh air at about 90% efficiency.

*Photo: Prewett Bizley Architects*

Because the floor area is very limited it was decided to use the insulation with the highest thermal performance in each location even if it does not have the lowest embodied energy as the potential lifetime energy savings are much higher. A photovoltaic array on the roof with a 1000 kWh output provides about half the annual electricity requirement. It has been calculated that after six years the energy saved will have offset the energy used to carry out the refurbishment.

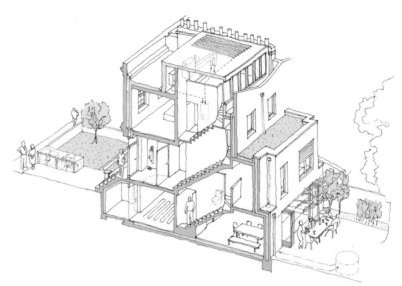

Sketch east–west section showing improvements carried out

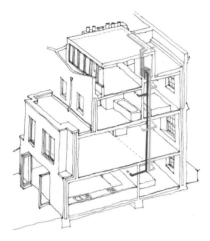

Diagram showing MVHR system

Upper ground floor plan – 1:150

Drawing labels:

1. Ground floor
Existing floor removed and ground excavated 150 mm.
20 mm ceramic screed replacement tile finish.
30 mm extruded polystyrene insulation with clip-in underfloor heating pipes.
100 mm extruded polystyrene insulation.
Liquid applied DPM (damp proof membrane).
150 mm reinforced concrete slab with edge upstand to support wall lining.

2. Front wall
Existing 330 mm stock brick wall with external stucco finish up to upper ground floor level.
15 mm sand/cement render applied to inner face to seal gaps.
Minimum 25 mm air gap ventilated via weepholes and airbricks.
25 mm aluminium top-hat sections screwed to brickwork at 400 mm centres.
12 mm OSB (oriented strand board) sheathing.
70 × 50 mm vertical rigid insulation spacer battens at 400 mm centres with glass mineral wool insulation in between.
18 mm OSB air-tightness layer with all joints taped.
70 × 50 mm horizontal rigid insulation spacer battens at 400 mm centres with glass mineral wool insulation in between.
12 mm OSB sheathing.
12 mm foil-backed plasterboard internal lining with plaster skim coat.

3. Front windows
New bespoke softwood sliding sash windows with four seals at all sash edges.
Micro-double-glazed units consisting of 4 mm outer, 6 mm argon-filled cavity and 4 mm low-e inner pane.

4. Window linings
18 mm WBP plywood box fixed to outside of window frames on all sides prior to installation and sealed with two silicone beads.

DPM liquid applied to rear face of plywood and window frames.
Inside edges of plywood sealed to surrounding construction with air-tightness tape.
Expanding foam to fill all gaps between frame and masonry.

5. First floor at front
150 × 20 mm tongued and grooved pitch pine floorboards secret-nailed to plywood.
18 mm tongued and grooved plywood screwed to joists.
203 × 102 mm × 23 kg UBs (universal beam) spanning between party walls.
Existing softwood joists cut off and hung off steel beam on joist hangers to eliminate cold bridge.
Two layers 12 mm plasterboard ceiling on softwood battens with plaster skim coat.

6. First floor in extension
Paired 203 × 102 mm × 23 kg UBs spanning between party walls.
150 mm reinforced concrete slab.
Floor and ceiling as 4 above.

7. Party wall linings
Existing stock brick wall.
15 mm sand/cement render to seal gaps.
50 mm light gauge steel studs screwed to wall at 400 mm centres with 50 mm glass mineral wool acoustic insulation in between.
18 mm OSB air-tightness layer with all joints taped.
12 mm plasterboard with plaster skim coat.

8. Air-tightness tape
Proprietary air-tightness tape to seal gaps between different materials.

9. Rear walls
102 mm reclaimed stock brick outer leaf.
200 mm glass mineral wool full-fill insulation impregnated with silicone for moisture resistance.
Basalt fibre wall ties to reduce cold bridging.
100 mm aerated blockwork inner leaf.
15 mm sand/cement render with skim coat finish.

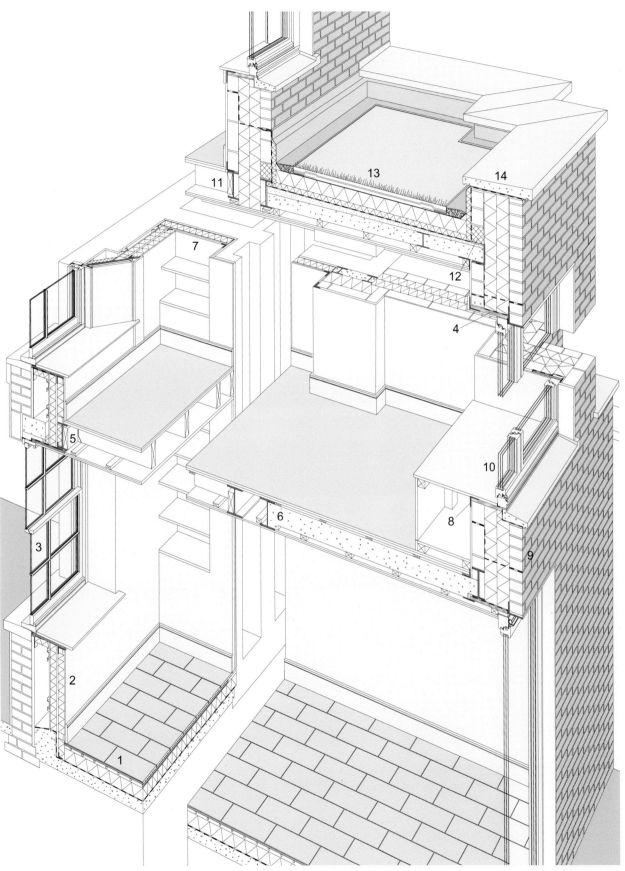

Cut-away section through front and rear façades

10. Rear windows
Laminated softwood framed windows.
Triple-glazed sealed units with argon filled
cavities and low-e coating.
Double seals on opening lights.
Concrete cills cast on site with DPC below.

11. Second floor structure
Paired 203 × 102 mm × 23 kg UBs spanning
between party walls and bearing on paired
100 × 100 mm H columns.
Existing joists re-used and hung off steel beam
on joist hangers.
Floor and ceiling as 4 above.

12. Insulation blocks
Single course of 115 × 100 mm foamglass
insulation blocks built into walls to eliminate
cold bridges.

13. Roof
Sedum planting in growing medium on
geotextile layer.
EPDM rubber waterproof membrane.
140 mm rigid urethane insulation.
50 mm insulation to upstands.
Polythene vapour barrier continued up masonry
walls to bond with DPCs.
Sand/cement screed laid to fall.
150 mm reinforced concrete slab.
12 mm plasterboard ceiling on softwood
battens with plaster skim coat.

14. Parapet
530 mm wide concrete copings cast
on site.

DPC over cement-fibre slate cavity closers.

*Photo: Nick Kane*

*Photo: Nick Kane*

*Photo: Nick Kane*

# Clay Field Housing
# Elmswell, Suffolk

Architect: Riches Hawley Mikhail Architects
Sustainability Consultant: Buro Happold

An affordable housing development in the Suffolk village of Elsmwell combines strategies for sustainable construction, lifetime energy use and landscape to achieve exemplary low levels of embodied energy and carbon emission. The 22 houses and four flats each have their own private garden and are grouped in threes around three communal gardens. Rainwater is collected to flush toilets and to water the gardens. The houses are oriented east–west to maximise solar gain and heat and hot water are provided by a shared biomass boiler.

*Photo: Riches Hawley Mikhail Architects*

The dwellings have timber frames that were partially prefabricated in sections off-site. The walls are raised off the ground slightly on masonry plinths to protect the timber from rising damp and there are ventilated voids beneath the timber floors. 12 mm Sasmox sheathing, a gyspum reinforced fibreboard, has been fixed on the inside to brace the frame. The walls are insulated with Hemcrete, a mixture of hemp, hydrated lime and a small amount of Portland cement as a binder to accelerate the curing process, which sets to form a rigid, breathable layer. The Hemcrete was mixed on site and sprayed onto the timber frames to ensure there are no gaps that might compromise air-tightness.

On the gable walls the Hemcrete has been finished with 20 mm of lime render. The window openings on the gable are lined with 25 mm Heraklith wood fibre boards to form a square reveal and the lime render is returned into the reveals. The north and south elevations are clad in cedar boards on timber studwork battens built out from the primary frame. Isonat, another hemp-base product made with recycled cotton fibre and a thermoplastic binder has been used to insulate the roof. The building control officer deemed that the cedar shingle roof constituted a risk for spread of flame so the rafters have been 'overdrawn' with a layer of calcium silicate board to provide 30 minutes' fire protection.

*Photo: Riches Hawley Mikhail Architects*

Curved walls provide privacy and enclosure to the gardens. They are built from unfired clay blocks rendered both sides with lime render and capped with a cedar shingle coping. There are three low-maintenance gardens which are seen as part of a wider village life, a wild flower meadow, allotments and an orchard of Suffolk apples.

Site plan – 1:2000

First floor plan of two bedroom
house – 1:200

Ground floor plan of two bedroom
house – 1:200

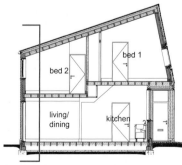

Section through two bedroom
house – 1:200

Drawing labels:

1. Foundations
450 mm wide × 1000 mm deep reinforced
concrete footings consisting of 50% GGBS
(ground granulated blastfurnace slag).

2. Ground below floor
Weak mix concrete blinding.
Polythene DPM (damp proof membrane)
dressed up plinth and bonded to blockwork
with double sided tape.
50 mm sand blinding.
Minimum 150 mm compacted hardcore.

3. Plinth
190 mm high × 215 mm wide concrete
blockwork inner leaf plinth.
DPC (damp proof course) bonded with
polythene DPM and dressed over blockwork
and up side of softwood floor structure.
140 × 32 mm treated softwood sole plate to
support floor joists.
215 mm high × 190 mm wide concrete
blockwork outer leaf plinth where retaining –
elsewhere 215 × 100 mm.
Five courses engineering brick with lime mortar.
Gap between inner and outer plinths filled with
50 mm polystyrene insulation and weak mix
concrete.
DPC below top course of brick dressed over
concrete and bonded to inner leaf DPM.

4. Ground floor
18 mm tongued and grooved particle board
floor.
Breather membrane.
194 × 50 mm treated softwood joists at 400 mm
centres.
Breather membrane stapled to tops of joists
and dressed down sides to carry insulation.
150 mm insulation made from hemp and
recycled cotton.
238 mm ventilation gap below joists.

5. Gable wall
Three coat limewash finish.
20 mm lime render outer finish.
250 mm Hemcrete sprayed onto prefabricated
panel.
Prefabricated structural wall panel consisting
of 140 × 50 mm softwood studs at 600 mm

centres with 12 mm gypsum reinforced
fibreboard internal lining infilled with sprayed
Hemcrete.
Paint finish internally.

6. Window in gable wall
25 mm Heraklith (magnesite woodfibre) board
fixed back to timber studwork on all four sides
to form opening in Hemcrete wall.
Laminated softwood window frame fixed to
timber studwork.
Double-glazed sealed units with low-e coating.
Pressed aluminium external cill fixed to frame
and to wood-fibre board with aluminium clips.
104 × 32 mm softwood cill and internal lining to
all four sides of opening.

7. North and south walls
142 mm shiplapped tapered western red cedar
boards fixed to battens with stainless steel
nails.
50 × 25 mm vertical treated softwood battens
at 600 mm centres.
Breather membrane.
75 × 50 mm horizontal treated softwood
battens at 600 mm centres.
75 mm Hemcrete sprayed between battens.
Prefabricated structural wall panel consisting
of 140 × 50 mm softwood studs at 600 mm
centres with 12 mm gypsum reinforced
fibreboard internal lining infilled with sprayed
Hemcrete.
Paint finish internally.

8. Roof
Western red cedar shingles.
50 × 25 mm treated softwood battens at
123 mm centres.
50 × 50 mm treated softwood battens at
400 mm centres forming ventilation gap.
Breather membrane.
100 mm insulation made from hemp and
recycled cotton between 100 × 50 mm treated
softwood battens.
9 mm calcium silicate board to provide fire
protection to structure below.
175 mm insulation made from hemp and
recycled cotton between 175 × 50 mm treated
softwood rafters at 400 mm centres.
Vapour barrier.
12.5 mm plasterboard ceiling with skim coat
and paint finish.

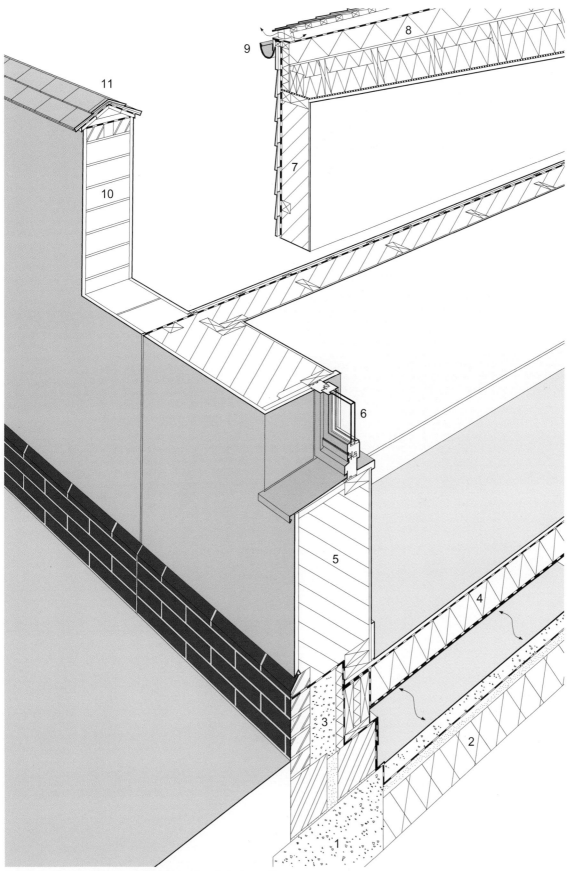

Cut-away section through gable wall, roof and garden wall

9. Eaves
120 × 22 mm cedar fascia.
Galvanised steel half-round gutter on brackets screwed to fascia.
Breather membrane lapped over DPC and dressed into gutter.
9 mm calcium silicate board returned to provide fire protection to eaves beam.

10. Garden wall
314 mm wide engineering brick cavity wall plinth with lime mortar.
DPC 150 mm above ground level.
Cavity filled with weak mix concrete below DPC level.

Solid wall above plinth made from 350 × 100 × 255 mm unfired wide earth blocks bedded in lime mortar.
20 mm lime render to both faces with three coat limewash finish.

11. Garden wall coping
Cedar ridge cap.
Two courses cedar shingles with minimum 50 mm lap over outer faces of wall.
Breather membrane.
Continuous triangular treated softwood block.
Continuous plywood.
DPC.
Top course of brick bedded in lime mortar.

Photo: Simon Lewis

Photo: Simon Lewis

Photo: Ioana Marinescu

Photo: Ioana Marinescu

# Chance Street Housing
# Bethnal Green, London

Architect: Stephen Taylor Architects
Stair Fabricator: Tin Tab Ltd

In Victorian times the Nichol was a dense East End slum consisting of tiny terraced houses suffering from horrendous overcrowding and poverty. Most of it was demolished in the late nineteenth century but the narrow streets and cobbled surfaces remain. This development of three new terraced houses fills the whole of a 12 × 9 metre plot previously occupied by a single storey industrial shed. A three-storey brickwork façade completes the urban block, reinforcing the hard edge and intimate character of the street.

Each house is only 4 metres wide but the terrace is ingeniously planned with a narrow courtyard at the back that allows each house a dual aspect. The 2 × 2 metre courtyards are fully glazed on two sides and the other two walls have an outer leaf of white clay bricks to reflect light down. The timber framed glazing has a combination of fixed panels and folding/sliding doors to allow the rooms to open up and appropriate the courtyard. Dining/kitchen spaces are located on the top floor to take advantage of the best light. A ground floor porch provides a buffer between each house and the street, protected by a folded 'curtain' of perforated metal that allows eastern sunlight to penetrate.

A laminated timber staircase twists its way up next to the light well bringing a sculptural finesse to the interior. The stair is made from a single material, laminated timber, CNC cut into a kit of panels which were assembled off site into several large pieces. 19 mm thick sheets were used for the treads and risers and 27 mm for all other pieces. A 20 mm gap was allowed on all sides for tolerance as the walls were already plastered and painted before the stair was installed. Stainless steel spacers were cut on site to suit and the bolt holes in the timber have been concealed with larch plugs. At ground floor the stair panels are birch-faced and stained dark like the brick on the main elevation facing the street. On the floor above, the stair has a knotty, strong-grained larch finish. The walls and ceiling are white so that looking up the stair you see a gradation from dark to light, enhancing the transition from the gritty street to the private domestic realm.

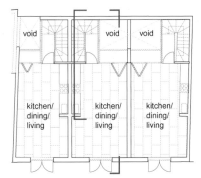

Second floor plan – 1:250

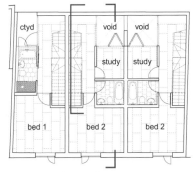

First floor plan – 1:250

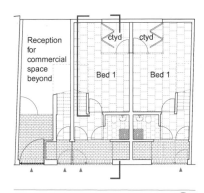

Ground floor plan – 1:250

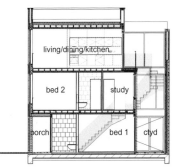

East–west section – 1:250

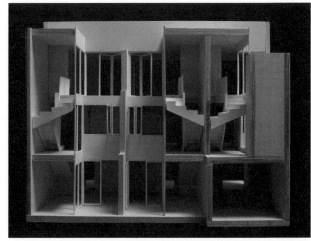

Sectional model through courtyards – David Grandorge

Drawing labels:

1. Foundations
Reinforced concrete piles.
600 × 400 mm deep concrete ground beams.

2. Ground Floor
500 × 500 × 20 mm tiles on adhesive bed.
5 mm flexible adhesive.
Electric underfloor heating.
50 mm polymer-modified cement/sand screed.
Polythene vapour barrier.
70 mm phenolic insulation.
Damp proof membrane.
225 mm thick reinforced concrete slab spanning between ground beams.
50 mm concrete blinding.
150 mm compacted hardcore.

3. External party wall
100 mm concrete blockwork outer leaf.
100 mm cavity.
100 mm concrete blockwork inner leaf.

4. Windows
Double 225 × 50 mm softwood joists at floor edges to support windows.
64 mm thick laminated timber windows.
Double-glazed sealed units.
Folded aluminium external cills.

5. Typical upper floor
1200 × 600 × 15 mm plywood panel floating floor.
Underfloor heating layer consisting of moisture barrier on carbon heating film on 6 mm insulation.
18 mm plywood deck.
225 × 50 mm softwood joists at 400 mm centres.
100 mm mineral wool insulation between joists.
12.5 mm plasterboard ceiling with skim coat and paint finish.

6. Internal partition
70 mm metal channel studs.

Mineral wool insulation between studs.
Two layers 12.5 mm sound insulating plasterboard to each side with skim coat and paint finish.

7. Ground to first floor staircase
27 mm tri-ply laminated timber stringer.
19 mm butt-jointed tri-ply treads and risers.
27 mm tri-ply balustrade with profiled softwood handrail.
Two layers 12.5 mm plasterboard fire resisting ceiling fixed below stair on isolating hangers.

8. First–second floor stair stringer
27 mm tri-ply laminated timber stringer.
Stair and landing stringers fixed to wall using 38 mm long M12 bolts screwed into 90 mm long × 25 mm diameter mild steel anchors chemically bonded into masonry.
Bolt heads concealed with larch veneer plugs.
Stringer held nominal 25 mm off plaster wall with 38 mm diameter stainless steel spacers.

9. First–second floor stairs
830 mm wide × 19 mm thick butt-jointed larch-faced tri-ply treads and risers.
Outer veneer of tread laps over riser to cover end-grain of riser.

10. First–second floor balustrades
27 mm thick larch-faced tri-ply balustrade panels fixed to stringers.

11. Second floor landing
27 mm thick larch-faced tri-ply stringers with 100 mm deep notches to accept joists.
850 mm wide × 200 mm deep × 27 mm thick larch-faced tri-ply joists glued into notches in stringers at 250 mm centres.
27 mm thick larch-faced tri-ply floor panel.

12. First floor desk
1800 mm wide × 600 mm deep × 27 mm thick larch-faced tri-ply desktop with 75 mm deep downstand along front edge.
Desktop jointed to 27 mm thick tri-ply stringer supporting stair above.

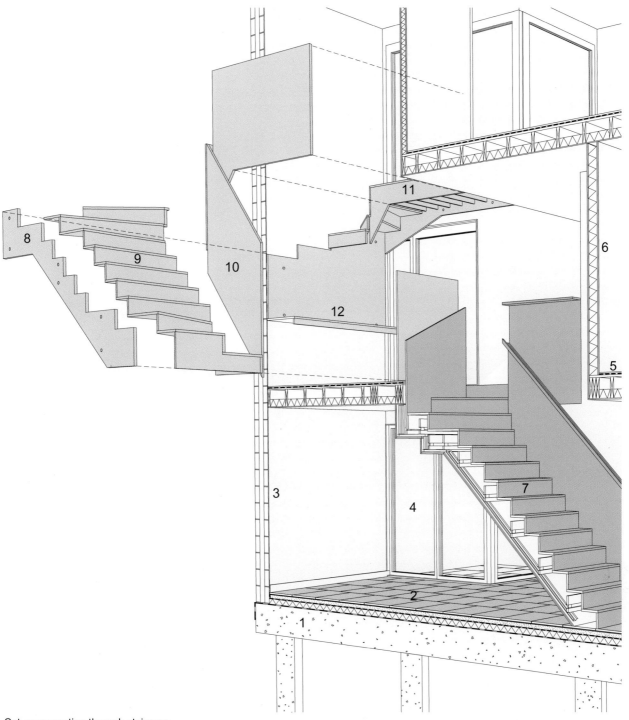

Cut-away section through staircase

*Photo: Edmund Sumner*

*Photo: James White*

*Photo: Edmund Sumner*

# Islington Square Housing, Manchester

Architect: FAT
Structural Engineer: Whitby Bird

The Cardroom Estate was a deprived community just to the east of Manchester's city centre that was suffering from depopulation and a lack of shops and services. In a plan drawn up by Alsop Architects, Urban Splash are completely redeveloping and rebranding the area as New Islington. The new community will eventually boast 1400 new homes. For this development of 23 social housing units, FAT have worked closely with the residents to make a strong urban street frontage using conventional construction techniques and incorporating symbolic references to the idea of home. The dwellings were designed to Lifetime Homes standards and achieve an EcoHomes rating of 'excellent'. The units are a mixture of two bedroom flats and three or four bedroom houses laid out in two parallel terraces with private gardens in between.

New Islington is an ex-industrial area so the canals and land have had to be treated to remove contaminates. Piled foundations support ground beams and load-bearing masonry cavity walls. The ground floor has a beam and block structure which is ventilated to the outside via telescopic vents. The first floor and roof are timber and the roof has an aluminium sheet finish. The street façade is brick, precisely set out by the architects in a criss-cross pattern using three different colours of brick. Timber windows are recessed with almost a full brick reveal and the variety of shapes and sizes makes a lively elevation.

The brick wall is capped by a glass reinforced plastic (GRP) parapet that swoops and dives along the street linking the Dutch gabled fronts of the houses in a continuous line. The GRP is prefabricated in 1–1.5 metre lengths and fixed to the masonry with metal clips. L-shaped steel wind posts concealed in the masonry walls and fixed into the roof structure help support the free-standing gables. Balconies at first floor are supported by steel beams tied back to the floor structure. The balustrade is made of 150 mm wide timber planks CNC cut with a pattern and screwed to the steel structure from behind. The motifs in the façades are abstract and diverse enough to avoid any fixed association, allowing the development to achieve an identity entirely its own.

*Photo: Tim Soar*

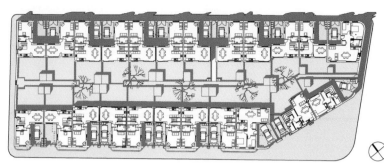

Two bedroom house first floor
plan – 1:200

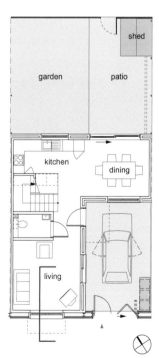

Two bedroom house ground floor
plan – 1:200

Drawing labels:

1. Foundations
Reinforced concrete ground beam.
Precast concrete driven piles.

2. Ground floor
70 mm thick sand-cement screed.
100 mm thick insulation.
Damp-proof membrane lapped over blockwork
into cavity and bonded to cavity tray.
155 mm deep precast concrete T-beams.
100 mm thick concrete block infill between beams.

3. Ventilation
Minimum 150 mm ventilated void between
ground and suspended floor.
Proprietary telescopic underfloor ventilation units
to give 1500 mm$^2$ airflow per metre length of wall.
Air bricks in outer leaf of wall.

4. External wall
103 mm face brick outer leaf.
60 mm air gap.
90 mm partial fill mineral wool insulation.
140 mm dense concrete blockwork inner leaf.
13 mm plaster internal finish.

5. First Floor
21 mm particle board deck screwed to joists.
150 × 50 mm softwood joists at 400 mm centres.
13 mm plasterboard ceiling with vapour barrier
fixed to softwood battens at 600 mm centres.

6. Window cill
Pressed aluminium cill polyester powder coated
to match window frame.
Mastic seal with backing rod at edges.
Painted softwood internal cill.
Insulated cavity closer with integral DPC.

7. Window head
Cavity tray with stop ends.
Weepholes in perpends at 450 mm centres.
180 mm wide galvanised steel T-lintel to outer leaf.
215 mm high × 100 mm wide galvanised steel
angle lintel to internal leaf.
Gap between lintels packed with mineral wool
insulation.
Lath welded to lintel and plaster returned
across internal reveal.

8. Window
2250 mm high softwood framed sliding patio
door with cold bridge insulated aluminium/
wood bottom rail.

26 mm thick double-glazed unit.

9. Balcony structure
2100 × 800 mm balcony made from
152 × 89 mm galvanised universal beams (UB)
on front and sides bolted to first floor joists.
150 × 50 mm treated timber joists spanning
between steel beams.
150 mm wide stained and treated timber board
decking.

10. Balustrade
50 × 50 mm galvanised steel rectangular hollow
section (RHS) posts in each corner.
50 × 50 mm galvanised steel RHS top and
bottom members spanning between posts.
150 mm wide treated and painted softwood
planks with CNC cut-out pattern screwed to
steel structure from behind.

11. Roof
175 mm high × 200 mm wide aluminium
upstand flashing with 25 mm insulation board
behind.
Pressed aluminium cover flashing polyester
powder coated to match parapet render with
mastic joint to render stop bead.
Profiled aluminium roofing laid to 1 in 40 fall in
400 mm width strips with standing seam lock
joints.
200 mm mineral fibre insulation compressed to
183 mm.
Thermally broken roof sheet brackets fixed
through plywood deck to joists below.
Vapour control and air-lock layer lapped up and
mechanically fixed to blockwork.
20 mm WBP plywood deck screwed to joists.
200 × 50 mm softwood joists at 400 mm
centres.
13 mm plasterboard ceiling with vapour barrier
fixed to softwood battens at 600 mm centres.

12. Windposts
L-shaped windpost frames welded up from
152 × 89 mm steel joists resting on steel beam
in blockwork leaf and tied into timber roof
structure.

13. Parapet
Prefabricated GRP (glass reinforced plastic)
coping units clipped over fixing brackets bolted
to top of masonry.
Butt straps between adjacent sections.

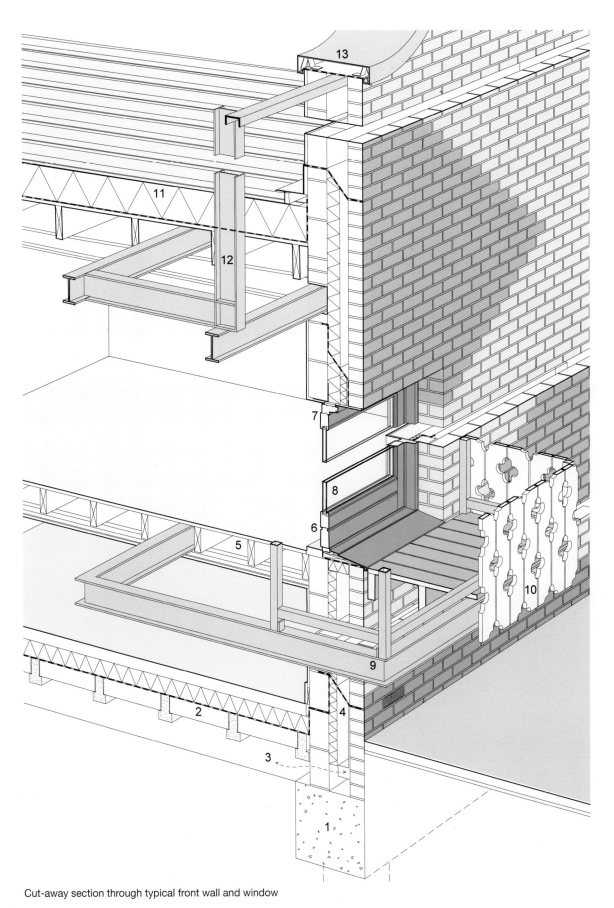

Cut-away section through typical front wall and window

Photo: Elena Marco

Photo: Elena Marco

Photo: Elena Marco

Photo: Empresa Municipal de la Vivienda

# EMV Social Housing, Vallecas, Madrid

Architect: Feilden Clegg Bradley Architects
M&E Engineer: Max Fordham LLP
Environmental Engineer: Emma s.l

Vallecas is a south-eastern suburb of Madrid. In a massive expansion over 26,000 new housing units are being built, a proportion of which will incorporate renewable sources of energy, the efficient use of power, recycling and landscaping. Northern European expertise in sustainable design was brought in to create an exemplary low-energy 139 unit housing scheme.

Cross-ventilation and stack ventilation are an integral part of the architecture reducing the need for winter heating and summer cooling. Each flat will have dual aspect to the street and to an internal courtyard. A combination of full height windows, balconies and sliding screens on the west, south and east sides allow high levels of control of cross-ventilation and sunlight. In addition, each flat will have its own dedicated ventilation chimney in a central core to draw air up to roof level using stack effect. The ducts work in a similar way to the shared light wells in traditional Spanish urban apartment blocks but without the problems of odours and acoustic privacy. The negative pressure generated as the wind blows across the chimneys aids the stack effect.

The ducts are sized according to the volume of each flat and the height of the ventilation chimney. The taller the shaft, the smaller its cross-sectional area. Air is drawn out of the flat via a grille with an acoustic damper in the hallway set to open automatically on a timer at night. Thermal modelling was used to size the ducts, openings in the external envelope and grilles in or above the doors to the hallway. The timer can be over-ridden manually. The chimneys are used primarily for night-time cooling of the thermally massive structure of the building. The chimneys project 5 metres above the top floor in clusters giving the building a distinctive silhouette.

The building fabric is insulated with 100 mm of polystyrene as opposed to the normal 30–40 mm on Spanish housing. Rainwater from the roofs and hard surfaces is used to water the plants in the courtyard. Photo-voltaic cells on top of the chimneys provide enough electricity to light the communal areas and 140 square metres of solar-thermal collectors will heat water for winter heating. Energy consumption and the emission of $CO_2$ is intended to be 70% lower than in a conventional residential building.

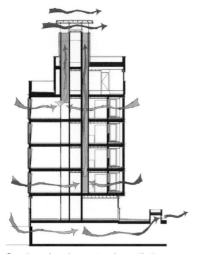

Section showing natural ventilation airflow

Typical three bedroom flat plan – 1:300

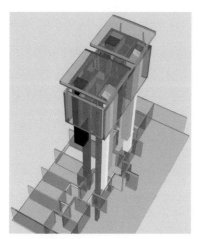

Diagram showing individual chimneys for each flat

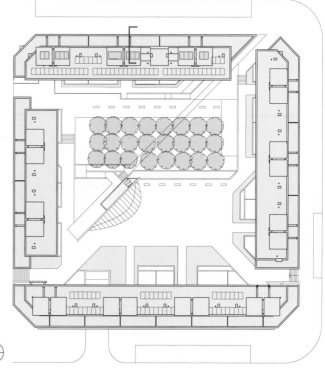

Roof plan – 1:1000

**Drawing labels:**

**1. Roof**
Curved galvanised steel roofing with standing seams at 450 mm centres.
18 mm plywood deck.
Galvanised steel edge flashings with continuous gap to ventilate roof void.
Softwood firrings to form fall.
150 × 50 mm softwood joists fixed to steel structure below.
12 mm calcium silicate soffit boards fixed to steel via timber battens.

**2. Chimney roof structure**
Four 100 × 100 mm rectangular hollow section (RHS) posts bolted to gutter channel below.
100 × 100 mm RHS horizontal frame bolted to posts.

**3. Bracing**
100 × 60 mm RHS bolted between horizontal roof frame members.
Steel cable braces bolted to RHS above and to masonry walls below.

**4. Gutter**
Galvanised 260 × 90 mm parallel flange channel (PFC) forming gutter bolted to masonry walls below.

**5. Central roof**
Curved galvanised steel roofing with standing seams at 450 mm centres.
18 mm plywood deck.
100 × 50 mm softwood joists fixed to PFC gutter channel on steel cleats.
12 mm calcium silicate soffit boards fixed to timber joists.

**6. External wall**
120 mm solid terracotta blockwork wall.

100 × 50 mm vertical softwood battens fixed to masonry.
100 mm mineral wool insulation between battens.
50 × 38 mm horizontal softwood battens forming ventilation gap.
Galvanised steel cladding panels on 18 mm plywood backing.

**7. Coping flashing**
Pressed galvanised steel coping flashing on 18 mm plywood on softwood battens.

**8. Mesh**
Rigid stainless steel mesh over duct openings to prevent ingress of insects and birds fixed to duct walls on stainless steel angle cleats.

**9. Internal duct wall**
120 mm solid terracotta blockwork wall, fair faced on duct side.
Plaster with paint finish to flat side.

**10. Typical floor**
70 mm terrazzo floor finish.
50 mm screed.
50 mm concrete structural topping.
250 mm deep terracotta pots spanning between concrete beams.
250 mm deep precast concrete beams at 800 mm centres spanning between main reinforced concrete beams.
25 mm plaster to ceiling with paint finish.

**11. Ventilation in flat**
0.5 square metre aluminium ventilation grille above cupboard in hall with motorised damper linked to automatic timer.

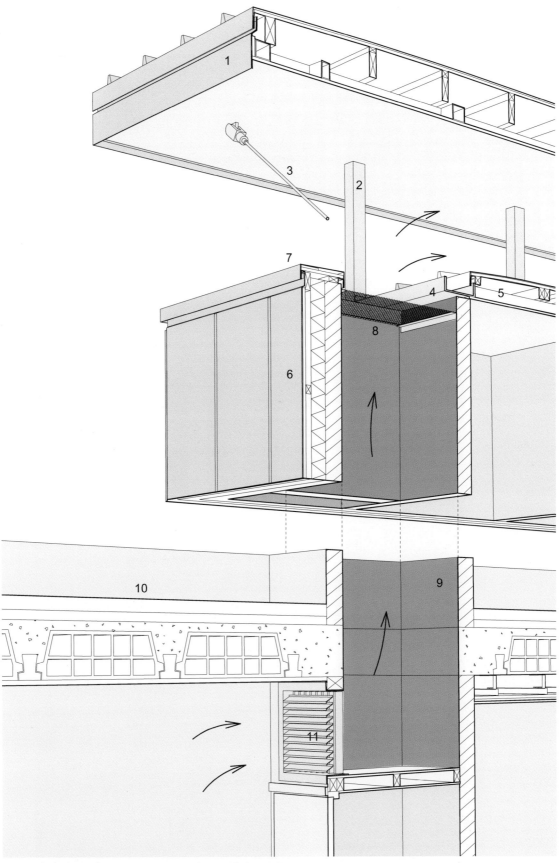

Cut-away section through chimney showing passive ventilation system

Photo: Allford Hall Monaghan Morris

Photo: Tim Soar

Photo: Allford Hall Monaghan Morris

Photo: Tim Soar

# The Johnson Building
# Clerkenwell, London

Architect: Allford Hall Monaghan Morris
Structural Engineer: Price & Myers

A dramatic atrium unites a refurbished 1930s building with a new concrete framed structure bringing natural daylight right down to the ground through a seven-storey office development in central London. Occupying the whole width of a city block in London's traditional jewellery quarter between Hatton Garden and Leather Lane the complex is actually a cluster of several buildings around a central courtyard. In addition to office space, Camden Council planners insisted that 14 apartments and a retail unit be provided, as well as a building dedicated for tenants in the jewellery trade.

The main office building is 37 metres wide so the atrium is essential for natural light at the centre of the plan. Daylight has been maximised by using a lightweight ETFE roof that requires much less structure than a glass roof. The ETFE is designed to be sacrificial in case of fire so that the atrium can be considered as an outdoor space, simplifying the fire escape strategy.

At each floor level, a concrete bridge connects the offices on both sides to a lift core. A precast concrete beam spans 7.5 m from side to side supporting four precast concrete floor panels. The beams have a profiled section to conceal lighting. The precast floor panels were installed with their trowelled surface uppermost as a non-slip finish. Glass lenses were fitted on site as the holes were required for lifting the panels into position. All the precast elements were installed in one day and required careful protection for the rest of the contract period.

The concrete walls either side of the walkways were formed with steel shutters that had all their welds ground off and were then bead-blasted so the concrete would have a fine matt finish. Timber panels on the atrium walls have been carefully jointed with 60 mm return pieces on three edges to appear like pieces of joinery rather than a thin veneer. The wall of the lift shafts facing the atrium is glazed and lit from behind with an 80% frit to diffuse the light evenly. The ghostly movement of the lifts behind adds life to the crisp serenity of the atrium.

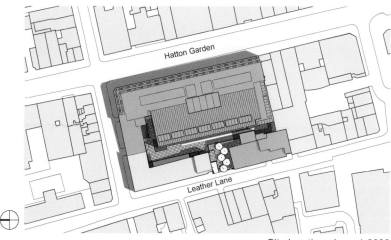

Site location plan – 1:2000

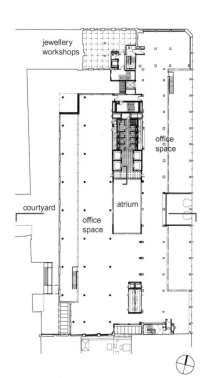

First floor plan – 1:1000

East–west section – 1:1000

**Drawing labels:**

**1. Lift lobby floor**
12 mm thick composite stone tile floor finish on adhesive bed.
25 × 25 mm brushed stainless steel edge trim angle with silicone sealant between tiles and precast floor slabs.
50 mm sand-cement screed.
150 mm thick reinforced concrete slab with 375 × 140 mm thick downstand at slab edge.
125 × 100 mm recess to carry walkway floor slabs.

**2. Walkway wall**
250 mm thick reinforced concrete shear wall cast with steel shutter.
All welds on steel shutter ground smooth and surface bead blasted to give matt finish to concrete.

**3. Walkway beams**
7500 × 575 × 350 mm precast concrete beam with recessed profile on walkway side.
Beam ends have T-profile to sit on 440 mm high × 350 mm wide reinforced concrete U-brackets cast as part of shear wall.
Continuous 150 × 90 × 10 mm rolled steel angle (RSA) with intumescent paint finish fixed with captive bolts to galvanised steel channel cast into bottom flange of beam to carry floor panels.

**4. Walkway floor**
2720 × 1865 × 150 mm thick ordinary Portland cement precast concrete floor panels spanning between RSA and lift lobby floor edge.
Glass lenses inserted on site bedded in tile adhesive.

**5. Walkway balustrade**
Continuous 200 × 100 mm painted steel T-bracket fixed with captive bolts to galvanised steel channels cast into concrete beam.
Balustrade formed from five 905 mm high toughened glass sheets bolted via 40 mm diameter stainless steel spacers to T-bracket with brushed pignose bolts and rubber isolation washers.
Cold cathode lighting tube fixed in recess below T-bracket.
Continuous brushed folded stainless steel capping rail silicone bonded to top edge of glass.

**6. Lift shaft glazing**
50 × 25 mm rectangular section polyester powder coated (PPC) aluminium support at base of glazing.
150 × 75 mm steel unequal angle (UA) bolted to concrete beam at head to restrain glazing frame.
50 × 25 mm PPC aluminium glazing frame with 28 × 22 mm aluminium angle glazing bead.
12 mm toughened glass with 80% fritted film.

**7. Bulkhead and ceiling**
One layer 12.5 mm plasterboard fixed to proprietary galvanised steel suspended ceiling track system.
Shadow gap beads at edges.
Plaster skim coat with painted finish.

**8. Typical office floor**
440 mm deep proprietary raised floor system.
275 mm thick reinforced concrete floor.
Sprayed plaster finish to soffit.

**9. Atrium walls**
2740 × 1115 × 12 mm thick elm veneered cementitious board cladding panels with concealed fixings on atrium side with sanded lacquer finish.
60 mm wide elm veneered cementitious board strips around lower and side edges on concealed fixings.
58 × 50 mm softwood battens.
590 high × 175 mm thick reinforced concrete upstand wall.
12.5 mm plasterboard with plaster skim coat on 25 mm battens on office side.

**10. Atrium glazing**
12 mm clear toughened glass.
50 × 25 mm PPC aluminium glazing frame with 28 × 22 mm aluminium angle glazing bead.
210 × 15 mm painted MDF cill screwed and plugged on timber packers at 600 mm centres.
120 × 70 mm continuous RSA glazing support bolted to concrete wall at cill.
70 × 70 mm continuous RSA glazing restraint bracket bolted to concrete soffit at head.
65 × 65 mm PPC aluminium angle subframe at head.

**11. Doors**
Glazed doors with 70 × 60 mm brushed stainless steel box section frames.

**12. Side panel**
High gloss lacquered 280 mw wide × 15 mm MDF panel at side of door to allow tenant to mount entry system.
Softwood studwork frame fixed to 75 × 75 mm RSA door jamb.

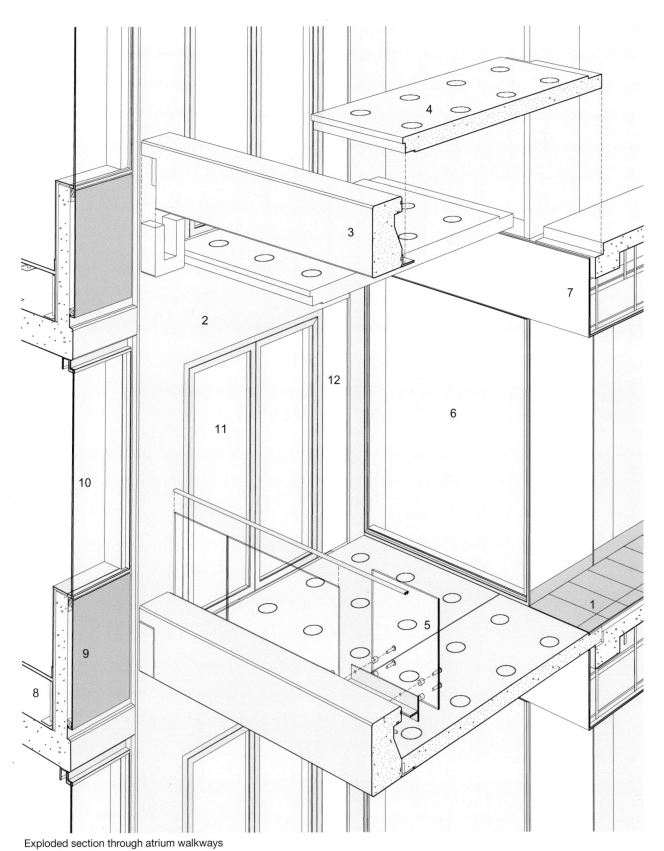

Exploded section through atrium walkways

Photo: Swanke Hayden Connell

Photo: Hélène Binet

# One Coleman Street, City of London

Architect: Swanke Hayden Connell in association with David Walker Architects
Structural Engineer: Arup
Precast Concrete Subcontractor: Decomo

Photo: Swanke Hayden Connell

Angular precast concrete cladding elements form a distinctive sculptural façade for this 20000 m$^2$ office building in the City of London. The area around London Wall was badly bombed during the Second World War and rebuilt in the 1950s and 1960s. One Coleman Street is part of a second phase of redevelopment which is seeing the post-war slab blocks replaced by more varied, sculptural forms.

Using precast concrete has allowed predictability of programme on site, and a very high quality finish that the planners were happy to accept instead of Portland stone. Despite the apparent complexity, a typical column/beam façade junction was designed to work for all the upper floors around the curved façade. Only three moulds were required for the precast elements: one for a ground floor column, one for the upper floor columns and one for a spandrel panel, although in fact two each were made of the upper floor column and spandrel panels to speed up fabrication.

Movable timber ends were slid along the steel shutters to account for the varying lengths of the pieces. Each piece was oversized slightly to allow 2–3 mm of polishing to the exposed surfaces. After inspecting over 25 samples a mix was chosen consisting of white cement and four different aggregates.

The slab edges have a faceted steel edge angle to follow the form of the backs of the precast panels and reduce the gap requiring fire stopping between floors. The column pieces bear on a concrete corbel and are restrained laterally by threaded bars between brackets on the steel frame and channels precast into the rear of the cladding element. Steel channels cast into the rear of the spandrel elements rest on two steel brackets on the perimeter steel beams. Slotted holes and a 30 mm packing zone allow tolerance and the gaps were dry packed with grout.

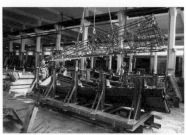

Photo: Swanke Hayden Connell

The windows have aluminium frames fixed via stainless steel brackets to channels cast into the precast spandrels. Around the edge they are clad in polished stainless steel. Reflections of the neighbouring buildings are broken up by the crisp frames and shifting polished planes of the cladding.

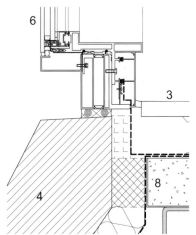

Detail section through typical cill – 1:10

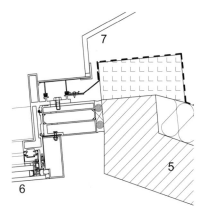

Detail plan through typical jamb – 1:10

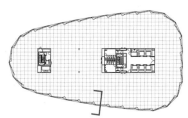

Typical floor plan – 1:1500

East–west section – 1:5000

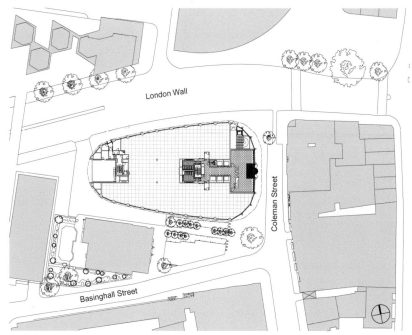

Gound floor site plan – 1:1500

Drawing labels:

1. Typical façade column
305 × 305 mm × 240 kg UC (universal column) steel column.
Two 780 mm long × 150 × 75 mm PFC (parallel flange channel) fixing brackets bolted to column on site.
200 mm long 305 × 305 mm × 240 kg UC stub shop-welded to column at floor level.

2. Typical façade beam
300 × 220 mm × 240 kg RHS (rectangular hollow section) steel beam.
Two steel plate brackets welded to beam, 450 × 330 × 300 mm approximately but varying depending on location.

3. Typical floor
Proprietary 600 × 600 × 40 mm raised access floor panels on 110 mm pedestals.
130 mm concrete slab on galvanised metal deck spanning between beams.
457 × 152 mm × 60 kg UB (universal beam) with circular cut-outs in web to coordinate with building services.
Polyester powder coated edge trim to plasterboard suspended ceiling.

4. Typical spandrel cladding element
Nominally 4570 mm long (varies from 4280–4725 mm) × 895 mm high polished precast concrete element.
Two 300 × 100 × 12 mm galvanised steel channels cast into rear of spandrel for bolting to steel beam brackets with M24 bolts and 50 × 50 × 8 mm packing shims.
Two further M27 bolts tighten against steel bracket for final adjustment.
30 mm vertical packing zone for tolerance filled with non-shrink grout once spandrel level in position.
Bolt holes in channels and brackets slotted in opposite directions to allow tolerance in both directions.
10 mm fall on top and bottom faces of spandrel.

Vented double external mastic seal within the 20 mm joints between adjacent precast elements.

5. Typical column cladding element
3725 mm high × 1400 mm wide polished precast concrete element with concrete corbel cast into rear to bear on steel stub on column.
Column element laterally restrained to steel column with M16 stainless steel threaded rods from PFC brackets to channels cast into rear of precast element.
65 mm rigid phenolic insulation fixed to rear of element prior to delivery.

6. Typical window
Nominally 4530 × 2790 mm polished stainless steel clad natural anodised aluminium window in each bay.
145 × 85 mm black satin anodised aluminium external frame to form 100 mm recess on all sides bolted in three places to top and bottom precast concrete spandrel.
20 mm gap between precast elements and frame for tolerance.
112 × 50 mm polished stainless steel cladding on all sides fixed to aluminium frame.
Double-glazed sealed unit consisting of 10 mm laminated outer pane, 16 mm argon filled cavity and 12 mm toughened inner pane with low-E coating.
Natural anodised aluminium internal frame bolted to precast concrete on top and bottom.
Roller blind at head.

7. Build-up behind precast column
Rigid phenolic insulation and vapour barrier to seal junction between precast column and window frame.
In-situ plasterboard linings to columns.

8. Build-up behind precast spandrel
Standardised steel slab edge tray cranked to follow profile of rear of precast spandrel to minimise gap for fire stopping.
Fire stop between slab edge and rear of spandrel.
Rigid phenolic insulation and vapour barrier between spandrel and raised floor and between spandrel and ceiling void.

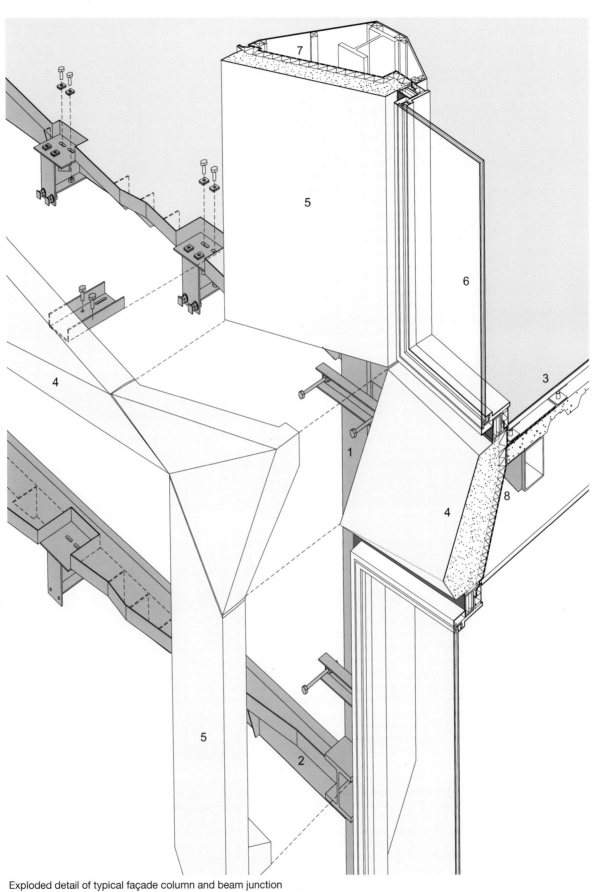

Exploded detail of typical façade column and beam junction

*Photo: Terry Pawson Architects*

# Vernon Street Offices
# Kensington, London

Architect: Terry Pawson Architects
Cast Stone Subcontractor: Histon Concrete Products Ltd

Crisply detailed cast stone gives a new office building for a soft toy company in west London a strong material presence on a street of yellow stock brick houses. The new building is linked to the redundant West London Magistrates Court next door, a red brick and Portland stone free classical style building from 1914 which was also refurbished as office accommodation as part of the project. Six of the original 38 prison cells have been retained in the basement, complete with steel doors and graffiti, not something you would normally expect to find in a high-spec office development.

Adjacent to the street a basement has been formed with reinforced concrete walls insulated and tanked externally. The new building has a concrete frame and cavity walls with a self-supporting cast stone outer leaf. The cast stone walls of the new building relate to the Portland stone details of the courthouse and the rendered lower stories of the near-by terraced houses.

Cast stone is effectively concrete with an aggregate of crushed stone, in this case Portland, and a carefully balanced mix of cement, super-plasticizers and accelerators to match the colour and texture of natural stone. 165 × 100 mm blocks were cast in several lengths from 1 to 2.2 metres. After being struck from the mould the faces to be exposed were acid etched to expose the aggregate. A blockwork inner leaf was built first with stainless steel cavity ties folded down so that the cast stone could be built later, reducing the time it had to be protected on site. Forty-two different shapes were made so that the quoins, cills, lintels and copings would be seamless with the walls.

A 6-metre long concrete slab clad in cast stone forms a porch over the entrance. The cast stone elements below are coffered to reduce weight and hung on stainless steel rods that pass through the concrete slab to be carried by plates above. The upper cladding elements fall towards a central stainless steel gutter to remove rainwater. In a similar way a cast stone cill in a recess on the street elevation slopes backwards channelling rainwater to a slot at the rear into a concealed gutter. Careful detailing reduces potential staining by concentration of water on the visible edges.

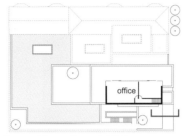

Second floor plan – 1:1000

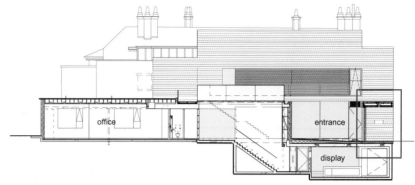

North–south section – 1:350

First floor plan – 1:1000

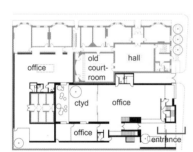

Ground floor plan – 1:1000

Basement plan – 1:1000

Drawing labels:

**1. Basement wall**
50 mm extruded polystyrene insulation.
225 mm reinforced waterproof concrete basement wall.
15 mm plaster internal finish.

**2. Entrance courtyard floor**
20 mm natural limestone stone paving.
25 mm sand/cement bedding.
Minimum 75 mm screed.
50 mm extruded polystyrene insulation.
120 × 125 mm stainless steel drainage channel.
275 mm thick reinforced waterproof concrete slab.
15 mm plaster internal finish.

**3. Entrance porch**
6735 × 2610 × 275 mm thick in-situ concrete slab spanning across entrance between concrete frame of main building and concrete columns in boundary wall.
50 mm thick cast stone elements with 30 mm ribs for stiffness fixed with stainless steel bolts to concrete slab.
25 mm slot between precast elements for drainage.
190 mm wide stainless steel central drainage channel falling to 75 mm diameter stainless steel downpipe in boundary wall.
Single ply waterproof membrane bonded to concrete and dressed into drainage channel.

**4. Abutment to wall**
Stainless steel masonry support angle on brackets bolted to channel cast into first floor slab edge.
Bronze strip folded around 38 × 38 mm softwood (sw) packer screwed to 38 × 28 mm stainless steel angle welded to masonry support angle to form shadow gap at first floor level.
White coloured damp proof membrane (DPM) bonded to inner leaf blockwork and dressed over masonry support angle.

**5. Entrance gates**
Galvanised head track channel fixed to concrete slab with resin anchor bolts.
100 × 50 mm polyester powder coated (PPC) steel rectangular hollow section (RHS) frame.
60 × 8 mm PPC flat bars at 120 mm centres.
Two 16 mm diameter vertical rods welded between flats.

Bronze bottom guide channel fixed into groove in cast stone paving.

**6. Base of wall**
190 mm wide × 360 mm high reinforced concrete haunch cast at top of basement wall to carry outer leaf of masonry.
Pea shingle and land drain adjacent to wall construction.
Compressible drainage board adjacent to cast stone wall.
Continuous 38 × 38 mm stainless steel angle to form slot between pavement and wall.

**7. Meeting room floor**
1200 × 600 × 20 mm thick lime stone paving slabs.
25 mm sand/cement bedding.
75 mm screed.
35 mm extruded polystyrene insulation.
275 mm reinforced concrete slab.

**8. External wall**
165 mm high × 100 mm thick cast stone blocks with stainless steel wall ties.
50 mm air gap.
50 mm rigid polyisocyanurate (PIS) insulation.
140 mm concrete blockwork.
12.5 mm plasterboard on 50 × 50 mm softwood studwork with plaster skim finish.

**9. Cill in recess**
Cast stone cill with fall to 30 mm wide drainage slot at rear.
1650 × 100 × 75 mm stainless steel gutter box fixed to underside of cill.
50 mm diameter insulated drainage pipe with trap connected into cast iron rainwater pipe internally.
Continuous cavity tray behind cill.

**10. Meeting room window**
Double-glazed sealed unit made up from 6.3 mm laminated inner pane, 16 mm cavity, 10 mm toughened outer pane.
51 × 38 × 6 mm angle carrier frame bonded to glass with structural silicone.
Continuous 156 × 6 mm flat subframe screwed to carrier frame and fixed back to blockwork inner leaf with aluminium restraint straps.
8 mm black silicone filled glass-to-glass corner joint.

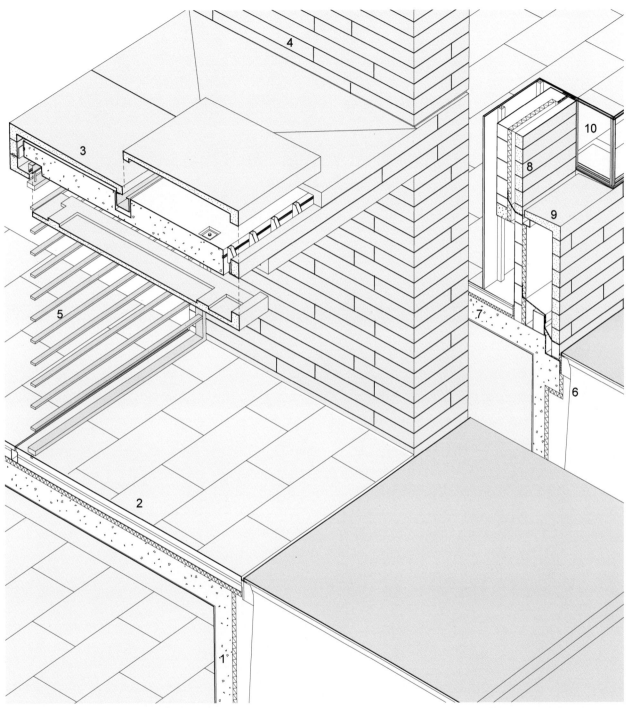

Cut-away section through front wall and entrance

Photo: Markus Bachmann

*Photo: John Gollings*

*Photo: Grimshaw*

*Photo: Grimshaw*

*Photo: Grimshaw*

*Photo: Grimshaw*

*Photo credit: John Gollings*

# Southern Cross Station, Melbourne Australia

Architect: Grimshaw Jackson JV
Structural Engineer: Winward Structures
Services Engineers: Lincolne Scott Australia

A roof of shimmering zinc-coated aluminium billows across the platforms of Southern Cross Station in central Melbourne. The station is part of an AS$350 Million redevelopment which unites the rail and bus terminals and was completed in time for the 2006 Commonwealth Games. The surrounding urban landscape has been re-configured so the station acts as a link rather than a barrier between the central business district and the docklands.

The undulating profile is designed to remove diesel fumes without the need for a costly mechanical system. Ventilation lanterns at the top of each dome allow the wind to draw out fumes by Venturi effect. Heat build up under a single skin metal roof would cause disturbance to the air flow, so an inner lining of faceted 200 mm thick triangular panels has been installed between the steel bracing to effectively insulate the roof. Air is drawn up through gaps between the ceiling panels into a void between the inner and outer layers.

The outer roof skin is curved in two directions using tapered strips of zinc-coated aluminium. Equipment was brought from Germany to roll the strip metal on site. To achieve the tight curves the strips were passed through the rollers four times in batches of five or ten strips, each batch with a slightly different tapered profile. This complex process was only possible because the roofing sub-contractor was appointed at the detailed design stage to develop fabrication details alongside the architects, a process Grimshaws say worked remarkably well.

The main structure is steel. Curved roof arches span up to 40 metres between trusses that are in turn supported on concrete filled steel columns. The long spans reduce the number of columns required allowing for future flexibility or re-arrangement of the platforms beneath. 900 mm wide gutters either side double as maintenance walkways. Above the trusses 20 metre long ETFE pillows provide natural light on the platforms. The ETFE is fritted to reduce heat gain from the summer sun bathing the platforms in a cool forest floor light.

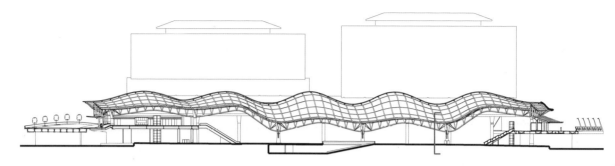

North–south section – 1:1750

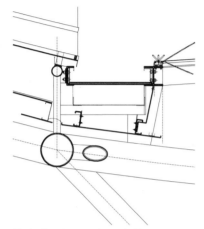

Typical gutter section – 1:40

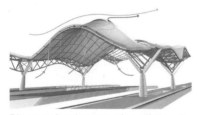

Diagram showing natural ventilation via roof cowls

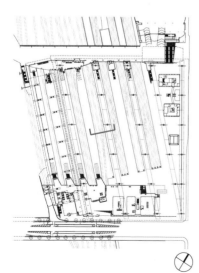

Level 1 plan – 1:5000

Drawing labels:

1. Typical column
10 mm thick circular mild steel (MS) column casing bolted down to concrete plinth.
Casing tapers from 2000 mm diameter at base to 1180 mm at top.
Height varies from 6 m to 12 m.
Casing filled with concrete by pressure pumping from base once bolted in place.

2. Wishbone column arms
Tapered arms made from varying thickness steel plates welded at edges with internal 6 mm thick diaphragm stiffening plates at 1250 mm centres.
1000 mm diameter × 16 mm thick circular hollow section (CHS) welded through base of arm for connection to column.
CHS connector located in column head and welded in place prior to filling column with concrete.

3. Spine truss
Steel truss brought to site in prefabricated 4-bay sections.
356 mm diameter curved top and bottom chords.
356 mm diameter curved top horizontal member.
273 mm diameter vertical members.
219 mm diameter horizontal diagonal braces.
168 mm diameter diagonal braces either side of column connection.
Three pin connections on truss prefabricated and site welded to each column arm.

4. Roof steelwork
356 mm diameter MS primary roof arches curved to form undulating roof profile.
168 mm diameter MS lateral struts bolted to cleats welded to arches.
168 mm diameter MS diagonal braces bolted to 356 mm diameter bosses welded to arches.
76 mm diameter MS posts with brackets to support roof panels and cladding rails welded to primary arches at maximum 1500 mm centres.

5. Ceiling panels
200 mm thick prefabricated triangular panels bolted between diagonal braces to cleats on MS posts.

Panel frame made from 150 × 75 mm galvanised light gauge steel channel sections.
Profiled galvanised steel top sheet.
Joints between panels covered with reinforced plastic strips.
1.5 mm thick polyester powder coated aluminium panels to underside to form finished ceiling.
100 mm gaps between ceiling panels above truss chords and primary arch to allow fumes to be drawn into roof void.
Bird mesh fixed to rear of ceiling panels over gaps.

6. Cladding support rails
114 mm diameter curved aluminium rails bolted to MS posts to support roof cladding.

7. Roof cladding
Tapered 1 mm gauge zinc-coated aluminium standing seam roof cladding clipped over proprietary supports.
Continuous void between roof cladding and ceiling panels to allow fumes to be drawn up to ventilation domes at tops of arches.

8. Gutter
200 × 75 mm parallel flange channel (PFC) and 200 × 200 mm universal column (UC) gutter frame bolted to steelwork at each primary arch.
930 mm width × 20 mm plywood gutter base bolted to steel frame.
Non-slip single ply membrane gutter lining to act as maintenance walkway.
4000 × 700 × 220 mm deep sump with two outlets at each column position.
Folded 2 mm aluminium vertical cladding to conceal gutter below rooflight.
Two 125 mm diameter rainwater downpipes running down each column arm and cast into concrete trunk of column.
One electrical conduit in each column arm running up into ceiling void.

9. Rooflights
20 metre long ETFE pillows running along full length of roof over spine trusses with 18 mm diameter white frit over 60% of surface.
Extruded aluminium perimeter clamp plate bolted to UC gutter structure.
Clamps at ends of ETFE pillows made from back-to-back angles to form expansion joint.

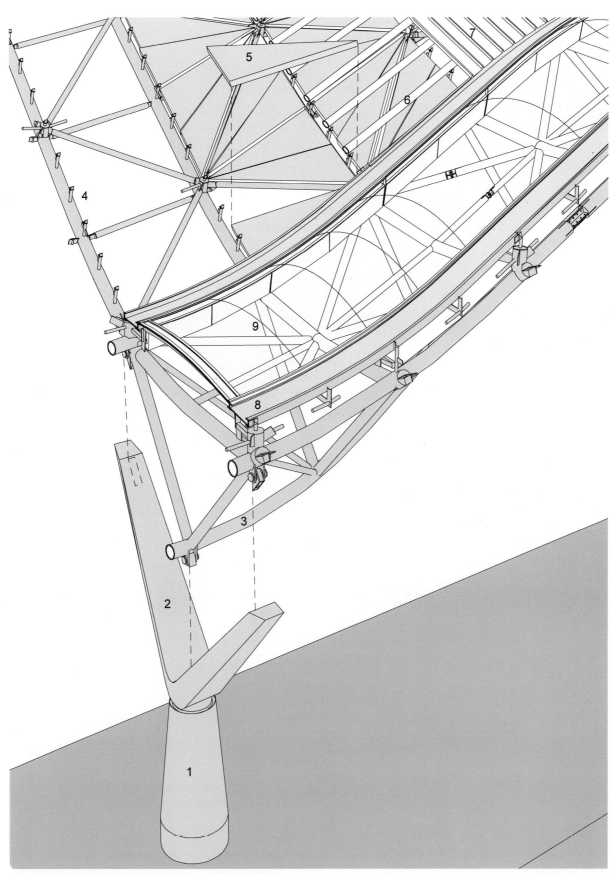

Cut-away view of typical column, truss, rooflight and roof

# Project Credits

The introduction and accompanying text for each project was written by Graham Bizley. The detail illustration for each project was drawn by Prewett Bizley Architects (Enrico Arrigoni, Graham Bizley, Joel Howland, Anurag Varma). All other drawings were supplied by the architects or engineers. I am grateful to the architects and clients for allowing their projects to be published in this book and for supplying the necessary information. The photographer for each image used is credited with the image and I am most grateful to them for allowing their images to be used.

## Individual Project Credits

### Royal Festival Hall, London

Completion: 2007
Construction cost: £117.9 million including new building, riverside retail and public realm
Gross floor area: 42,010 sq m

Client: Royal Festival Hall, Southbank Centre
Architect: Allies & Morrison
Structural Engineer: Price & Myers
M&E Services Engineer: Max Fordham and Partners
Quantity Surveyor: Davis Langdon LLP
Auditorium Acoustic Consultant: Kirkegaard Associates
Theatre Designer: Carr and Angier
Lighting Consultant: Speirs and Major
New building Executive Architects: BDP Architects
Landscape Architects: Gross Max
Planning Supervisor: PFB Construction Management
Planning Consultant: RPS Planning Plc
Project Management: Bovis Lend Lease Consulting
Masterplanning Architect: Rick Mather Architects
Fire Consultant: Faber Maunsell
Access Consultant: David Bonnett Associates
Pedestrian flow: Space Syntax

Contractors and selected suppliers:
Main refurbishment Contractor: ISG InteriorExterior
New building Contractor: Taylor Woodrow
Auditorium seating: Race Furniture
Auditorium joinery & WC Fit Out: Taylor Made Joinery
Specialist sliding screens: SpArt Andersen & Copenhagen
Suspended ceilings: Clark & Fenn Skanska Ltd
Stage machinery: Delstar Engineering Ltd
Organ refurbishment: Harrison & Harrison Ltd
Carpet and soft floor finishes: Loughton Contract Carpets Ltd
Borehole Consultants: Parsons Brinkerhoff

French polishing: SJM (French Polishers) Ltd
Stage machinery: Stage Technologies Ltd
Tapestry/panel restoration: Textile Conservation
Scaffolding: TRAD Scaffolding Company Ltd

Photographs:
Dennis Gilbert/VIEW
Allies & Morrison

### Neues Museum, Berlin

Completion: 2009
Construction cost: €200 million approx.
Gross floor area: 21,500 sq m

Client: Stiftung Preußischer Kulturbesitz
Architect: David Chipperfield Architects
Restoration Architect: Julian Harrap Architects
Consultant/site supervision (restoration): Pro Denkmal GmbH
Structural Engineer: Ingenieurgruppe Bauen
Quantity Surveyor: Nanna Fütterer
Site supervision: Lubic & Woehrlin GmbH
Project management: Ernst & Young Real Estate GmbH
Heating, ventilation & sanitary engineer: Jaeger, Mornhinweg & Partner Ingenieurgesellschaft
Electrical and security: Kunst und Museumsschutz Beratungs- und Planungs- GmbH
Lighting Consultant: Kardorff Ingenieure Lichtplanung
Building physics: Ingenieurbüro Axel C. Rahn GmbH
Landscape Architect: Levin Monsigny Landschaftsarchitekten
Exhibition design: Architetto Michele de Lucchi S.r.L

Photographs:
Ute Zscharnt
Christian Richters

### Newlyn Art Gallery, Cornwall

Completion: 2007
Construction cost: £950,000
Cost per sq m: £2110
Gross floor area of new building: 138 sq m
Gross floor area of existing building: 267 sq m

Client: Newlyn Art Gallery
Architect: MUMA
Structural Engineer: Dewhurst Macfarlane
M&E Engineer: Buro Happold

Quantity Surveyor: Davis Langdon LLP
Project Manager: Cyril Sweet
CDM Co-ordinator: Davis Langdon
Access Consultant: Lisa Foster Associates
Slate Consultant: Viv Stratton, Cornwall College
Camborne

Contractors and suppliers:
Main Contractor: Cowlin Construction (Truro)
Slate Supplier: Mill Hill Quarries Ltd, Tintagel
Slate Subcontractor: Forrester Roofing, St. Austell
Zinc cladding: J.E. Gibbings, Bristol
Glazing: Solaglass (Portsmouth)
Soffit grilles: Component Developments
Fair-faced concrete: Cornish Concrete Products, Bissoe
Concrete formwork: Luscombes
Concrete flooring: Permaban, Devon
Screed flooring: Sika
Architectural metalwork: Ferguson Engineering, Newton Abbot
M&E Subcontractor: EIC (Redruth)
Gallery lighting: Concord/Selux
Ironmongery: Allgood
Counters/shopfitting: WFC, Newton Abbot
Hard landscaping: Mid Cornwall Landscaping, St. Austell

Photographs:
Allan Williams


### The North Wall Arts Centre, Oxford

Completion: 2007
Construction cost: £2,665,000

Client: St Edward's School
Architect: Haworth Tompkins
Structural Engineer: Price & Myers LLP
M&E Engineer: Max Fordham LLP
Acoustic Engineer: Paul Gillieron Acoustic Design
Theatre Consultant: Charcoalblue Ltd
Quantity Surveyor: Bristow Johnson & Partners
Planning Supervisor: PFB Construction Management Services Limited
Fire Engineer: Safe Consulting Ltd
Access Consultants: Tom Lister Associates

Contractor and Subcontractors:
Main Contractor: Benfield & Loxley (Oxford) Ltd
Mechanical services installation: F.G. Alden Limited
Electrical services installation: Lowe & Oliver Ltd
Electrical: Oxford Sound & Media
External windows: Specialist Cladding Services Ltd
Theatre staging: Steeldeck
Ironmongery: Yannedis Ltd

Photographs:
Philip Vile
Haworth Tompkins


### Regent's Park Open Air Theatre, London

Completion: 2008
Construction cost: £640,000
Cost per sq m: £2850
Gross floor area: 225 sq m
Contract: GC Works

Client: The New Shakespeare Company Ltd
Architect: Prewett Bizley Architects
Landscape Architect: Colvin & Moggridge
Structural Engineer: Price & Myers
M&E Services Engineer: Fulcrum Consulting
Project Manager: Rider Levett Bucknall UK
Quantity Surveyor: Rider Levett Bucknall UK
CDM: Rider Levett Bucknall UK
Arboricultural Consultant: CBA Trees

Contractor and Subcontractors:
Main Contractor: Ashe Construction Piling: Hill Piling
Steel frame: County Construction Ltd
Groundworks: Cara Plant Ltd
Steel decking: Richard Lees Ltd
Carpentry: Newman Martin Construction
Roof coverings: Russell Trew
Mechanical installation: Primary Plumbing Services Ltd
Electrical installation: Astra Electrical Ltd
Roller shutters: Kenrick Door Systems Ltd
Resin Floors: McDaid Screeding
Folding screen in bar/rehearsal area: AGB Narib Ltd
Fencing: Metalwood Contracts Ltd
Landscaping: A1 Landscaping
Sign writer: John Pope

Suppliers:
Roofing: Permanite
Windows: Rationel
Doors: Humphrey & Stretton
Roller shutters: Eurotherm by Shutter and Door Components Ltd
Tilly Triboard linings and cubicle partitions: MCI Timply (now UCM Timber) Phenolic faced plywood linings: FinnForrest
Resin Floors: Flowcrete
Entrance mats: Jaymart
Sanitaryware: Ideal Standard
Infra-red controls: Cistermiser
Translucent & opaque woodstain: Sikkens by Akzo Nobel
Paint: Dulux by ICI
External surface finish: Natratex by Bituchem
Fencing: Expamet Security Products
Pendant luminaires: Concord:marlin
Fluorescent batten luminaires: Philips
Emergency luminaires: Thorn
Fairy lights: Light projects

Photographs:
Kilian O'Sullivan/VIEW
Prewett Bizley Architects

## The Bluecoat Arts Centre, Liverpool

Completion: 2008
Construction cost: £9.5 million
Cost per sq m: £2000
Gross floor area: 4720 sq m

Client: The Bluecoat
Architect: Biq Architecten
Executive Architect: Austin-Smith:Lord
Conservation Architect: Donald Insall Associates
Landscape Architect: Austin-Smith:Lord
Project Manager: Buro 4
Structural Engineer: Techniker
M&E Services Engineer: Ernest Griffiths
Cost Consultant: Tweeds
Planning Supervisor: CDM Planning Supervisors
Main Contractor: Kier North West

Photographs:
Stephan Muller
Biq Architecten

## Ruthin Craft Centre, Denbighshire

Completion: 2008
Construction cost: £3.1 million
Cost per sq m: £1980
Gross floor area: 1566 sq m

Client: Denbighshire County Council
Architect: Sergison Bates Architects
Client's Consultant: MN Arts
Landscape Architect: Pat Brown with Landscape Interface Studio
Structural Engineer: Greig-Ling Consulting Engineers
Services Engineers: BDP
Lighting Consultants: BDP Lighting
Project Managers: Turner & Townsend
Quantity Surveyors: Smith Turner
Main Contractor: Pochin Contractors Ltd
Artists/makers (furniture): Jim Partridge and Liz Walmsley
Artists/makers (gates): Brian Podschies

Photographs:
Ioana Marinescu
Dewi Tannatt Lloyd

## Siobhan Davies Dance Centre, London

Completion: 2005
Construction cost: £2.4 million
Cost per sq m: £3042
Gross floor area: 789 sq m

Client: Siobhan Davies Dance Company
Architect: Sarah Wigglesworth Architects

Structural Engineer: Price & Myers
Building Services Engineer: Fulcrum Consulting
Quantity Surveyor: Boyden & Company
Project Manager: Jackson Coles
Acoustic Consultant: Paul Gilleron Acoustic Design
Theatre lighting & sound: Charcoal Blue
Access Consultant: All Clear Design
Main Contractor: Rooff Ltd

Photographs:
Peter Cook/VIEW
Sarah Wigglesworth Architects

## Rich Mix, Bethnal Green, London

Completion: 2006
Construction cost: £12.5 million
Cost per sq m: £1830
Gross floor area: 6000 sq m

Client: Rich Mix Cultural Foundation
Architect: Penoyre & Prasad
Structural Engineer: Arup M&E
Services Engineer: Arup
Quantity Surveyor: Peter Gittins Associates
Project Manager: Bovis Lend Lease
Planning Supervisor: Arup
Acoustic Consultant: Paul Gillieron Acoustic Design
Main Contractor: Mansell Construction Services Ltd

Photographs:
Morley von Sternberg
Penoyre & Prasad

## MIMA, Middlesbrough

Completion: 2006
Construction cost: confidential
Cost per sq m: confidential
Gross floor area: 4000 sq m

Client: Middlesbrough Council
Architect: Designed by Erick van Egeraat
Structural Engineers: Buro Happold M&E
Services Engineer: Buro Happold
Quantity Surveyor: Gardiner & Theobald
Project management: Turner & Townsend
Civil engineer: White Young Green
Landscape Architect: West 8
Planning Supervisor: PFB Consultants
Artists and collaborating designers: Graham Gussin
Cafe design Consultant: Gijs Bakker
Shop design Consultants: Andy Miller and Colin Williams Design
Main Contractor: Miller Construction
M&E Contractors: Hayden Young

Photographs:
Christian Richters/VIEW
Designed by Erick van Egeraat

*Multi Purpose Hall, Aurillac, France*

Completion: 2008
Construction cost: £6.5 million
Cost per sq m: £1235
Gross floor area: 5265 sq m

Client: Communauté d'agglomération du bassin d'Aurillac
Architect: Brisac Gonzales
Structural Engineer: VP Green
Theatre Consultant: Ducks Sceno
Acoustic Engineer: Xu acoustique
M&E Services Engineer: INEX
Quantity Surveyor: Lucigny Talhouët et Associés

Photographs:
Brisac Gonzales

*ARC, Hull*

Completion: 2005
Construction cost: £550,000
Cost per sq m: £2500
Gross floor area: 220 sq m

Client: ARC
Architect: Niall McLaughlin Architects
Structural Engineer: Price and Myers 3D Engineering
Services Engineer: XCO2 Conisbee
Quantity Surveyor: E.C. Harris
Project Supervisor: Cameron Jemison

Contractor and Subcontractors (all local firms):
Main Contractor: Wright Construction
Steelwork: J&A Structural Services Ltd
M&E: Neville Tucker Heating Ltd
Roofing and cladding: RSR Cladding
Glazing: Glass and Framing Solutions
Security: Initial Electronic Security

Main Suppliers:
Aluminium roof panels: Eltherington Aluminium Ltd
Roofing Material: Brett Martin Daylight Systems
Blue caravan paint: Holliday Pigments (donated all the high build paint free of charge)
Caravan windows: Swift Group (donated windows and wheels free of charge)
Sanitary ware: Ideal Standard/American Standard (donated all sanitary ware free of charge)
Wood Pellet Boiler: The Organic Energy Company
Solar panels: Solar Century
Wind turbines: Windsun
Flooring: Sealand Flooring Ltd

Photographs:
Niall McLaughlin Architects

*Resource Centre, Grizedale Forrest Park, Cumbria*

Completion: 2008
Construction cost: £1.2 million

Client: Forestry Commission
Architect: Sutherland Hussey Architects
Project Manager: Turner Townsend
M&E Services Engineer: David Eley
Quantity Surveyor: Johnstons
Structural Engineer: Burgess Roughton
Main Contractor: Conlon Construction

Photographs:
Sutherland Hussey Architects

*Thermae Bath Spa, Bath*

Completion: 2006
Construction cost: confidential
Cost per sq m: confidential
Gross floor area: 3650 sq m

Client: Bath & North East Somerset Council & Thermae Development Co
Architect: Grimshaw Architects
Conservation Architect: Donald Insall Associates
Structural Engineer: Arup
M&E Services Engineer: Arup
Energy Consultant: Arup
Façade Engineer: Arup
Quantity Surveyor: Bath & North East Somerset Council, Gleeds, Gardiner and Theobald
Project Manager: Focus Consultants
Lighting Consultant: Speirs & Major Associates
Hydro-geological Consultant: Dr G. Kellaway, Dr Simon Kilvington

Contractor and Subcontractors:
Main Contractor: Capita Symonds
Services Subcontractor: Skanska
Water treatment: Thermelek Engineering Services
Glazing Subcontractor: MAG Hansen
Stone Subcontractor: Bath Stone Group
Lift Subcontractor: Otis Ltd
Kitchen Subcontractor: Lockhart
Glazed partitions: Prospec
Metalwork: McGrath Group
Ironmongery: Yannedis Ltd
Interior stone: Bröls Natuursteen BV

Photographs:
Edmund Sumner/VIEW
Grimshaw Architects

## Civil Justice Centre, Manchester

Completion: 2007
Construction cost: £110 million
Cost per sq m: £3235
Gross floor area: 34,000 sq m

Project Instigator: Her Majesty's Court Service
Tenant: Ministry of Justice (North West)
Developer: Allied London Properties
Architect: Denton Corker Marshall
Structural Engineer: Mott MacDonald
M&E Services Engineer: Mott MacDonald
Fire Engineer: Mott MacDonald
Façade Consultant: Mott MacDonald
Landscape Architect: Hyland Edgar Driver
Acoustic Consultant: Sandy Brown Associates
Stone Consultant: Harrison Goldman
Façade access Consultant: REEF Associates

Contractor and Subcontractors:
Main Contractor: Bovis Lend Lease
Façades: Josef Gartner GmbH
Mechanical Subcontractor: Axima
Electrical Subcontractor: Hills
Controls: Honeywell
Fit-out including pods, concourse balustrading, concourse panelling, joinery, fitted furniture and equipment: Mivan Ltd
Internal glazing: Clestra Hauserman
Demountable partitions: Clestra Hauserman
Blinds: Claxton Blinds
Paving: English Landscapes Ltd
Raised access floor: Kingspan Access Floors
Architectural metalwork: Shawton
Engineering Roofing: Topek (BUR) Ltd
Stone flooring: Q Flooring Paint: Johns of Nottingham
Roller shutters/smoke curtains: Bolton Gate Company
Building maintenance unit: Cento
Dry linings and partitions: Horbury Building Services
Slipform concrete: PC Harrington
Steelwork: William Hare Ltd
Lifts: Thyssenkrupp
Kitchen equipment: Tribourne
Suspended ceilings: Clark and Fenn Skanska Ltd
Blockwork: Irvine Whitlock
Carpet Subcontractor: John Abbot Flooring Ltd
Fire protection: R&S Dri-wall Ltd
Signage: WSi Ltd
Cafe sun-shade: Fabric Architecture

Suppliers:
Ceilings: Armstrong
Carpets: Interface
Drywall: British Gypsum
Doors: Leaderflush Shapland
Door hardware: Allgood
Sanitaryware: Duravit

Toilet partitions: Amwell Systems
Glass balustrades: Alurail
Interior metal panelling: Mercantile Met Tech
Lighting: Zumtobel
Raised access floors: Kingspan
Demountable office partitions: Clestra Hauserman
Blinds: Mechoshade
Roof waterproof membrane: Permaquick 6100
Roof paving: Marshalls
Flat roof insulation: Dow Roofmate
Concourse seating: OMK Design, Trax

Photographs:
Tim Griffith
Denton Corker Marshall

## Sean O'Casey Community Centre, Dublin

Completion: 2008
Construction cost: €7.9 million
Gross floor area: 2319 sq m

Client: Dublin Docklands Development Authority
Architect: O'Donnell + Tuomey
Structural Engineer: Casey O'Rourke Associates Ltd
M&E Services Engineer: RPS Group
Quantity Surveyor: Cyril Sweet
Project Manager: Cyril Sweet
Landscape Architect: Howbert and Mays
PSDP (Health & Safety co-ordinator): OLM Consultancy
Fire Consultant: OLM Consultancy
Kitchen Consultant: QA Design

Contractor and Subcontractors:
Main Contractor: P.J. Hegarty & Sons
Concrete Subcontractor: Tricastle Ltd
Mechanical installation: Walsh Mechanical Engineering Ltd
Electrical installation: Harry Sheils
Landscape: Avondale Landscapes Ltd
External joinery: Woodfit
Internal joinery: Essexford
Specialist fitted furniture: Gem Group
Fitted furniture: Brogan Jordan Homestyle Ltd
Mondo turf pitch: Clive Richardson
Metalwork: Hentech
Specialist light fittings: Charles Furniture
Lift: Otis Ltd

Photographs:
Michael Moran
O'Donnell + Tuomey

## Bellingham Gateway Building, Lewisham, London

Completion: 2006
Construction cost: £1.26 million

Cost per sq m: £1930
Gross floor area: 650 sq m

Client: London Borough of Lewisham Community
Department, Bellingham Surestart and BECORP
(Bellingham Recreation Project)
External Funding Body: Active England – Sport England
Architect: Cottrell & Vermeulen Architecture
Structure Engineer: Engineers HRW
M&E Services Engineer: Downie Consulting Engineers
Project Management: Mace Ltd
Quantity Surveyor: Mace Ltd
Planning supervisor: Mace Ltd

Contractor and suppliers:
Main Contractor: Buxton Building Contractors Ltd
Extensive green roof system: Bauder
Polycarbonate: Rodecca
Profiled glass reinforced plastic: Brett Martin
Profiled fibre cement: Eternit
Windows: SWS
Windows: Velux
Sports flooring: Junckers
Lining board: Sasmox

Photographs:
Anthony Coleman
Cottrell & Vermeulen Architecture

## Maryland Early Years Centre, Stratford, London

Completion: 2007
Construction cost: £500,000
Cost per sq m: £1760
Gross floor area: 284 sq m

Client: London Borough of Newham
Key Stakeholders: Maryland Primary School, Sure Start
Forest Gate Plus and Early Years Newham
Architect: Fluid
Structural Engineer: Conisbee and Associates
Quantity Surveyor: London Borough of Newham

Contractor and Subcontractors:
Main Contractor: Framework CDM
Mechanical Subcontractor: Shires Building Services
Electrical Subcontractor: Rivendell

Suppliers:
Panelised timber building system: Framework CDM
GRP cladding: Filon
EPDM roof: Prelasti – AAC Waterproofing
Windows & curtain wall glazing: AM Profiles Ltd
Rainwater goods: Alumasc
Rooflights: Whitesales
Vinyl floor finish: Altro
Underfloor heating: Underfloor Heating Now
Ironmongery: Lloyd Worrall Ltd

Sliding door: Geze
Lighting: Dextra
Whiteboards & projectors: Promethean
Washroom systems: Armitage Venesta
Acoustic ceiling tiles: Ecophon
Soft Internal linings: Sundeala
External paving: Marshalls
Impact absorbing play surface: Playtop
Artificial grass: Evergreens

Photographs:
Morley von Sternberg
Fluid

## Emmaus School, Wybourn, Sheffield

Completion: 2007
Construction cost: £3.6 million
Cost per sq m: £2030
Gross floor area: 1770 sq m

Client: Diocese of Sheffield
Architect: DSDHA
Structural Engineer: Price & Myers
Services Engineer: Atelier 10
Quantity Surveyor: Davis Langdon LLP
Landscape Architect: Watkins Daly
Acoustic Consultant: Tim Lewers Acoustics
Main Contractor: Allenbuild Ltd (Derby)

Photographs:
Hélène Binet
Morley von Sternberg

## Bedford School Music School, Bedford

Completion: 2007
Construction cost: £2.1 million
Gross floor area: 1131 sq m

Client: Bedford School
Architect: Eric Parry Architects
Structural Engineer: Adams Kara Taylor
M&E Services Engineer: White Young Green
Acoustic Consultant: Paul Gillieron Acoustic Design
Quantity Surveyor: Davis Langdon & Everest
Planning Consultant: Phillips Planning Services
Fire Consultant: Fisec Consultants Ltd

Contractor and Subcontractors:
Main Contractor: T & E Neville Ltd
Structural steelwork: Convoy Structural Services Ltd
Roof Subcontractor: Sterling Building Systems Ltd
Fixed glazed panels: Solaglas Saint Gobain UK
Blinds and shutters: Levolux
Cladding supplier: Falzinc Metal
Acoustic floor/strip supplier: CDM-UK

Electical Subcontractor: Landhurst Electrical Services

Photographs:
Hélène Binet


*Sanger Building, Bryanston School, Dorset*

Completion: 2007
Construction cost: £5.1 million
Gross floor area: 3500 sq m

Client: Bryanston School
Architect: Hopkins Architects Ltd
Structural Engineer: Buro Happold
M&E Services Engineer: Cundall Johnston & Partners
Quantity Surveyor: Turner Townsend
Acoustic design: Buro Happold
Contractor: Dean & Dyball Construction Limited

Photographs:
Anthony Weller


*Scitec, Oundle School, Northamptonshire*

Completion: 2007
Construction cost: £8 million
Cost per sq m: £2469
Gross floor area: 3240 sq m

Client: Oundle School
Architect: Feilden Clegg Bradley Architects
Structural Engineer: Jane Wernick Associates
M&E Services Engineer: Max Fordham LLP
Project Manager: Davis Langdon LLP
Quantity Surveyor: Davis Langdon LLP
Landscape Architect: Churchman Landscape Architects
Planning Supervisor: Davis Langdon LLP
Fire Consultant: Fire Design Solutions
Access Consultant: Colin Moore
Building Control: Approved Inspector Services Ltd

Contractor and Subcontractors:
Main Contractor: Willmott Dixon Construction
Concrete frame Subcontractor: J. Reddington
Stone Subcontractor: Ketton Architectural Stone and Masonry
Glazing Subcontractor: Deane and Amos

Photographs:
Amos Goldreich


*Ann's Court, Selwyn College, Cambridge*

Completion: 2005
Construction cost: confidential

Cost per sq m: confidential
Gross floor area: 2641 sq m

Client: Selwyn College
Architect: Porphyrios Associates
Structural Engineer: Hannah Reed
M&E Services Engineer: Max Fordham LLP
Project Manager: Davis Langdon LLP
Quantity Surveyor: Davis Langdon LLP
Landscape Architect: David Brown Landscape Design

Contractor and Subcontractors:
Main Contractor: Bluestone
Specialist stone masons: Ketton Architectural Stone & Masonry

Photographs:
Morley von Sternberg
Porphyrios Associates


*Wolfson Building, Trinity College, Cambridge*

Completion: 2006
Construction cost: £4.7 million
Cost per sq m: £1,336
Gross floor area: 3555 sq m

Architect: 5th Studio
Structural Engineer: Cameron Taylor (now Scott Walker)
M&E Services Engineer: Roger Parker Associates
Quantity Surveyor: Gleeds
Client Representative: Bidwells
Planning Supervisor: AFP Construction Consultants
Contractor and Subcontractors:
Main Contractor: SDC Builders Ltd
M&E Subcontractors: Dodd Group (Eastern) Ltd
Lift: ThyssenKrupp Elevator UK Limited
Frameless Glazing to Hanging Rooms: F.A. Firman (Harold Wood) Ltd
Stair and Undercroft Glazing: J. Street and Co
Windows: Alco Beldan Ltd
Joinery: Janes and Albone Carpentry Ltd
Steelwork: B and D Willett Fabrications Ltd
Photo Voltaic installation: Equinox Energy
Roofing: Cambridge Asphalt Co Ltd
Ironmongery: Allgood
Photographs:
David Stewart
5th Studio


*Information Commons, University of Sheffield*

Completion: 2007
Project cost: £23 million
Cost per sq m: £2210
Gross floor area: 11,500 sq m

Client: University of Sheffield
Architect: RMJM
Structural Engineer: Whitby Bird & Partners
M&E Services Engineer (pre-novation): RMJM
M&E Services Engineer (post-novation): Operon
Quantity Surveyor: Turner Townsend
Project Manager: Turner Townsend
Landscape Architect: Land Landscape
Planning Supervisor: RLF
Acoustic Consultant: Sharps Redmore Partnership
Fire Consultant: Safe & Buro Happold
Approved Building Inspector: Sheffield City Council

Contractor and Subcontractors:
Main Contractor: HBG Construction
Concrete void formers: Hanson Cobiax

Photographs:
Hufton & Crow
Broadstock Office Furniture

## St John's Therapy Centre, Wandsworth, London

Completion: 2006
Construction cost: £6.7 million
Cost per sq m: £1899
Gross floor area: 3529 sq m

Client: South West London Health Partnership, on behalf
of Wandsworth Primary Care Trust
Architect: Buschow Henley Architects
Structural Engineer: Price & Myers
M&E Engineer: Whitbybird
Quantity Surveyor: Davis Langdon LLP
Building Control: MLM Building Control
Main Contractor: Willmott Dixon Construction

Photographs:
Nick Kane

## Christchurch Tower, City of London

Completion: 2006
Construction cost: £1.1 million
Cost per sq m: £4400
Gross floor area: 250 sq m

Client: Kate Renwick
Architect: Boyarsky Murphy
Structural Engineer: Alan Baxter & Associates and Greig
Ling Consulting Engineers
M&E Services Engineer: McDonnell Langley Associates
and Max Fordham LLP
Planning Consultant: Washburn Greenwood Development
Planning
Historic building Consultant: Chris Miele
Building Control: JHAI Ltd

Contractor and Subcontractors:
Main Contractor: KoruBuild Ltd (Brockham)
Stonework: Paye Stonework & Restoration
Lead roofing: Able Waterproofing
Window supplier: Senlac, Windows & Doors
Window manufacturers: Jansen and Crittall
Window glazing: Pilkington Building Products UK
Front door: MSJ Joinery
Internal sliding door gear: Hafele UK
Glass balustrades and floor panels: Sharder Glass
Spiral staircases: Spiral Staircase Systems
Timber panelling & joinery: KoruBuild Ltd
Limestone flooring: Stone Age
Slate flooring: Delabole
Floor wax: OS hardwax oil by OSMO Ostermann &
Scheiwe GmbH
Smooth masonry finish: Johnstones
Ironmongery: Allgood
Lighting: Lightgraphix, Bega, Erco, Kreon, SKK
Lighting controls: Panasonic
Lift: IMEM Ascensores SL

Photographs:
Hélène Binet

## Halligan House, St Albans

Completion: 2007
Construction cost: £312,400
Cost per sq m: £1360
Gross floor area: 230 sq m

Client: Private
Architect: Simon Conder Architects
Structural Engineers: Built Engineers
Main Contractor: Dunworth Builders

Photographs:
Tom Ebdon
Steve Ambrose

## Herringbone Houses, Wandsworth, London

Completion: 2007
Construction cost: £1.63 million
Cost per sq m: £2200
Gross floor area: 2 × 400 sq m

Client: Private
Architect: Alison Brooks Architects
Structural Engineer: Price & Myers
M&E Services Engineer: Peter Deer and Associates
Quantity Surveyor: Carruth Marshall Partnership
Planning Consultant: FPD Savills
Project Manager: Brian White
Planning Supervisor: Peter Deer and Associates
Building control: Wandsworth Council
Land Surveyors: W.P.G. Surveyors

Party wall Consultant: BLDA Consultancy
Archaeology: Compass Archaeology
Arboricultural Consultant: Quaife Woodlands
Main Contractor: Cobalt Green Construction Ltd

Suppliers:
Cladding: Ipe timber by Tradelink Wood Products
Roofing membrane: Sarnafil
Breather membrane: Tyvek
Insulation: Kingspan
Aluminium windows: Fineline
Oak flooring: HFL (Hardwood Flooring London)
Precast concrete planks: Bison floors
External render: Weatherby Insulated Render Systems
Underfloor heating: Warmafloor Underfloor Heating
Closets: Oval Workshop
Staircase & glass balustrades: Fastrac Joinery
Kitchen: Kitchen Clinic

Photographs:
Cristobal Palmer
Alison Brooks Architects

### GreenHouse, BRE, Watford

Completion: 2008
Construction cost: confidential
Cost per sq m: confidential
Gross floor area: 133 sq m

Client: Barratt Developments PLC
Architect: Gaunt Francis Architects
Structural Engineer: Arup (Newcastle)
M&E Services Engineer: Arup (Newcastle)
Acoustic Engineer: Arup (Newcastle)
SAP/Sustainability Consultant: BRE
BREEAM assessor: Arup (London)
Building regulations inspector: NHBC

Contractor and suppliers:
Main Contractor: Barratt North London
Aircrete wall panels: H&H Celcon
Precast floor slabs: Millbank
Thermally broken slab connections: Schöck
SIP roof panels: Smartroof Ltd
Windows: Nordan
Window sealant system: Tremco Illbruck Ltd
Doors (main entrance and roof terrace): Russell Timber Technology
Sunpipe: Monodraught Ltd
Thermal insulation: Kingspan Insulation Ltd
Vacuum insulation panels: Va-Q-tec through Passive House Solutions Ltd
Roof coverings: Bauder Ltd
Photovoltaic panels: Solarcentury
External render: Weber building solutions
Copper cladding: KME UK
External cladding: Trespa U Ltd

Automatic sliding shutter gear: Hawa AG through Häfele
Internal ceiling plaster: Knauf UK
Internal thin coat spray plaster: Alltek UK
Dry lining: British Gypsum
External paving: Hanson
Sockets & switches: LeGrand
Kitchen: Symphony Kitchens
Sanitaryware: Ideal Standard
WC wall mounting system: Grohe
Taps & showers: Bristan

Photographs:
Denis Jones
Peter White
Gaunt Francis Architects

### Focus House, Finsbury Park, London

Completion: 2006
Construction cost: confidential
Cost per sq m: confidential
Gross floor area: 120 sq m

Client: Private
Architect: bere:architects
Structural Engineer: Techniker
Landscape design: Declan Buckley Design
Lighting design: John Cullen Lighting

Contractor and Subcontractors:
Contractor: Vision Build Ltd
Timber structure: KLH UK (massivholtz GmbH)
Zinc cladding & roofing: PMF Roofcraft
Bespoke furniture: Contrax Furniture

Suppliers:
Structural timber: KLH Massivholz GmbH
Zinc: VM Zinc UK
Insulation: Pittsburgh Corning UK Ltd
Gas fired hot water boiler: Viessmann
Solar panel and hot water storage: Viessmann
Whole house ventilation & heat recovery: Ubbink UK Ltd
Flooring: Hutchison Flooring Ltd
Drainage: Geberit UK
Oak flooring: Hutchinson Flooring Ltd
Timber windows external: Scandinavian Window Systems Ltd
Aluminium windows & front door: Isaacs Glass Co Ltd
Internal (non-fire rated) doors: Timbmet Group Ltd
Ironmongery: Franchi Locks & Tools Ltd
Tiles: Domus Tiles
Entrance matting: Gradus Ltd
Bath top: DuPoint Corian
Hand basins & WC pans: Duravit UK Ltd
Shower units: Grohe Ltd
Bath: Bette GmbH & Co
Sealant: Adshead Ratcliffe
Drainage slot channels: ACO drain

Floor drains in shower: Dallmer
Water softener: The Fresh Filter Co. Ltd
Steel column radiators: Caradon Stelrad Ltd
Towel radiators: Bisque Radiators
Under floor heating: Warmfloor (GB) Ltd
Electrical accessories: MK Electric Ltd
Taps: Vola UK

Photographs:
Jefferson Smith
bere:architects

## 80% House, De Beauvoir Town, London

Completion: 2009
Construction cost: £240,000
Cost per sq m: £1370
Gross floor area: 175 sq m

Client: Private
Architect: Prewett Bizley Architects
Structural Engineer: Nabeii Consultancy
Building control approved inspector: JHAI

Suppliers:
Wall and roof insulation: Knauf
Insulated wall studs: Knauf
Perinsul blocks: Foamglas
Teplo wall ties: MagmaTech
Roofing membrane: Prelasti
Sash windows: Soundcraft
Double glazing (for sash windows): Slimlite
Triple glazed timber windows: Bayer supplied through Double Good
Front door: Soundcraft
Pitch pine flooring: Lawson's Timber
Timber stairs: Tidy joinery
Handrail: Haldane
MVHR box: Itho supplied through Green Building Store
MVHR ducting: Lindab
Airtightness tapes and seals: Proclima supplied through Green Building Store

Photographs:
Prewett Bizley Architects

## Clay Field Housing, Elmswell, Suffolk

Completion: 2008
Cost per sq m: £1300
Gross floor area: 2072 sq m

Client: Orwell Housing Association
Architect: Riches Hawley Mikhail Architects
Structural Engineer: BTA Structural Design Ltd
Sustainability Consultant: Buro Happold
M&E Services Engineer: Inviron

Quantity Surveyor: Hyams and Partners
Landscape Architect: J&L Gibbons LLP
Civil Engineer: Scott Wilson incorporating Cameron Taylor

Contractor and suppliers:
Main Contractor: O. Seaman and Son Ltd
'Hemcrete' Suppliers: Lime Technology & Lhoist
'Hemcrete' Subcontractor: Quickseal
Window Suppliers: Scandinavian Window Systems & The Rooflight Company
Cedar supplier: John Brash
Roofer (cedar shingles): Nigel Maguire

Photographs:
Nick Kane
Riches Hawley Mikhail Architects

## Chance Street Housing, Bethnal Green, London

Completion: 2007
Construction cost (new houses): £643,500
Cost per sq m (new houses): £1950
Gross floor area (new houses): 330 sq m

Client: Rebecca Collings
Architect: Stephen Taylor Architects
Project Manager: Davis Langdon LLP
Quantity Surveyor: Measur
Structural Engineer: Paul Hardman Structural Engineers
M&E Services Engineer: Intengis

Contractor and Subcontractors:
Main Contractor: Charter Construction
Stair construction: Tin Tab Screens: J&R Fabrications

Photographs:
Ioana Marinescu
Simon Lewis

## Islington Square Housing, Manchester

Completion: 2006
Construction cost: £2.3 million
Cost per sq m: £1100
Gross floor area: 21,000 sq m

Client: Manchester Methodist Housing Group
Architect: FAT
Structural Engineer: Whitby Bird
Eco Homes Assessor: Pozzoni Group
Employer's agent: Simon Fenton Partnership
Quantity Surveyor: Simon Fenton Partnership

Contractor and suppliers:
Main Contractor: Richardson Projects
Windows: Rationel
Bricks: Baggeridge
Roof: Kalzip

Render: Alumasc

Photographs:
Tim Soar
James White
Edmund Sumner

### EMV Social Housing, Vallecas, Madrid

Completion: 2005
Construction cost: £8.5 million
Cost per sq m: £646
Gross floor area: 13,150 sq m

Architect: Feilden Clegg Bradley Architects
Local Architect: Ortiz Leon Arquitectos
Environmental Engineer: Emma s.l, Madrid, Spain
M&E Services Engineer: Max Fordham LLP
Structural Engineer: Integral

Photographs:
Empresa Municipal de la Vivienda
Elena Marco

### The Johnson Building, Clerkenwell, London

Completion: 2006
Construction cost: £22.2 million
Cost per sq m: £1133
Gross floor area: 19,587 sq m

Client: Derwent London plc
Architect: Allford Hall Monaghan Morris LLP
Structural Engineer: Price and Myers
Project Manager: Buro4
Quantity Surveyor: Davis Langdon LLP
M&E Services Engineer: ARUP M&E
Lighting Design: GIAEquation
Fire Engineer: Exova Warringtonfire
Landscape Designer: BBUK
Landscape Architecture Access Consultant: All Clear Design
CDM Coordinator: Jackson Coles

Contractor and Subcontractors:
Main Contractor: E. Bowman & Sons
Concrete Superstructure and Fair Faced Concrete: Duffy Construction
Brickwork: Irvine Whitlock
Roofing: WWR
ETFE Atrium Roof: B&O Hightex
Windows and Glazing: WRC
Atrium Timber Cladding: LSA Contracts
Stone floors: Harper and Edwards
Architectural Metalwork: Steel Arts
Stone and Brick façade refurbishment: PAYE Stonework and Restoration Ltd

Reception Desk: Benchmark

Photographs:
Tim Soar
Allford Hall Monaghan Morris

### One Coleman Street, City of London

Completion: 2008
Construction cost (shell & core): £35.32 million
Cost per sq m: £1648
Gross floor area: 21,203 sq m

Developer: Stanhope plc
Property owner: Union Investment Real Estate AG
Architect: Swanke Hayden Connell in association with David Walker Architects
Structural Engineer: Arup
M&E Engineer: Arup
Quantity Surveyor: Davis Langdon LLP
Construction Manager: Stanhope plc

Contractor and Subcontractors:
Main Contractor: Bovis Lend Lease
Concrete sub-structure and super-structure: John Doyle Construction
Precast concrete Subcontractor: Decomo, Belgium
Stent aggregate supplier for concrete: Bardon Aggregates

Photographs:
Hélène Binet
Swanke Hayden Connell

### Vernon Street Offices, Kensington, London

Completion: 2006
Construction cost: £3.5 million
Cost per sq m: 1600
Gross floor area: 2200 sq m

Architect: Terry Pawson Architects
Structural Engineer: Barton Engineers
Services Engineer: Max Fordham LLP
Quantity Surveyor: Bucknall Austin
Construction Management: Acuity Management Solutions
Garden/Courtyard Design: Gatacre Garden Design
General Builder: Pexhurst Services Ltd
Cast Stone Subcontractor: Histon Concrete Products Ltd

Photographs:
Terry Pawson Architects

### Southern Cross Station, Melbourne

Completion: 2005
Construction cost: confidential

Cost per sq m: confidential
Gross floor area: 60,000 sq m

Client: State Government of Victoria
Architect: Grimshaw Jackson JV
Joint venture Architect: Jackson Architecture Pty Ltd
Structural Engineer: Winward Structures
Services Engineer: Lincolne Scott Australia P/L
Environmental engineer: AEC (Advanced Environmental Concepts)
Quantity Surveyor: DCWC Pty Ltd
Pedestrian flow Engineer: Scott Wilson Irwin Johnston Pty
Rail & civil Engineers: Maunsell Australia
Signalling Engineer: GHD
Access Consultant: Blythe Saunderson
Security Consultant: Honeywell
Acoustic Consultant: Marshall Day
Roof Shop Detailing: Precision Design

Contractor and Subcontractors:
Main Contractor: Leighton Contractors Pty Ltd

Suppliers:
Ground Floor Accommodation (Precast Concrete Panels): Bianco Constress
Escalator and Lift Metal Cladding (Alucobond): Red Earth
Ticket Office Cladding (Glass Reinforced Concrete): Glenn Industries
Pod Cladding (Formawall): HH Robertson

Soffit Panels (Luxalon): Schiavello
Steel Spine Trusses: Geelong Fabrications, AJ Mayer and Haywoods
Primary arches, secondaries, diagonals: Alfasi and Riband Steel, Riband Steel
Roof sheeting (Kalzip standing seam aluminium roof-sheet): Unison/BSI JV
Ceiling panel supply (aluminium panels): Unison
Skylights (ETFE cushions): Vector Foiltec
Columns (steel composite columns and arms): Shearform
Roof erection Subcontractor: Rigweld P/L
Spencer St & Collins St Glazed Façades Aluminium & glass façades: Riband/Clipfit
Bourke St Bridge & Western Glazed Façades Aluminium and glass façades: Alfasi/Clipfit
Main Station Entrance Doors: Airport Doors
Balustrades and Handrails: Applied Manufacturing
Concourse and Platform Seating (Downforce seats): Aura
Active Pedestrian Information Systems: Honeywell
Wayfinding: Bentleigh Signs
Heating/cooling systems: Entire
Lighting and Electrical: Downer
Paint: Ameron, Jotun
Paving: Bluestone, Bamstone

Photographs:
John Gollings
Markus Bachmann
Grimshaw

# Project Details

| Project | Architect | Page no. | Gallery or museum | Theatre or dance | Cinema | Live music | Civic | Sport or leisure | Nursery | School | Higher education | Health |
|---|---|---|---|---|---|---|---|---|---|---|---|---|
| | | | Building use | | | | | | | | | |
| Royal Festival Hall, London | Allies & Morrison | 17 | | | | ● | ● | | | | | |
| Neues Museum, Berlin | David Chipperfield Architects | 21 | ● | | | | ● | | | | | |
| Newlyn Art Gallery, Cornwall | MUMA | 25 | ● | | | | ● | | | | | |
| North Wall Arts Centre, Oxford | Haworth Tompkins Architects | 31 | ● | ● | | | | | | | | |
| Regents Park Open Air Theatre, London | Prewett Bizley Architects | 37 | | ● | | | | | | | | |
| Bluecoat Arts Centre, Liverpool | Biq Architecten | 41 | ● | ● | | ● | ● | | | | | |
| Ruthin Craft Centre, Denbighshire | Sergison Bates Architects | 45 | ● | | | | ● | | | | | |
| Siobahn Davis Dance Centre, London | Sarah Wigglesworth Architects | 49 | | ● | | | | | | | | |
| Rich Mix, Bethnal Green , London | Penoyre & Prasad | 53 | ● | | ● | | ● | | | | | |
| MIMA, Middlesbrough | Designed by Erick van Egeraat | 57 | ● | | | | ● | | | | | |
| Multi Purpose Hall, Aurillac, France | Brisac Gonzales | 61 | | | | ● | ● | ● | | | | |
| Arc, Hull | Niall McLaughlin Architects | 65 | | | | | ● | | | | | |
| Resource Centre, Grizedale Forrest Park, Cumbria | Sutherland Hussey | 69 | | | | | | ● | | | | |
| Thermae Bath Spa, Bath | Nicholas Grimshaw & Partners | 75 | | | | | | ● | | | | |
| Civil Justice Centre, Manchester | Denton Corker Marshall | 81 | | | | | ● | | | | | |
| Sean O'Casey Community Centre, Dublin | O'Donnell + Tuomey | 85 | | | | | ● | ● | ● | | | |
| Bellingham Gateway Building, Lewisham, London | Cottrell and Vermeulen Architecture | 91 | | | | | | ● | ● | | | |
| Maryland Early Years Centre, Stratford, London | Fluid | 95 | | | | | | | ● | | | |
| Emmaus School, Wyebourne, Sheffield | DSDHA | 99 | | | | | | | | ● | | |
| Bedford School Music School, Bedford | Eric Parry Architects | 105 | | | | | | | | ● | | |
| Sanger Building, Bryanston School, Dorset | Hopkins Architects | 111 | | | | | | | | ● | | |
| Scitec, Oundle School, Northamptonshire | Feilden Clegg Bradley | 115 | | | | | | | | ● | | |
| Ann's Court, Selwyn College, Cambridge | Porphyrios Associates | 121 | | | | | | | | | ● | |
| Wolfson Building, Trinity College, Cambridge | 5th Studio | 125 | | | | | | | | | ● | |
| Information Commons, University of Sheffield | RMJM | 129 | | | | | | | | | ● | |
| St Johns Therapy Centre, Wandsworth, London | Buschow Henley Architects | 133 | | | | | | | | | | ● |
| Christchurch Tower, City of London | Boyarsky Murphy | 137 | | | | | | | | | | |
| Halligan House, St Albans | Simon Conder Architects | 141 | | | | | | | | | | |
| Herringbone Houses, Wandsworth, London | Alison Brooks Architects | 147 | | | | | | | | | | |
| GreenHouse, BRE, Watford | Gaunt Francis Architects | 151 | | | | | | | | | | |
| Focus House, Finsbury Park, London | Bere Architects | 155 | | | | | | | | | | |
| 80% House, De Beauvoir Town, London | Prewett Bizley Architects | 159 | | | | | | | | | | |
| Clay Field Housing, Elmswell, Suffolk | Riches Hawley Mikhail Architects | 165 | | | | | | | | | | |
| Chance Street Housing, Bethnal Green, London | Stephen Taylor Architects | 171 | | | | | | | | | | |
| Islington Square Housing, Manchester | FAT | 175 | | | | | | | | | | |
| EMV Social Housing, Vallecas, Madrid | Feilden Clegg Bradley | 179 | | | | | | | | | | |
| Johnson Building, Clerkenwell, London | Allford Hall Monaghan Morris | 183 | | | | | | | | | | |
| One Coleman Street, City of London | David Walker Architects in association with Swanke Hayden Connell | 187 | | | | | | | | | | |
| Vernon Street Offices, Kensington, London | Terry Pawson Architects | 191 | | | | | | | | | | |
| Southern Cross Station, Melbourne | Nicholas Grimshaw & Partners | 195 | | | | | | | | | | |

| Private house | Housing | Offices | Transport | < £1 Million | £1 – 5 Million | £5 – 15 Million | £15 – 50 Million | > £50 Million | < £1500 | £1500 – 2000 | £2000 – 3000 | > £3000 | New build | Refurbishment | Extension | Work to listed building/landscape | Concrete | Steel | Masonry | Timber | Brick | Stone | Concrete | Render | Glass | Timber cladding | Metal cladding | Metal screens/louvres | Polycarbonate or GRP cladding | Other cladding |
|---|---|---|---|---|---|---|---|---|---|---|---|---|---|---|---|---|---|---|---|---|---|---|---|---|---|---|---|---|---|---|
|  |  |  |  |  |  |  |  | • |  | • |  |  |  | • |  | • | • |  |  |  |  | • |  |  |  | • |  |  |  |  |
|  |  |  |  |  |  |  |  | • |  |  |  | • |  | • |  | • | • |  | • |  | • | • |  |  |  |  |  |  |  |  |
|  |  |  |  | • |  |  |  |  | • |  |  |  | • | • | • | • | • | • |  |  | • |  |  |  |  |  |  |  |  | • |
|  |  |  |  |  | • |  |  |  | • |  |  |  | • | • | • | • | • |  | • |  | • |  |  |  |  | • |  |  |  |  |
|  |  |  |  | • |  |  |  |  | • |  |  |  | • |  | • | • |  | • |  | • |  |  |  |  |  | • |  |  |  |  |
|  |  |  |  |  |  | • |  |  | • |  |  |  | • | • | • | • | • |  | • |  | • |  |  |  |  |  |  |  |  |  |
|  |  |  |  |  | • |  |  |  |  | • |  |  | • |  |  |  | • |  |  |  |  |  |  | • |  |  |  |  |  |  |
|  |  |  |  |  | • |  |  |  |  |  |  | • |  | • |  |  |  |  | • | • |  |  |  |  |  |  |  |  | • |  |
|  |  |  |  |  |  | • |  |  | • |  |  |  | • | • | • |  | • |  | • |  |  |  |  |  |  |  | • | • | • |  |
|  |  |  |  |  |  | • |  |  |  |  | • |  | • |  |  |  |  |  | • |  |  |  | • |  | • | • |  |  |  |  |
|  |  |  |  |  |  | • |  |  | • |  |  |  | • |  |  |  |  |  | • |  |  |  | • |  |  |  |  |  |  |  |
|  |  |  |  | • |  |  |  |  |  |  | • |  | • |  |  |  |  |  | • |  |  |  |  |  |  |  |  | • | • |  |
|  |  |  |  |  | • |  |  |  | • |  |  |  | • | • | • |  |  | • | • |  | • |  |  | • | • | • |  |  |  |  |
|  |  |  |  |  |  |  | • |  |  |  | • |  | • | • | • | • | • |  |  |  |  | • |  | • |  |  | • |  |  |  |
|  |  |  |  |  |  |  |  | • |  |  | • |  | • |  |  |  |  |  | • |  |  |  |  | • |  | • |  |  |  |  |
|  |  |  |  |  |  | • |  |  |  |  | • |  | • |  |  |  | • |  |  |  |  |  | • | • | • |  |  |  |  |  |
|  |  |  |  |  | • |  |  |  |  |  | • |  | • |  |  |  |  |  | • |  |  |  |  |  |  |  |  |  | • |  |
|  |  |  |  | • |  |  |  |  |  |  | • |  | • |  |  |  |  |  |  | • |  |  |  |  |  |  |  |  | • |  |
|  |  |  |  |  | • |  |  |  |  |  | • |  | • |  |  |  |  |  | • |  |  |  |  | • |  |  |  |  |  |  |
|  |  |  |  |  | • |  |  |  |  |  | • |  | • |  |  |  |  |  | • |  | • |  |  |  |  |  | • |  |  |  |
|  |  |  |  |  |  | • |  |  |  |  | • |  | • |  |  |  |  |  | • |  | • |  |  |  |  |  |  |  |  |  |
|  |  |  |  |  |  | • |  |  | • |  |  |  | • |  |  |  | • |  |  |  |  | • |  |  |  |  |  |  |  |  |
|  |  |  |  |  |  | • |  |  | • |  |  |  | • |  |  |  |  |  | • |  | • | • |  |  |  |  |  |  |  |  |
|  |  |  |  |  | • |  |  |  | • |  |  |  |  | • | • |  | • |  |  |  |  |  |  | • |  |  |  |  |  |  |
|  |  |  |  |  |  | • |  |  |  |  | • |  | • |  |  |  | • |  |  |  |  |  |  |  |  |  |  | • |  |  |
|  |  |  |  |  |  | • |  |  |  | • |  |  | • |  |  |  | • |  |  |  |  |  |  |  |  |  |  |  |  | • |
| • |  |  |  |  | • |  |  |  |  |  |  | • | • | • |  | • |  |  | • |  |  | • |  |  |  |  |  |  |  |  |
| • |  |  |  | • |  |  |  |  | • |  |  |  | • |  |  |  |  |  | • | • |  |  |  | • | • | • |  |  |  |  |
| • |  |  |  |  | • |  |  |  |  |  | • |  | • |  |  |  |  |  | • |  |  |  |  | • | • |  |  |  |  |  |
| • |  |  |  | • |  |  |  |  | • |  |  |  | • |  |  |  | • |  | • |  |  |  |  | • |  |  |  | • |  |  |
| • |  |  |  | • |  |  |  |  |  |  | • |  | • |  |  |  |  |  | • |  |  |  |  | • |  |  |  | • |  |  |
| • |  |  |  | • |  |  |  |  | • |  |  |  | • | • | • |  |  |  | • |  | • |  |  |  |  |  |  |  |  |  |
|  | • |  |  |  | • |  |  |  | • |  |  |  | • |  |  |  |  |  |  | • |  |  |  | • |  | • |  |  |  |  |
|  | • |  |  | • |  |  |  |  |  |  | • |  | • | • |  |  |  |  | • |  | • |  |  |  |  |  |  |  |  |  |
|  | • |  |  |  | • |  |  |  | • |  |  |  | • |  |  |  |  | • | • | • | • |  |  | • |  |  |  |  |  |  |
|  | • |  |  |  |  | • |  |  | • |  |  |  | • |  |  |  | • |  |  |  |  |  |  | • |  |  |  | • |  |  |
|  |  | • |  |  |  |  | • |  | • |  |  |  | • | • | • |  | • |  |  |  | • |  |  |  |  |  |  |  |  |  |
|  | • |  |  |  |  |  | • |  |  | • |  |  | • |  |  |  |  | • |  |  |  |  | • |  | • |  |  |  |  |  |
|  |  | • |  |  | • |  |  |  |  |  | • |  | • | • |  |  | • |  |  |  |  |  |  | • |  |  |  | • |  |  |
|  |  |  | • |  |  |  |  | • |  |  | • |  | • |  |  |  |  | • |  |  |  |  |  |  |  |  |  | • |  |  |